BOLDLY
BELONG

Julie **HARRIS**

BOLDLY BELONG

The Power of Being **YOU** in a Disabling Society

WILEY

Published by John Wiley & Sons, Inc., Hoboken, New Jersey.

Published simultaneously in Canada.

For general information on our other products and services or for technical support, please contact our Customer Care Department within the United States at (800) 762-2974, outside the United States at (317) 572-3993 or fax (317) 572-4002.

Wiley also publishes its books in a variety of electronic formats. Some content that appears in print may not be available in electronic formats. For more information about Wiley products, visit our web site at www.wiley.com.

Library of Congress Cataloging-in-Publication Data Is Available:

ISBN 9781394251353 (Cloth)
ISBN 9781394251360 (ePub)
ISBN 9781394251377 (ePDF)

COVER DESIGN: PAUL MCCARTHY
SKY10080513_072524

Contents

Introduction

MY STORY STARTS at age 20 when I passed out, hit my head, and lost memory of my entire life up to that point. Only a few minutes before, I had received a phone call from my sister telling me that one of my brothers was in the hospital in critical condition, so I immediately went to see him. As the medical staff was telling my sister and me the status of our brother, he was wheeled into the room. He had no skin on his back and was otherwise not in great shape. This led me to pass out. Instead of crumpling to the ground as is typical, I fell straight back hitting my head on the emergency room floor. My sister describes the sound as the loudest crack she had ever heard. Blood immediately started to come out of my ears and nose as I went into a 40-minute seizure. My parents, who were still on their way to see one child in critical condition, got a second call that another child was in critical condition in the same hospital. Both kids were possibly going into surgery, and all they could do was continue driving.

One of the three times my mom has seen my dad cry was while I was still having seizures after my parents finally arrived to the hospital. My brother ended up being released in six days, while I remained in various hospitals for three months. I went in with the brain of a young adult and left with brain function that more closely resembled that of a child's. In addition to the physical damage and related behavior changes, I lost all memories from before the brain injury and didn't

1

develop or retain any memories for weeks after. Everything I told you up to this point and everything I know about my childhood, history, and social norms is what I have learned secondhand from others. While this part of the story matters for you to understand what happened, it is the least significant part of the story as far as my experience, memories, and perspective are concerned.

The Aftermath and What I Learned

The most significant part of my story isn't the fall itself but the aftermath, relearning the world through the understanding of a child but with the mental capacity of an adult. Infants come into this world free of stigmas, learned biases, and most fears. They don't care about judgment or the expectations of others. I forgot everything, so I came into the world as an adult free of stigmas, learned biases, and fears that typically accrue by this age. I wasn't yet hindered by external expectations and judgments. Because I didn't have those influences, I saw the world in a completely new way.

Lesson #1: Needs Are a Priority

Because my first memories were in a hospital where meeting my needs was literally the priority, I learned that I was entitled to my needs getting met. I learned to communicate my needs and was actively asked what my needs were. I was taught how I could meet my own needs and what to do when I needed external support to get my needs met. All of my needs were respected by doctors, nurses, family, and visitors because my life and health depended on it. As far as I knew, the world revolved around me. If people were in my room, it was to visit me. If doctors or nurses were in my room, it was to check on me to support meeting my needs. Since this was the only experience I remembered, it became deeply instilled in me to ask for my needs to be met and to expect that they would be met. Nurses would even support me when I was getting tired or overstimulated and tell people to leave the room if my asking wasn't enough. Even after I was discharged from the hospital, my family continued to meet my needs without question and helped advocate for me when necessary.

Later, I learned that having my needs respected to even a fraction of this degree was not the norm. I learned that many people do not have families or environments that are this accepting of their needs. I learned that having my needs accepted directly related to having my difference accepted, which directly related to me feeling that I belonged. I don't remember any disability-related judgment from my parents or siblings ever. They may have had judgments, and may have even voiced those judgments away from me, but they never treated me differently. They never treated me as if I were inferior in any way. I didn't realize it until years later, but I think this was the most significant difference in my disability experience and the common disability experience. I lived the first few years of my life after the brain injury completely accepted. Because I was treated as if my needs mattered no matter who I was or what I was capable of, I didn't question if I was enough. I didn't question if I was too much. And that is a rare trait in the disability community.

Lesson #2: All the Rules Are Made Up

I left the hospital and learned that all the rules I learned about behavior in rehab were made-up rules that were only followed in certain situations. In rehab, I worked with occupational therapists, physical therapists, and speech therapists, who all supported me in learning how to better engage with people and society. I had no tact, no sense of respect, no idea what should or shouldn't be said, how it should be said, or how to interpret or consider others' feelings.

I remember using flash cards of facial expressions and the corresponding emotion the expression portrayed. I remember the matching games where I was to match emotions to certain scenarios. I learned the rules of "please," "thank you," and "you're welcome." I learned that you don't play on your phone while people are visiting. I learned that you don't just say, "I don't want you here anymore" but should make it a bit kinder, to consider the other person. Even when I don't understand it, I can accept that it is a rule to be followed.

Then I went out into the real world and learned others weren't applying these rules. When I would raise the question of why someone wasn't following the rules, they would explain why that specific situation didn't merit following the rule in the same way. They would explain that because of an imperceptible (to me) nuance, a completely different rule applied. I learned that trying to follow the rules just for the sake of following the rules led to me applying them inappropriately. When I didn't catch the nuance of the situation (or I caught the nuance but was completely wrong in my interpretation), I would apply the rules inappropriately. Either way, I seemed to be wrong in my behavior no matter how hard I tried.

I then learned that expectations of following certain rules changed depending on the person. I learned that what one person perceives as respectful and kind another could perceive as invasive. I learned that people love to project their interpretation of the rules onto everyone else with the assumption that their own rules are right.

What this experience taught me is that all of the rules are made up. Even the rules that seem very clear aren't. Even rules that seem to always apply, don't. There is always nuance that can change the applicable rule, or the interpretation of the applicable rule.

So I stopped following rules except the ones that I made up for myself based on my needs and values.

Lesson #3: People Settle

When I met new people and learned to listen about their life, it was more common than not to hear complaints. When somebody would talk about being unhappy in a job or marriage I would say, "Just get a new one." The person would explain to me that isn't how the world works. You can't just do what you want when you want. This confused me significantly because I did what I wanted every day. Sure, I was limited in some ways by my health and my circumstances, but within my control I did what I wanted. I didn't know enough to know that my situation was unique, but it just didn't make sense why so many people were living a life they didn't like and not making the basic changes to improve it. People were settling—and explained it with the assumption that it's the way it had to be.

Tie in lessons one and two, and it explains why. People don't prioritize their basic needs. People don't ask for their needs to be met and often don't even *know* their needs. The reason why typically lies in prioritizing the external made-up rules over their basic needs. When an assignment is due in school or work, it is expected to risk sleep to finish it. Somehow deprioritizing sleep and risking the very real health consequences is more acceptable than not prioritizing a made-up deadline with made-up consequences. When a marriage is full of unhappiness, stress, and fighting that leads to health issues, there is often an expectation to stay in it. Staying unhappy and unhealthy is more acceptable than getting a divorce if your family or religion or culture looks down on it. Attitudes around this have relaxed since I initially saw the pattern, but the point remains. People have convinced themselves that external expectations and judgments are hard rules that must be followed. They further convince themselves that those made-up rules take priority over the very real needs of the human body and mind. So, although I learned that rules don't matter at all, I also learned they simultaneously matter all too much.

Lesson #4: Society Itself Is Disabling

People with disabilities were very obviously treated "less than." I realized I was different pretty early on and started to feel the stigma before I even knew what stigma was or that the word "disabled" applied to me.

I learned that people viewed anything different as less than and talking about anything different as taboo. It didn't make sense to me because people aren't any less for being different—especially neutral differences in appearance and functioning that people can't control. It just made no sense at all.

My first job after my brain injury was serving the disability community in the form of being a support worker. I got better results with people I served than anyone else, so fairly quickly I became a manager. The people I served as a manager had immediate and startling improvements that caught the attention of the president of the company. Because of this success, I was asked to develop and deliver training for the entire company on my methodology. Turns out treating people with basic respect, allowing them some autonomy over their lives, and working with them instead of around them was quite effective.

What seemed common sense to me was a novel idea to most whom I worked with, including those who founded and led the company.

This was the first example where I recognized that people's perceptions, treatment, and the environment are far more disabling than disabilities themselves. This isn't to say that there aren't real limitations inherent with each disability, but those limitations can be accommodated for if external attitudes and environments allow for it.

The more I paid attention to this pattern, the more I found that not only did the stigma and environment limit existing disabilities, but stigma and discrimination even cause disabilities. The impacts of discrimination and stigma on mental health and stress can exacerbate or lead to depression, anxiety, and many stress-based diseases.

Being discriminated against is disabling. Having needs denied is disabling. Being denied autonomy over your own life is disabling.

Lesson #5 Brains Function as Designed

As a way to cope with my injury, I started studying the brain. I was frustrated by the lack of explanation around my injuries and symptoms, so I started to study all I could. While most of my study was geared toward brain injury, amnesia, seizures, my specific brain injuries, and recovery from brain injury, I also studied neuroscience in general. Basic education taught me that the brain does what it does for a reason. The brain sends signals to the rest of the body prompting certain responses, and most of it isn't our choice. The brain functions how it was designed to function, and even when it doesn't, it functions as expected given its circumstances. How does that make sense? Well, each part of the brain has specific functions, so when part of the brain is damaged, related functions are affected. In my case, my right frontal and temporal lobes were damaged. The right frontal lobe influences judgment, impulse control, and social-emotional recognition among other things. The right temporal lobe influences certain types of memory and regulation of some emotions. Anybody who visited me in the hospital would tell you it was incredibly obvious that those functions were severely affected. For example, I was known to tear out my IVs on a regular basis because I didn't understand how it contributed to my safety, didn't like the feel of it, and had no inhibitions. Even when my brain wasn't functioning as a brain was initially designed to, it was functioning as was expected for a brain with damage to the affected areas.

In addition to brain functioning based on structure, the brain's biggest priority is safety. Dissociative amnesia occurs as a protective response to a traumatic event. Certain emotional reactions are protective actions that are also guided by the brain. The brain always has a reason for doing what it is doing, and most of it is completely outside of our control.

However, that does not mean we have no control. When released from the hospital, I was told that I couldn't do certain activities because it would harm my brain but that I should eat and drink certain things to support my brain. It became obvious from those suggestions that internal and external input directly affects the brain. I later learned that it not only affects the brain, but external and internal stimuli is what guides the brain to do what it does. While I can't control my brain, I can control the input. So I started tracking everything. I tracked what I ate, how much, and when. I tracked what lights were on in the house and for how long. I tracked the duration of social interactions, who was involved, and the moods that they caused. I tracked how long I did puzzles or math or how long I read. I tracked seizures, irritability, and pain. I had a lot of free time as all I was doing was healing, so I tracked absolutely every factor I could.

What I learned was significant and has guided my life ever since. I learned that certain foods give me headaches every single time. I learned all of the ways my brain becomes overwhelmed and at what point that occurs. I learned what activities decrease feeling overwhelmed and increase calm. I learned that as long as I took care of my basic needs I could decrease the likelihood of seizures, but if I neglected two or more basic needs, I was asking for a seizure. I could successfully navigate loud environments as long as I had adequate sleep and properly nourished myself, but if I didn't, I was asking for a seizure. I learned that I could neglect a basic need in one area for a few days before it starts to affect everything else even when all other needs are being met.

Further research showed me that what I learned was nothing that hadn't already been discovered about the brain.

Food, sleep, sensory input, mental and emotional stress, and everything you do directly affects your mental functioning, mood, and actions. Like most people, you may believe you are in control of your actions in the moment, but you aren't. What you surround yourself with, the habits you build, and how you provide for your body's needs affect who you are and what you do far more than choices in the moment. Even choices that seem conscious and in the moment are dictated by past experiences, how the brain interpreted the external stimuli, and the cognitive health of the brain at the time.

This leads me to why I am writing this book. Because people believe that you can choose how you act in any given moment, they think that people who are disabled can just try harder, choose to be happier, and otherwise push through in specific moments. People who aren't disabled often think it is a choice to be miserable or limited. Because disabled people and anyone who is on the receiving end of stigma or discrimination know society's treatment directly affects mental health, which directly influences physical health, it's easy to think you can make no improvements until society itself improves.

You can't just push through and choose to not be disabled. And you don't have to be at the whim of society's treatment. By learning that your needs are a priority and that external rules, judgments, and expectations are not a priority, you can stop settling. You can recognize that society is disabling, and proactively choose to provide your brain with better input. You can stop living a life dictated by society's treatment of you. You can learn a new way of living, and you don't even have to have a brain injury and retrograde amnesia to do it.

THROUGHOUT THIS BOOK, the words "disabled" and "disability" are used frequently. This was done very intentionally to reduce stigma, to normalize the words, and to use the words that are most accurate.

Before getting into the book, I want to directly address what the word "disability" actually means free of stigma.

Many believe that the words "disability" and "disabled" are inherently negative. They aren't. The most common argument in the English language is that the prefix "dis-" makes them inherently negative. However, a grammatical negative does not have any inherent moral, ethical, or value implication. It simply is a tool to make a word mean its opposite, much like a mathematical negative makes a number its opposite.

There are multiple grammatically negative prefixes that are used at different times to denote different things. If you *disable* something, you make something that could work, no longer able to work. An external action is required. If something is *unable*, it is simply not able. That could describe its intrinsic lack of capability or an inability due to an external force. The word itself doesn't specify the cause, if any, just that it is not able. "Inability" describes the state of being unable, without implying whether the lack of ability is inherent or a result of an external cause.

In contrast, a *disability* does inherently mean that capabilities were limited or taken away by external factors—whether that's an injury, illness, genetic condition, or lack of accommodating environments and systemic barriers.

"Disability" is a neutral descriptor perceived to be morally, ethically, and value negative by stigma.

All of us are inherently unable to do some things. All of us are made unable to do some things. Maybe you were unable to access your office because your key card was disabled. Then you discovered an inability to contact your coworkers because your phone was disabled.

It is accepted that "unable," "disabled," and "inability" are not bad words when used in this context. They are accurate descriptors to describe certain situations. The word "disability" does not suddenly mean "less" just because the *inability* is related to a physical or mental difference. "Disability" and "disabled" are accurate and neutral descriptors.

PART

I

Stigmas Lie

THIS SECTION (CHAPTERS 1–3) serves as an introduction to the prominent points introduced in the book. You will learn what it means to live life on your terms and how it is possible no matter who you are. You will learn the difference between fitting in versus belonging and how prioritizing the former leads to losing yourself, while prioritizing the latter leads to real connection and acceptance.

You will learn how your identity has been developed over time and how it is largely influenced by beliefs learned through others' treatment of you. You will learn how consistent acceptance or lack thereof has affected how you see yourself, the world, and others. You will learn how your beliefs shape your behaviors, which shapes your identity, which shapes your beliefs. You will learn how to stop that cycle to change your beliefs, identity, and behavior.

After you learn how belief systems shape how you see yourself and the world, you will learn to identify who you really are, the process to become who you really are, and how that affects your life. You will learn how the feelings of belonging only come as a result of knowing and accepting who you are, in turn allowing others to accept you as you are.

You may have been taught that parts or all of you is unacceptable or less than, but that simply isn't true. Regardless of others' ability to accept you or not, you do not have to hide who you are to fit in. In fact, doing so will only ensure that you never feel that you truly belong. This section is designed to give you hope in what is possible while outlining how you can get there.

1

Live Life on Your Terms

HAVE YOU EVER worked really hard to improve yourself according to someone else's preference only to still be not enough? Have you ever tried to fit in only to still be rejected? Have you ever hidden your needs to be less needy only to end up being seen as needy anyway?

When being different feels like a threat, it is easy to prioritize acceptance from others while deprioritizing the value of maintaining your true identity. When rejection occurs consistently, it is easy to blame yourself and your differences as the problem to be fixed. When true acceptance doesn't seem feasible, it is easy to settle for fitting in while convincing yourself it isn't settling at all.

When all of this adds up, it seems as if the only way to live life is by following the rules dictated by others. Whether it is family, religion, employers, or culture, there are expectations that define acceptable behavior, what traits and accomplishments are rewarded, and what traits and accomplishments (or lack thereof) are criticized and rejected. When so many people abide by a specific set of rules and perpetuate the beliefs that those rules are rooted in, societal norms are created. It becomes normal to believe that following the rules to fit in is the best option. Add safety risk, whether real or perceived, and it solidifies the belief that there is only one option—to attempt to live according to all the external expectations in order to avoid the stigma associated with being different.

The problem is, attempting to meet all the external expectations doesn't mitigate the stigma-associated issues it attempts to resolve or avoid. You can try to meet all the external expectations and still be rejected. You can meet all the external rules to qualify for safety yet still be at risk. You could do absolutely everything expected of you and still have your needs denied when what you require doesn't fit into the societal model of acceptability.

Living life on your terms may seem as realistic as a rainbow-colored unicorn. When you don't see how it could be possible, it is normal to doubt that it is possible at all. But it is possible. I did it after my brain injury when I knew the least about social norms and was the least socially acceptable. Many of my clients have also accomplished living life on their terms to some degree regardless of disability, profession, experience, race, gender, religion, or age. Living life on your terms isn't an all-or-nothing thing, and it is possible to some degree for everyone.

Are there external parameters that you still have to work within? Yes. But far fewer than it seems. Those who take the risk of living life on their own terms may struggle more in the short term but live a much happier and healthier life in the long term.

Living life on your terms isn't inherently selfish, and it isn't only about doing grand things that go against what everyone else wants. It is much more simple than that. It is making choices based on you in every moment instead of prioritizing external factors. It is asking for your needs to be met even when it makes someone else uncomfortable. It is wearing the clothes that you want even when it isn't what is in style. It is using your mobility device even when it may attract attention, even judgment. It is doing all of this in line with your own values and goals. While any of the above examples can be done in selfish ways or with disrespect, living life on your terms is doing all of these things in line with your own values and goals, which for most is not going to be intentionally selfish or disrespectful. Choosing you in these little moments is living life on your terms. Conversely, denying yourself in these moments is losing yourself moment by moment, decision by decision to the expectations of others.

Your Choices Set Your Terms

Living life on your terms may seem impossible if it means changing in drastic and lofty ways such as abruptly quitting your job, becoming fully independent, or suddenly not being sensitive to rejection. It may seem impossible if it means not having a part of your life that you can't control such as a disability, familial judgments, or the current state of the economy. Living life on your terms doesn't mean changing in drastic and lofty ways, nor is it denying or attempting to change factors outside of your control. It is made up of subtle yet consistent choices that are within your control and aligned with who you are and what you want.

Living life on your terms doesn't mean changing in drastic and lofty ways, nor is it denying or attempting to change factors outside of your control. It is made up of subtle yet consistent choices that are within your control and aligned with who you are and what you want.

Small actions such as ending a conversation, stimming without shame, or asking for time to process new information without apologizing are all living life on your own terms. Respecting your body's needs rather than pushing through in the name of productivity is living life on your own terms. Taking a call while on a walk or while knitting to improve focus regardless of external judgment is living life on your own terms.

Stimming—or self-stimulatory behavior—is repetitive body movements or noises. Stimming might include hand and finger movements or whole-body movements, for example, finger flicking and hand-flapping, or rocking back and forth while sitting or standing. It could also be repetitive throat clearing or repeating certain sounds or words. While everyone stims, prominent stimming is common among autistic and other neurodivergent people.

Pushing back against unfair expectations and staying true to who you are despite pressure to change is acting on your own terms. Prioritizing your values, goals, and needs consistently in any capacity when the world asks you to prioritize the comfort of others is living life on your own terms. Using masking as a strategy rather than as a go-to coping skill is living life on your own terms.

While it isn't always easy, especially if you aren't used to it, the cumulative impact of choosing you over external expectations adds up. It strengthens your mental resolve, self-trust, and confidence, while freeing up mental energy that was previously occupied by constant monitoring of external indicators of acceptability.

Belonging Is the Goal

Advice around building confidence, getting a job, or getting accepted into a group is often based on how to present yourself in line with current standards, how to follow the latest trends, or how to be more like others to be accepted. It is easy, even natural, to think that becoming more like others is the antidote to rejection. After all, doesn't it make sense that fitting in leads to belonging? Except the side effect of becoming more like others is becoming less of yourself. Acting to avoid others' judgments may lead to fitting in but never belonging. Fitting in and belonging are not the same.

Fitting in is conforming to the norms of a group with the hopes of acceptance. The goal is to avoid rejection by improving likeness to others. Alternatively, belonging is finding genuine connection and acceptance by presenting yourself as you truly are. The goal is to be included as your true self, not as someone else expects you to be.

Beyond definition, fitting in and belonging have crucial distinctions.

- Fitting in is short-term; belonging is long-term.
- Fitting in requires constantly monitoring and realigning to the ever-changing "acceptable" standards. Belonging allows you to be you without conforming or self-censoring.
- Fitting in relies on *modifying* who you are, while belonging relies on *embracing* who you are.
- Fitting in prioritizes others' judgments of you, while belonging prioritizes your own values and goals.
- Fitting in relies on your ability to maintain the likeness of the group. If it isn't natural, eventually you are likely to show your true self, showing that you don't actually fit in and never did, leading to your inevitable rejection. Belonging isn't based on your presentation or your perfection; it is based on who you are at your core.

Fitting in does not always contradict belonging, and sometimes it has benefits. If you want to go to a formal event, it is reasonable for you to wear appropriate attire and act in an appropriate manner even if it means dressing and acting in ways that are outside of your norm. In situations such as job interviews, it is appropriate to use certain language, avoid certain topics, and present your best even if that is outside of your norm. Funerals, weddings, and religious ceremonies all have specific standards for behavior. In these situations, conforming to the norms of the group is not only expected but respectful. Following some external standards in these situations is not being fake in an attempt to fit in but adapting to the situation. In the short term, this is appropriate. In the short term, this can be done in line with who you are and without losing who you are. It is when attempting to fit in by changing who you are for the long term that it becomes harmful.

Attempting to fit in over the long term requires suppressing parts of yourself permanently. It requires conforming to standards that do not support or allow who you truly are. Attempts to fit in are usually with the goal of eventual belonging but instead make belonging impossible.

Hiding your identity as a result of not being accepted for who you are severely damages your mental health and self-esteem over time. Fitting in requires knowing what is expected of you, instead of knowing who you are. It leads to a suppression of self that not only erodes your self-esteem but your sense of self entirely. It isn't just hiding who you are from others but also hiding who you are from yourself.

Worthwhile Changes Are Rarely Easy

To find where you belong requires the exact opposite of what is required to fit in. Belonging in the long term requires showing up as you are. It requires showing the parts of you that may be different from the group. It requires showing the parts of you that are most often rejected. It requires risking rejection from people and environments where you don't belong in order to find the people and environments where you do.

When fitting in is primarily done to avoid rejection, acting in ways that might invite more rejection is not the easy or obvious choice. Beyond the discomfort that can accompany vulnerability, other internal and external barriers exist. Stigma is real. Discrimination is real. Threats to safety are real. Also real is the fact that not every environment is for every person. Nobody likes everybody, just as nobody is liked by everybody. Rejection does not reflect a personal failing but a natural part of being human. Add in the realities of unjust stigma and discrimination, and any rejection can act as a painful reminder that part of you is deemed unacceptable by many.

Years of attempting to conform, to push through, or to hide create inner beliefs that encourage the temporary comfort of fitting in over belonging. These inner beliefs include:

- Beliefs that you must people-please, be perfect, or be hyper-independent to be accepted;
- Beliefs that you will never be accepted, so there is no hope in trying;
- Beliefs that you inherently aren't good enough (which can lead to depression, hopelessness, and anxiety).

Acting against these beliefs creates discomfort of its own. There is discomfort in the form of more judgment from others when you stop people-pleasing and stop conforming to their expectations. There is discomfort in the form of not knowing who you are and a related discomfort of not knowing how to act separate from others' expectations. There is discomfort in the form of fear—one of the strongest discomforts of all. With all of these discomforts it is no wonder that many resort to masking and conforming. While that may feel like the easier or only option, there is a better option. And that is accepting that there will be rejection and discomfort *either* way and then preparing for the discomfort you will encounter on the only path that leads to true acceptance and belonging.

Understanding where stigma and judgment originate, understanding who you are without stigma and external judgment, and using that knowledge to build strength against rejection is key. By knowing and accepting yourself deeply, you develop a strong sense of self. It is through this process that external judgments start to lose their power.

By accepting that people make judgments based on how their own brains work, not based on you, their judgments lose their power. By recognizing someone's judgment as untrue or irrelevant, it hurts less, if at all.

Developing a strong sense of self and strength against rejection isn't easy, but it is possible. The result, even if nothing else in the world changes, is increased confidence, improved mental wellness, and joy, with decreased fear, depression, and insecurity. With an increased sense of self and resistance against rejection, you will view yourself differently, and you will make different choices. Instead of choices based on fear and shame, you will make choices based on confidence and desire. With different actions and beliefs, your world will inevitably change. Stigma, discrimination, and inaccessibility may not change, but how you respond to it and your willingness to tolerate it will.

Pushing through the resistance may seem daunting, but it eventually leads to a life where you no longer find it necessary to hide the parts of you that you used to believe were unacceptable. It can lead to a life where you know you aren't a burden, or broken, or unworthy of acceptance. Sure, you may not perfectly believe those things, but you will start to believe them more often than not. You will find where you belong, and you will realize that you always did.

I strongly believe that stigma and stigma-led actions, beliefs, and systems can and must change. Much of my work is geared toward helping organizations and leaders make the necessary changes to become more accepting and inclusive of mental and physical differences. While that change is important and ongoing, you do not have to wait for external changes to find peace, joy, and belonging. You can find it now. You deserve to find it now.

2

How Belief Systems
Shape Identity

HAVE YOU EVER really looked up to somebody and you view everything they do as amazing? Even if they do something less than ideal, you can easily understand, justify, or defend it?

What about on the opposite end of the spectrum, have you ever really disliked somebody, and every single thing they do just reinforces how selfish, disrespectful, or annoying they are? Even if they do something seemingly kind, you just know there is an ulterior motive behind it?

Everybody does this to some degree. You tend to attribute positive meaning to the actions of people you view in high regard and negative meaning to the actions of people you view in low regard. Even if two people do the exact same thing with the exact same intention, it is natural to tie different meanings based on your existing beliefs about the person.

The same principle applies to how you view and judge yourself. If you view yourself as less intelligent than others, you might interpret any mistake as further evidence of your supposed lack of intelligence even if it has nothing to do with intelligence. If you see yourself as forgetful, you might see mistakes as evidence of your forgetfulness even if they had nothing to do with memory. If you believe your worth is dependent on perfection, any mistake may feel like a threat to your self-image and competence.

If you view yourself as capable overall, you are more likely to not think much of your mistakes, address them quickly, and then move forward without tying meaning to them.

Your self-assessment is heavily influenced by existing beliefs about yourself, which are heavily influenced by external influences. Your self-perception is based in part on learned belief systems that taught you what traits and actions were acceptable versus those that weren't. If others accepted you, you learned that you were acceptable. If others consistently criticized or labeled you, you may have internalized that as truth even if it wasn't an accurate reflection of who you are. If you were surrounded by people who believed people with disabilities were weak, helpless, and should be pitied, you may have accepted that belief about yourself. Alternatively, you may have rejected it and acted in defiance of the belief. Either way, external factors including others' judgments and behavior shape self-perception.

This is exacerbated when you have traits that are commonly stigmatized by society. Stigma, a negative and unfair belief imposed by society on people with characteristics deemed "unacceptable," can lead to negative views of yourself. Stigma can be strong and run deep throughout entire societies. Stigma will lead you to believe that the stigmatized part of you is unacceptable and should be fixed, removed, or hidden. (I discuss stigma in much more detail in Part II of the book.) While it starts out as a belief external from you, eventually you learn to hide to stay safe from stigma-based judgments and interactions. The more you hide, the more you wonder whether the belief is true. The more you start to believe that it may be true, the more you start to feel shame. Even if you didn't internalize the belief initially, the *act* of hiding shows your brain that there is something *worthy* of hiding. In hiding the stigmatized trait, stigma is reinforced internally whether or not it is ameliorated externally. Whether you logically believe the stigma or not, surviving in a world that makes your safety and acceptance dependent on hiding leads to feelings of shame and a pervasive sense of inadequacy that permeates your identity as a whole.

Belief-Identity-Behavior Cycle

Beliefs influence identity, which influences behavior, which influences beliefs, creating a cycle. If you believe you aren't capable of traveling, you will make decisions and take actions to avoid travel, which reinforces your identity as someone who can't travel or doesn't like to travel. You can let the cycle continue as is, or you can choose to change course. By choosing to give your brain new information whether through changing your behavior, identity, or beliefs, the cycle is disrupted. The new behavior challenges old beliefs or creates new beliefs, which influence your identity, which cements the new actions as the preferred actions. If you decided to change your behavior and instead of immediately turning down opportunities to travel, you ask whether there are ways to make it accessible, you then open yourself up to new information and experiences that lead to new beliefs. There are three steps that change any part of the belief-identity-behavior cycle: awareness, acceptance, and action.

1. **Awareness:** Develop awareness of the cycle. It is through awareness that you identify the relevant pieces to shift. You may first gain awareness of a behavior that you don't like and then use that to gain awareness of the beliefs and identity that are related. Or you may first identify a belief that is holding you back and use that to identify the related identity and behaviors that enforce that belief. No matter where it starts, awareness is the first step.

2. **Acceptance:** Accept the beliefs, behaviors, and identity that have led to and perpetuated the cycle. Acceptance doesn't mean you are allowing it to continue; it means you aren't judging it and, thereby, not judging yourself. (I discuss more about acceptance and non-judgment in Part III.) Recognizing each belief, behavior, and identity as it is, and nothing more, puts you in a prime position to start making desired changes.

3. **Action:** Action can be internal or external. Action can be advocacy, taking accountability, changing habits, thoughts, or beliefs, or a combination. Actions do not have to be big to be significant.

Because all parts of the cycle feed off each other, whether you act on your identity, your beliefs, or your behaviors, the cycle will shift. Sometimes it is most effective to poke holes in the beliefs that directly affect the related actions. Sometimes it is most effective to replace a behavior with one that you know is more productive, even though you still hold the root belief. The different behavior shows your brain something that conflicts with the existing identity, which then decreases the strength of the root belief. Continuing the new cycle eventually enforces the new identity and decreases the strength of the old belief enough that a new belief takes its place. Sometimes, the identity piece will be most effective to break the cycle. For example, instead of seeing yourself as incapable of traveling, you may recognize the very real barriers in traveling while disabled as separate from your capability. In tying the travel barriers to external factors instead of your identity, you shift your identity to being more capable, which will then give rise to new beliefs and behaviors. Changing your identity directly can be the most challenging route initially but once done, can make the most significant and lasting changes.

How Identity Affects Perception

It is a natural cognitive function to confirm what you already believe. It is also a natural cognitive function to fill in the blanks of what you don't understand. When you don't know why someone did something, your brain is likely to make up a story based on what you already believe of the world and that person. Your brain filters everything others do through the beliefs you already hold to be true. Everything that you do is similarly viewed through the lens of who you believe yourself to be, or your identity.

If your identity is that you are a good leader deserving of a raise, your brain will allow yourself to recognize the ways you have excelled and eventually ask for a raise. If you have a strong belief that you aren't a good leader and only good leaders qualify for raises, your brain won't allow you to advocate for a raise or even see the areas where you are doing well.

Your actions are influenced far more by your beliefs about yourself than the objective truth.

If you believe that you are inherently less valuable than others, you may constantly apologize, strive to prove that you have some value through people-pleasing, or other actions that stem from a belief that you are low value.

If you believe you are just as valuable as others, however, you will show up to conversations expecting equal respect and leave when it isn't given.

Your identity protects you from others' judgments and treatments that aren't aligned with the way you view yourself. If somebody treats you as if you weren't worthy of respect but your identity says that you are, then you will see their judgment as *their* problem, not *your* problem. If somebody judges you in a way that doesn't align with your identity, you may not even recognize it as the judgment or insult it was intended to be. I have been criticized on dog trails, in airports, and in grocery stores for looking "normal" but having a service dog. Unless the insult is blatantly obvious, I often simply reply, "Thank you" or smile and keep walking not realizing I had been insulted. I only realize it when the person criticizing me gets mad that I didn't react how they thought I should. Being oblivious to insults can be a great strength, and it is possible when your identity is such that insults (at least on certain topics) aren't allowed in.

This works the other way, too. If someone is kind to you and shows acceptance but your identity says that you are not worthy of acceptance, then you will question their motives, interpret their kindness as pity, or otherwise doubt their sincerity. This extends to gratitude, compliments, and other complimentary acts. If you don't believe your identity aligns with the gratitude, compliment, or kind act, you may dismiss it, question it, or not recognize it altogether. Your identity can lead your brain to protect you from incongruent judgments and actions, even those that are positive. Your identity can lead your brain to believe complimentary words or behaviors or to disregard complimentary words or behaviors altogether.

Your identity influences every aspect of life from your perception of others' treatment of you to your decisions. Your identity may have been largely created by others' treatment of you, or your own judgments of you, but you don't have to accept that identity forever. You can also internalize compliments when they support what you believe to be true about yourself, while disbelieving insults when they are incongruent with what you believe about yourself. The difference lies in what you believe to be your identity.

External vs. Internal Locus of Control

Not being accepted, having stigmatized traits, and basing your safety on the acceptance of others creates a profound sense of powerlessness. Especially when young or when medical needs require support from others, acceptance may very well dictate whether or not needs are met. Experiences such as these can foster a belief that having your own needs met is dependent on external factors outside of your control.

This concept is defined as an *external locus of control*. Taken to its extreme, it is a belief that no matter what you do, you have no impact on what happens to you. Instead, you believe it is a combination of how you were born, your environment, society, others' judgments, and luck that dictates the outcomes of your life.

On the opposite end of this model is an *internal locus of control*. Taken to its extreme, it is a belief that you are in control of your behavior and outcomes in your life, regardless of external factors.

Most people lie somewhere between the two extremes. You likely recognize there are some areas where you have control over what happens to you and some external factors that you have no control over that do affect your life, well-being, and opportunities. Regardless of what is true, your belief of what is true defines where you fall on the locus of control model. Whether you lean more toward internal or external control has a strong influence on how you view yourself and the world.

The more necessarily dependent you are on others, the more there is a tendency to lean toward the external locus of control perspective. After all, it is quite literally other people who you depend on to provide for your needs and whose acceptance or rejection of you dictates your needs being met. Even with no other influences, this dependence on others can lead to a sense of loss of control. Add in mistreatment, discrimination, denial of needs, or consistent rejection, and then the feelings of powerlessness are likely to increase. It is that sense of powerlessness that can lead to an external locus of control, which reinforces the sense of powerlessness.

Those who have an external locus of control are more likely to feel helpless, have decreased motivation, and take less initiative. They tend to prioritize social compliance and meeting external expectations, leading to a loss of their sense of self. Living with little or no sense of control leads to depression, anxiety, and behaviors such as people-pleasing in attempts to fit in and survive. Instead of excessive conformity, some with an external locus of control may act in harmful ways because they believe there is no point in trying to be good when their actions don't have any impact on the outcome anyway.

However, the external locus of control isn't the inevitable or only perspective. There are people who have been in the most horrible situations who had very little control but had a belief that they did have some control, even if it was only over their perspective and behaviors. There are many who have gone through the worst horrors in history, who have had the most painful or debilitating disabilities yet still found confidence, joy, and meaning in life. It is these people who exemplified the impact of an internal locus of control even in situations where external, non-controllable circumstances had significant influence over their lives.

Viktor Frankl, a revered psychiatrist, neurologist, and Holocaust concentration camp survivor is a great example of someone who went through horrendous experiences yet maintained an internal locus of control. He also professionally believed and taught these principles both before and after his time in concentration camps and losing all of his family and previous life (The Viktor E. Frankl Institute of America n.d.). He believed that "between stimulus and response there is a space. In that space is our power to choose our response. In our response lies our growth and our freedom."

Those who have an internal locus of control tend to be more pro-active, tenacious, and better at stress management. They are more likely to set and achieve personal goals and have greater life satisfaction and well-being. They are more likely to persist and less likely to feel hopeless in the long term. A feeling of control over their lives leads to an improved mental state overall. This is true regardless of the actual control they have over their life. Viktor Frankl is one of the most vivid examples as one who had less control over his life for a few years than most of us will ever experience.

There are people who have more control over their lives than most others yet still believe everything in their life is a result of external factors. There are people who have very little control in their lives who still believe they can influence outcomes. What is true doesn't matter as much as what you believe to be true.

Why Identity Matters

Your identity is what your brain uses to interpret information, filter out relevant opportunities, and decide what actions to take. In a world where identity is often diminished to just your disability or difference, it is vital to develop your own unique identity free of stigma. Doing so ensures that the lens you use to interpret the world isn't as faulty as the lens others use to view and judge you. If you don't develop your own identity, you allow others to develop it for you.

Whether you ever think about it intentionally or not, you have beliefs about yourself that make up your identity. Having an identity that you are capable, valued, and worthy leads to drastically different actions than an identity based on self-doubt and shame. One allows you to recognize the kindness and acceptance of others as well as the goodness and value in yourself, while the other won't allow you to see it even in its most pure state.

You possess far more power over your life than it may seem. A core identity built on acceptance and compassion rather than shame and stigma can change every aspect of your life.

3

Identify Who You Are Free of Stigma

You ARE WHO you are today for a reason. No matter how you think, act, or move, it is somehow explainable by experiences, environment, brain function, beliefs, and experiences with others. Regardless of the reasons for who you are today, are you who you want to be? Or are you who others wanted you to be? Or who you think you have to be to stay safe? Are you a version of you that is filled with shame? Or is it a version of you that you are proud of?

You can change how you perceive yourself at any moment. If you don't know who you are or if you aren't a version of yourself that you want to be, you can identify the version of you that you *do* want to be, and then start acting accordingly, watch your identity shift, and find belonging. Identifying who you are in a world that hasn't accepted you as you are requires intentional effort. It takes courage, self-reflection, and determination regardless of external judgments. It takes effort, risk, and some discomfort, but so does trying to fit in and meet others' expectations. While both options entail effort, risk, and discomfort, only one leads to a real possibility of belonging and true acceptance from yourself and others.

Identifying who you are can be exciting. You get to replace what matters most to others with what matters most to you. You get to replace what you believe you *should* achieve with what you desire and *choose* to achieve. You get to replace your schedule built from obligation with a schedule built around desire. You get to prioritize your needs, health, and comfort over others' comfort.

You get to let go of the parts of your identity that came from adaptation and replace them with the parts of your identity that have been there all along but suppressed. You get to finally feel what it feels like to be you.

Knowing who you are enables you to be proactive about belonging rather than reactive in attempts to fit in. Because fitting in is dependent on others' judgment, it requires being hypervigilant so that you can quickly react appropriately when a judgment occurs. It places a sense of urgency around every judgment, whether it is relevant or not. With this belief system, a judgment indicates a potential threat that requires you to assess the situation and identify how to change to prove that you are still acceptable.

Knowing who you are enables you to become who you are. Becoming who you are allows you to gain confidence in who you are. Gaining confidence in who you are improves mental health, decreases stress, and reduces stress-related impacts on physical health.

Learn to Trust Yourself

To know who you are requires trusting yourself. You don't find who you are by searching externally. It is by looking inward, identifying parts of your identity that were never yours to begin with, and replacing them with who you have always been at your core.

This requires becoming aware of the faulty belief systems that currently serve as the foundation of your identity. Once you have identified the faulty beliefs, you are able to deconstruct them so they can be replaced with more accurate belief systems (covered in depth in Part II). As awareness increases, you will naturally start to recognize how many of your old beliefs have led to protective behaviors that did more harm than good. As you start prioritizing your own inner knowing and more accurate belief systems, you will start to recognize how you knew what was right for you all along.

When survival depended on others' acceptance of you, you likely learned to focus on others' input over your own. Every time you were told to just push through, stop being so dramatic, or to try harder, you learned to disregard your own body's communication signals. If ever you were called needy, it just reinforced that suppressing your needs was the right thing to do. But this is false. Your body knows what it needs, and it knows how to communicate that to you. If there is a part of your body that can't communicate its need, you can accommodate that accordingly while learning to trust the parts of your body that do still communicate to you. Rebuilding trust in your body starts with listening to your body's needs and taking initiative to provide for those needs.

Beyond trust in your body is regaining trust in yourself. If your body doesn't feel safe to rely on you, it will protect itself as necessary. If you say that you'll do something but then don't do it, you lose trust in yourself just as you would lose trust in someone else who did the same thing. Keeping promises to yourself and meeting your own needs is even more important than others keeping promises to you and meeting your needs. While the specifics may look different for everyone, rebuilding self-trust is a priority in recognizing and deconstructing faulty beliefs and then identifying and becoming who you truly are free of stigma.

Don't Fight Against What Is

To identify who you truly are, you must build self-acceptance around who you are without the influence of shame, guilt, and inadequacy. This means not fighting against what is. When you've been consistently shamed, belittled, and otherwise made to feel less than, it is easy to fight against who you are in efforts to be who others want you to be or who you think you should be. But this is a losing battle. It doesn't mean you can never improve, but improvement happens when you accept what is (including even the shamed and stigmatized parts of who you are) and then use what is as parameters for improvement.

Fighting against who you are is fighting against human nature. Fighting against human nature is a fight never won. It is human nature to act according to what is most natural and offers the least resistance. Nowhere is this more obvious than with desire paths. These are physical paths that are unplanned but developed by repeated human or animal traffic over the same area. Desire paths are sometimes created in areas where no paths previously existed, and they are created even when clearly marked paths exist but do not follow the most natural path.

Robert Mcfarlane described *desire paths* as paths made over time by the wishes and feet of walkers, especially those paths that run contrary to design or planning. Also seen as free-will ways (Mcfarlane 2013).

This phenomenon reflects a fundamental aspect of human behavior that humans will do what is most natural and convenient despite efforts to guide behavior another way. When urban planners plan walkways, it is often by taking into consideration best practices, what would look best, and budget, among other factors. Some who consider human behavior try to predict what they *think* will happen or what *should* happen. Creating walkways based on what looks best rather than natural human movement patterns often results in ineffective pathways. It certainly results in tension between natural versus prescribed behavior. It shows that no matter how much you want a human to behave a certain way and no matter how much infrastructure you build to guide them to behave that desired way, people will seek the most straightforward, natural, and convenient route.

Then there are urban planners who build paths after watching where paths are naturally formed. Some city parks, school and work campuses as well as hospitals and business parks have walkways that were put in after waiting to see where the desire paths were naturally created. Those urban planners who are most successful consider and accept natural human behavior patterns rather than trying to fight against them.

This behavior isn't limited to physical pathways but includes various aspects of human behavior and decision making. You naturally gravitate toward choices that offer the least friction. If your body or brain works differently from the average, what offers the least friction for you may differ from what offers the least friction for others. Recognizing and accepting *your* natural inclination can guide you to know who you are free of stigma and to more effective belief and behavior change.

The key is accepting who you are, not who you think you should be. It is accepting how you tend to act, not how you think you should act or how you wish you would act. Trying to be someone you're not only leads to frustrations when you inevitably return to what is natural for you. Trying to force yourself to use a solution that works for someone else without considering your unique tendencies will result in self-blame and frustration.

However, accepting your natural inclinations and building habits around them will support you in being the best version of you while facilitating acceptance. Becoming who you are isn't a matter of ignoring who you are to become who you want to be. It is a matter of accepting who you *already* are and identifying the easiest next step to becoming who you want to be.

Not fighting against what is also applies to external factors including environments, uncontrollable events, and others' behaviors, beliefs, and judgments. It doesn't mean you accept these things in your life as a permanent fixture, but accepting what is rather than fighting against it allows you to identify the most effective way forward.

Advocate for Yourself

The final step is acting aligned with who you identified yourself to be, advocating for your needs to be met in a way that is aligned with your values, and moving forward as you are, regardless of others' judgments. Throughout this book, you will learn not only how to be you when things are easy but also how to maintain who you are even when things really suck. You will learn how to maintain who you are amid judgments, failures, and pain. The more you become who you truly are, the easier it gets to be you, and the easier it gets to reject irrelevant external input. Continued self-advocacy is what enables you to be who you are regardless of inaccessibility or others' judgments and discomfort.

After years of hiding or denying certain needs, advocating for yourself can feel daunting. Long-held habits of people-pleasing and minimizing yourself will surface. Acting according to your newly developed identity instead of your old beliefs is uncomfortable at first simply because it is unknown. Advocating in ways you previously didn't will feel uncomfortable, maybe even out of character. But the discomfort of the unknown with hope on the other side is far preferable to the discomfort of being someone you're not and still not being accepted. Advocating for your needs and for your newly identified values and goals sends signals to your brain that will further support you in becoming and maintaining the authentic you—free of stigma and shame. Every action you take to support the new, more true you reinforces the new beliefs while weakening the old beliefs, habits, and identity.

PART

II

Deconstruct Faulty Belief Systems

IF YOU LIVE with a mental or physical disability, whether you call it a disability or not, you know how society can judge you and treat you differently based on disability or diagnosis alone. You know all too well the experience of discrimination that comes as a direct result of judgments around mental health and disability. You know how related views perpetuated by society are harmful. But what I have found is common, and what I experienced myself is that we don't see all the ways we have internalized some of those stigma-based belief systems ourselves.

Have you ever thought to yourself, "But I'm not disabled because I'm not like them" or "I don't have a real disability"? Or have you refused to take medicine or use an assistive device because it would be admitting that you are weak? Or have you actively rejected the use of the word "disability"?

Do you feel shame or the need to hide some part of your disability? Do you resort to people-pleasing, perfectionism, or hyper-independence to prove your value or to be accepted despite your disability?

If you have, you aren't alone. Everyone with any mental or physical difference goes through the experience of reconciling how society treats and views disability with what that means about them.

In this section, we go in depth on stigma, what it is, where it originates, and the flawed and biased beliefs that serve as the foundation. We go in depth into how stigma affects the individual, both externally and internally. We identify how stigma can be a real or perceived threat to survival and how the brain responds to keep you safe. We go in depth on some of the most common survival skills you may have developed as a result. We recognize how the survival skills served a purpose at one point, while also recognizing that they may be more harmful than helpful now.

By the end of this section, you will see the flaws in the most pervasive beliefs around disability and mental health, how you may have internalized some of those beliefs, and the obvious and not so obvious ways those beliefs have affected you, your life, and your health.

This section is not just to point out how certain belief systems are wrong and harmful but also how to identify the purpose they are serving and how to identify a new replacement belief system that meets that purpose more effectively. It helps you understand why stigma exists, why you have developed certain responses to it, and how you can free yourself of it moving forward.

4

Disability Stigma

LIVING WITH A disability means living with inaccurate and unfair judgments by others. For people with more apparent disabilities, it results in the consistent need to prove your ability and competency. For people with less apparent disabilities, it results in the consistent need to prove your need and disability. For all of us, it is a consistent desire to be seen as a whole human with both needs and abilities.

Treatment rooted in inaccurate judgments can be intentionally malicious, but most often it is people attempting to be kind. It is the belief that disability has a look that is evident when someone attempts to compliment you by saying, "You don't look disabled." It is the belief that disabled people can't be capable; this is evident when a stranger helps you, unsolicited, because they assumed you can't do it yourself. It is the belief that disabled people can't travel as evidenced by a manager who thinks they are being helpful by removing the travel part of your job unsolicited.

There are times mistreatment comes in the form of policies based on inaccurate assumptions. It is requiring multiple forms to be filled out for basic needs to be met. It is the invasive questioning of personal medical information to be believed. It is depending on someone who has never met you and doesn't have a medical background to decide whether you meet the criteria to get support.

The commonality in all of these situations is stigma. When you have a disability, stigma affects every area of life and eventually how you see yourself. The key to deconstructing any belief is uncovering the root of that belief. So this chapter does just that.

Stigma is a negative and unfair belief imposed by society on people with characteristics deemed "unacceptable."

- Stigma has negatively influenced perceptions, expectations, and judgments across eras and cultures.
- Stigma perpetuates misconceptions, biases, and unjust treatment.
- Stigma presents itself socially in unwarranted assumptions, stereotypes, and externally imposed limitations.

Why does something so negative and harmful even exist? Where did it originate?

The answer lies in our biology. Human brains do not like what we don't understand, beliefs that conflict with our own, or when we encounter something different than us. Our brains especially don't like discomfort.

It is human nature to meet what we don't understand with fear and avoidance. It has been hypothesized that the greatest fear a human mind can experience is uncertainty. To protect us from that fear, the brain does whatever it can to avoid feeling uncertain (Adolphs 2013). This includes making judgments and assumptions to fill in the gaps in our understanding, essentially creating stories that give us a sense of certainty. Studies have shown that we believe such stories, even when they're not true (Raub 2022). For example, when your boss asks to meet but doesn't specify why, the uncertainty may be so much that your brain goes into high alert concocting a story about how you're going to be reprimanded or even fired. Regardless of actual evidence to support that, you may believe it to be inevitable until the moment that the meeting goes a different way. Even uncomfortable stories that actually undermine you are more comfortable than uncertainty. These stories are developed so quickly by our brains that we often don't realize they are not based in fact but subconscious judgments and assumptions.

It is also human nature to meet opposing beliefs with resistance. When presented with a conflicting belief, it is natural to defend and justify our belief, protecting our comfort, and cementing our existing (albeit incorrect) belief more deeply. All of us have experienced someone increasing in adamance when they were wrong, and at times we do it, too. It is also human nature to categorize what is different than us. At a biological level, we categorize things into similarities and differences. We find safety in those like us and distrust in that which is different. We find safety in the familiar and distrust the unfamiliar.

All of this is true with anything confusing, conflicting, or different but especially when it threatens our fundamental beliefs about what it means to be human. Disability does just that. Disability forces us to confront the uncomfortable truth that uncertainty, fragility, and limitations are inherent with having a human body. Disability forces those who are not yet disabled to confront the uncomfortable truth that they may also become disabled one day.

At a biological level, our brain's priority is to keep us safe. Discomfort feels like the opposite of safe. Making up an explanation for what we don't understand makes us feel safe amid uncertainty. Denying conflicting truths by telling ourselves stories that confirm our beliefs makes us feel safe amid conflicting beliefs. Categorization makes us feel safe by quickly assessing for safety and threat amid that which is different from us. The unknown, conflicting, and different threatens safety, so our brains protect us against it, sometimes even making up lies. Spread these faulty beliefs across entire groups, and you have stigma. This is how stigmas originate.

Stigma is what we apply to those whose existence is confusing, different, and threatens what it means to be an "acceptable" or "safe" human. Stigma is the foundation that influences all beliefs and behavior toward disability and people who are disabled.

Stigma is not rooted in fact but in fears. How we interpret and respond to those fears is defined by the societal norms and power structures of the time. This is why attitudes toward people with disabilities vary depending on the era and cultural values of a given society. The social construct of stigma lies with the observer, not the observed (though the observed can also be the observer, as we will address later when we discuss internalized stigma in Chapter 5).

Historical Perceptions and Attempts at Change

Stigma related to differences in people has existed as long as humanity has existed. Early writings show stigmatized views of disability, including the Greek philosopher Plato, who argued for infanticide in *The Republic*, saying "that is clearly the best thing both for the patients and for the state." Or Plutarch, who argued that those who were disabled should be excluded from warfare and politics.

While violence, cruelty, and stigma are as old as humanity, so is compassion and care. In multiple areas of the world, bones of children, teenagers, and adults who had various disabilities have been found. One notable case is that of a young adult whose skeleton was found in Vietnam. The skeleton had fused vertebrae, which likely resulted in complete immobility below the waist, and significantly limited upper body mobility consistent with the congenital disease Klippel-Feil syndrome. From the skeleton alone, we can be certain he needed assistance to live and was at least partially paralyzed for a decade preceding his death (Oxenham et al. 2009). While the existence of skeletons from disabled bodies doesn't tell us how the individuals were viewed or accepted, we can be certain they were cared for, or otherwise they wouldn't have lived as long as they did.

These are examples of the earliest evidence that historical perceptions and treatments of disability were dependent on the attitudes of the time and culture.

Ancient Views of Disability

The Greeks had a very specific view of the ideal body and believed in a strong connection between the mind and body. If one wasn't right, they judged the other to be lacking, as well. This directly influenced society's view of those who were disabled, physically or mentally. Disabilities of certain types were seen as divine punishment, so infants with disabilities were left outside to die, leaving their survival up to "divine will." People with disabilities who were allowed to live were often viewed as a burden to society. Certain disabilities, mental illness (as it was perceived at the time) especially, were viewed as a moral failing and a result of divine punishment. Hippocrates, known as the father of medicine, challenged that perception by explaining the origin of mental illness in the same way as physical disability—that it originated in the body, specifically the brain. He also believed that mental illness was often a result of environmental factors. He rejected the religious explanation of disability and instead approached disability in a scientific way, creating the first widely known medical model of disability. This new perspective on disability and mental illness resulted in diagnoses, treatment models, and increased acceptance. Now that there was a scientific explanation for the differences, mental and physical disabilities were not as easily explained as divine punishment that indicated a moral failing.

During the same time period, the Romans viewed physical difference of many types as a mark of inferiority, disability included. Despite this, there were some people with disabilities who were more accepted than others and even excelled. The disability type, how and when the disability was acquired, the social status and the skills of the individual all influenced how the disabled person was judged. For example, while many were ostracized and left to fend for themselves, one disabled man, Claudius, even became emperor.

> The Roman emperor Claudius suffered from a wide range of physical tics and disabilities. Many scholars have explained these symptoms by hypothesizing that Claudius suffered from cerebral palsy (Murad 2010).

It is believed that Claudius was only made emperor because he was viewed as weak and easy to manipulate due to his disability. Those who put him in power underestimated his competence and strength, and he had a fairly successful reign. It was customary for Roman emperors to be deified after death, and Claudius was treated no differently in this way despite his disabilities. After his deification, a satirical document was authored with the sole purpose of making fun of Claudius's disabilities while questioning his competence, reign, and deification. Even an emperor with a successful reign couldn't escape stigma-based criticism in life or after death.

While progress was made regarding disability inclusion in some regards during the Greek and Roman Empires, the fall of the Roman

Empire and the rise of Christianity resulted in additional changes about the beliefs and views of disability. While it was again considered an acceptable explanation that disability was a result of divine intervention, the rise of Christianity also resulted in a more compassionate and caring view of disability. Infanticide by exposure was no longer an accepted solution for infant disabilities. While some people with disabilities were viewed as better than human or angelic, other disabilities were viewed as signs that the person was possessed by demons or had sinned. Even so, killing disabled people wasn't as acceptable as it was during the Greek and Roman Empires, but it also wasn't acceptable to have disabled people mingle with the greater public. As a result, they were frequently committed to asylums.

In addition to the ancient Christian view, there are a number of theological models of disability. In some religions, the reason for the existence of disability at all had to be explained theologically because the understanding of who God is—an omnipotent being who doesn't make mistakes—contradicts the notion of pain inflicted unnecessarily, as well as perceived bodily imperfections. Disabilities couldn't be easily explained as something created by God, so as with anything that contradicts our existing beliefs, human brains developed an explanation. The justification was born that blamed the human for their own disability.

But what about a baby born with a disability? If humans are to be blamed for disability, what could a baby have done to deserve such a horrible punishment? Once again, the human brain created an explanation to reconcile conflicting beliefs. The story was created that people born with disabilities are angelic and closer to God, and if they die it's only because they are too good for this earth. Variations of these stories have existed in some of the oldest religions, and they continue today.

A commonality in the medical and religious models of disability is that there is an established norm, and anything that differs from that norm must be explained. This goes back to the basic biology of our minds—we are naturally inclined to develop an explanation for anything that differs from our norm or that we do not understand. The explanation from the medical model is that there is a difference in the body that must be treated to return to the norm (as it is perceived) or as close to the norm as possible. Sometimes this is true. If you have a cold, you probably want to get back to the established standard of health. If you have something more serious and life-threatening such as cancer, you almost certainly want to get back to the established standard of health. However, the medical model takes it further to say that almost any difference is a medical condition to be cured or fixed.

While these are only a few examples of historical beliefs, they underscore how the prominent beliefs of the time influence how we as humans are able to reconcile conflicting beliefs, uncertainty, and the unknown.

Modern Views of Disability

If we jump forward quite a bit to the 1700s, we find the first examples in this time period of schools being created specifically for the education of people with disabilities, especially those who were deaf. In France, the inhumane treatment of those with mental illness was recognized by Phillippe Pinel and Jean-Baptiste Pussin, who proposed treating mental illness with psychological counseling instead of abuse and constraint by shackles and chains. In 1817, after success in Europe with deaf schools, the first school for deaf students was built in the United States by Laurent Clerc and Thomas Hopkins Gallaudet. In 1829, the first raised point alphabet was invented by Louis Braille.

Despite these acts of progress, there were soon steps backward. In the late 1880s, it was decided (by people who weren't deaf) that oral learning was superior to signing, and all deaf schools in the United States were to replace deaf teachers with those who taught orally. This resembles the earlier beliefs that getting disabled people to function as close to "normal" as possible is the goal.

Through the early 1900s eugenics in the United States rose in popularity as people increasingly believed that evolution should be controlled by sterilizing people who were perceived to have defective genetics, including people with disabilities. This was funded by prominent foundations, and laws were enacted that prohibited disabled people from marrying and mandated sterilization.

All of this is to portray how fickle the view and treatment of disabilities can be and how it is all made up and dependent on the views of the people who have the power at the time.

Despite the regressive steps as outlined above, efforts continued to provide support and increase inclusion for the disabled population.

In the United States, the League of the Physically Handicapped was created in 1935 to help disabled people fight for employment. In 1945, curb cuts were implemented as a pilot program to aid the employment of veterans with disabilities and ended up benefiting many who weren't disabled. In 1946, President Truman signed the National Mental Health Act, which called for the creation of a National Institute of Mental Health.

Sit-ins occurred in the 1970s including a 25-day sit-in where a group of disabled people took over the fourth floor of a federal building in San Francisco. Disability rights started to be seen as civil rights.

Demonstrations were made including what is known as the Capitol Crawl in 1990. A group of disabled people traveled to the Capitol Building in Washington, DC, left their mobility device at the bottom of the steps, and crawled or pulled themselves up the steps to demonstrate the very real barriers that people with disabilities face. This led to the signing of the Americans with Disabilities Act on July 26, 1990. Following this act, many countries around the world signed similar laws, and in 2006 the United Nations adopted the Convention on the Rights of Persons with Disabilities, which led to even more countries adopting related laws. As of 2023, most countries have disability laws of some sort, especially in regard to education and employment where all but 22 countries have laws regarding disability rights in education, and all but 33 countries have laws regarding rights for people with disabilities in the workforce (World Policy Analysis Center 2023).

While this is all significant progress, stigma is still a prominent influence. Legal rights are hindered when those responsible for interpreting, implementing, and enforcing the laws are viewing it through a lens distorted by stigma. Laws themselves can't and won't change the overall views of people with disabilities. Most of the rights that were fought for in the 1900s are still being fought today, over 70 years later.

As long as stigma is an underlying societal driver, efforts cannot be fully realized.

Seeds of Change

Attempts to change views on disability have existed as long as disability has existed. Very rarely do these changes take the intended effect of improved treatment and inclusion of people with disabilities. Positive intentions do not always result in the intended impact as long as the underlying stigma has remained.

An example that is increasingly evident in more recent years are the attempts to change language related to disability. These attempts typically seek to remove stigma by making the words used for disability more palatable and less negative. It is an attempt to remove the stigma by changing the word. The terms "special needs," "person with a disability," "handicapable," etc., have all been introduced in attempts to improve on the word "disability." But the problem is that it isn't the word "disability" that is inherently negative; it is the associated cultural stigma. And that stigma won't change by changing a word that isn't the problem.

"Disability" is not a bad word. If you are uncomfortable with the word alone, how comfortable can you possibly be with a disabled person? How comfortable can you be working next to someone with a disability, hiring someone with a disability, or working for someone with a disability?

Although using euphemisms such as "special needs" or "differently abled" may make the speaker more comfortable, it minimizes the disabled person's experiences and reminds them that they make others uncomfortable by simply existing. Pushing euphemisms to replace the words "disability" and "disabled" is damaging instead of helpful, no matter how well intentioned. The euphemisms are steeped in negative stereotypes and only serve to further perpetuate stigma. Acknowledging the reality of disability is to acknowledge that some of it may be uncomfortable. But trying to evade discomfort through verbal gymnastics leads to ignoring the parts of the human that most need support and acceptance.

The term "special needs" unnecessarily and inaccurately others the disabled, including neurodivergent populations. The needs aren't different—they are basic human needs that every person shares.

> The term "neurodivergent" refers to people whose brain function differs from conventional norms, processing and engaging with the world in distinctive ways. These natural variations in brain functioning include distinct methods of processing information, emotions, and sensory inputs, as well as distinct communication styles. Neurodivergence can be congenital or acquired.

What is different is the way in which these needs are met, which is also a difference inherent to being human. Needs aren't "special" just because they are tied to a disability. We all need to intake nutrients, communicate, move, connect, and learn. We all do it in various ways. People with disabilities are human. Our needs are human needs, too.

Because of the stigma tied to disability, disability needs weren't seen as human needs to the extent that laws were required to give people with disabilities the legal right to have their basic needs met. In the United States, the Americans with Disabilities Act was one of these laws. Among other things, it legalized the right to reasonable accommodations necessary to participate in the workforce. "Accommodation" isn't a word specific to the disability community. "Accommodation" isn't inherently a legal term. Accommodation and accommodating are basic tenets of being human. Accommodations are granted every day by every human because we all have different ways of getting our needs (or even preferences) met. When we ask for someone to give us directions, or to withhold a certain ingredient, we are asking for an accommodation. When we tell someone we are going to be late, we are asking for an accommodation. (Or when we don't communicate it and just show up late, we are expecting an accommodation.)

As humans, we accommodate others and ask others to accommodate us. Accommodations support our humanity. Denying necessary accommodations to people with disabilities is to deny meeting basic human needs. Reasonable accommodations and other rights granted by law are not giving special treatment to the disability community; they are simply basic human rights already granted readily to others that had long been withheld from people with disabilities.

As long as fear-based stigmas take precedence over fact, perception and treatment of disability won't change. Even laws that are meant to ensure improved treatment and inclusion of people with disabilities are ineffective so long as those in charge of abiding by and upholding the law are led by stigma.

Disability and Self-Perception

Past views of disability inform the current debates and issues that affect people with disabilities including:

- Definition and classification;
- Perceived causes and prevention;
- Diagnosis and treatment;
- Rights and responsibilities; and
- Roles and representation.

Beyond the societal level, past views of disability also inform others' expectations and judgments of us on an interpersonal level.

But disability stigma does not have to inform our beliefs about ourselves. The point of this chapter is to show just how fickle and made up it all is. Is it real in the sense that it directly affects our lives? Yes. But is it real in that it is true? No. Is it real in that it is something that we need to take as fact and internalize? No.

As exhibited throughout this chapter, history reveals inconsistencies and fallacies that challenge the entire premise and validity of disability perception, beliefs, and treatment. The chapter shows how fears and societal beliefs, not fact, shape perspectives and dictate who is accepted and who is rejected. This influences even our personal identity. The purpose of analyzing and presenting how these perceptions ebb and flow through time is to clearly portray deeply embedded biases, irrational fears, and misplaced assumptions—and that we do not need to internalize them ourselves. These stigma-based beliefs projected onto us by society and those around us can easily overshadow who we are at our core, causing us to believe the distorted views ourselves.

Even if we don't believe them, we often change or hide parts of ourselves to avoid the discomfort of it all. Dismantling these faulty root beliefs allows us to reconsider our own attitudes toward disability and ourselves.

In a world that stigmatizes disability, embracing a mindset that questions, challenges, and rejects the externally imposed limitations is a bold act. Being who you are despite being stigmatized is a bold act. Choosing not to allow your perception of yourself to be limited and confined by other narratives is a bold act. While it may be scary at first, it results in a more liberated and self-assured person who can actually belong.

But how?

Now that we have effectively delegitimized disability stigma, you are better equipped to recognize and appreciate the impact that stigma has had on you at an individual level. You can identify where you have internalized stigma and where you have changed who you are to accommodate stigma. You can identify where you have allowed less than ideal treatment in fear of the repercussions of stigma, and where you have denied yourself the opportunity to belong as you are.

This is the first step in boldly being you despite all the external influences that try to change who you are. Your core is stronger than any external force.

5

Impact of Stigmas on Self

WHEN YOU AREN'T hired, included in groups, invited to parties, or given the same opportunities as others, you may start to wonder whether you aren't good enough. You may start to wonder whether it really is you that is the problem. You are the common denominator, after all. Right? Right?! Wrong. The common denominator is stigma. The common denominator is a mindset unwilling to see the value in people who look, think, move, or talk differently. But none of this means it is true. Many who don't understand the effort it takes simply to exist with a disability may believe and comment that you are exaggerating, being dramatic, being lazy, or just trying to get others to do things for you. They might even make comments about how nice it must be to receive special treatment when really all you're asking for are the basic accommodations you need to live in this world.

On the surface, you probably understand that these external beliefs are rooted in fallacy. Yet, you may internalize them and ask yourself whether you really do need accommodations or is it special treatment. Are you being lazy and should just try harder? In many ways, you start making the unwanted and dismissive comments to yourself before anyone else has the chance. In attempts to avoid these comments by others, you act as if they were true. While it makes sense to some degree as a survival tactic, it ends up hurting you more than helping. Beating yourself up like this is one of the first steps to becoming your own greatest bully.

There is a social experiment sometimes done in corporate or group settings meant to show how interactions with others affect an individual's behavior, belief about themselves, and overall demeanor. In this exercise, each person gets a descriptor placed on their back, not knowing what the descriptor is until the end of the exercise. The participants are then directed to interact with other participants according to the descriptors on each participant's back. The descriptors may range from "CEO of a Fortune 500 company" to "person who was just fired" or from "famous singer" to "person with really bad body odor." While the participant with the "famous singer" descriptor may experience people asking for photos or autographs, the "person who was just fired" may experience a lot of sympathy, judgment, or tips on what they should do next. The CEO of a Fortune 500 company may receive sales pitches, or requests for job opportunities, while the person "with bad body odor" may experience insults, disgusted facial expressions, or people staying far away from them.

It is only a few minutes into this exercise before you start to recognize the change in each participant's demeanor based on how they are being treated. The people who are getting praised, told how great they are, and always having someone wanting to talk to them start acting more confidently. Those who experience people pitying them, avoiding them, or constantly correcting them start to retreat from the group. Even though it is all based on fake personas and the participants know they are participating in an exercise, the external responses to the individual's descriptor have a very real impact on the individual's internal state. After the exercise, some are immediately able to return back to their original behavior and belief of who they are, while others remain affected by the external perceptions. This exemplifies that interactions with others, even in completely fabricated exercises, impact human feelings about the self, consciously or subconsciously.

Continuous interactions rooted in stigma can lead even the most rational and confident people to question themselves, despite logical knowledge of their worth. Not only do stigma led interactions undermine your self-confidence and existing beliefs, but they also replace them with a new belief system born from the very stigma you are trying to avoid. Rarely does this change happen consciously—it is a subtle process that eventually influences your entire reality.

Internalized Stigma

Stigma acts as a weasel that weaves its way into areas it isn't invited or welcome, yet it builds a home there. Despite being an uninvited guest, external stigma-based attitudes are eventually adopted as your own. This process is called *internalization*. While not specific to stigma, internalization occurs when any external belief system is adopted as one's own, especially subconsciously.

When you deal with stigma every day, it's impossible to not internalize some of it. It seeps in at varying degrees and in various ways, but no one avoids it completely. Internalized stigma isn't just a fleeting experience but a powerful psychological process that permeates the way you think, the way you perceive yourself within the world, and who you perceive yourself to be at your core. This faulty belief system rooted in self-stigma then affects everything from your confidence, your decision making, how you present yourself, and how you ask (or don't ask) for your needs to be met.

Just as the stigmatized beliefs of others affect their treatment of you, your self-stigma affects your treatment of yourself. To protect yourself, you do the very things that others do to you. They don't accept you, they deny your needs, they ask you to conform or hide the different parts of you to be accepted. So you don't accept who you are, you deny your needs, and you conform and hide the different parts of you in hopes of being accepted. Doing it to yourself isn't actually the self-preservation your survival brain thinks it is. It just means you are inflicting the pain on yourself instead of receiving it from others. And somehow that makes it all more bearable. By doing this, you likely don't realize that you have become your own biggest bully.

When you're first born, you act without hesitation. You are who you are. Then you start to learn and change your behavior accordingly. One of the ways you do this is by observing and then conforming to what is most acceptable to others. You identify what is most acceptable by observing what behaviors, interactions, or presentations of yourself and others receive positive versus negative feedback. This is how you learn the basic skills necessary to survive as a living being in society. These are fundamental and instinctive ways of learning that exist throughout the animal kingdom. Your brain was designed to learn from experience in this way. Except your advanced human brain isn't just adapting by learning to avoid certain behaviors that are unsafe or unacceptable; you start hiding fundamental parts of who you are in ways that actually perpetuate harm.

Impact of Internalized Stigma

The emotional and psychological impact of internalized stigma can be greater than the direct effects of disability itself. Every time you act from a place of internalized stigma, it chips away a little bit more from who you really are. It influences your self-esteem, self-efficacy, and your entire outlook on life. It often results in a distorted self-image and a false definition of your identity.

Societal stigmas and biases influence how people with disabilities define themselves, often emphasizing perceived limitations over skills or potential (Haft, Greiner De Magalhães, and Hoeft 2022). In this way, stigma shapes not just broad perceptions but the construction of individual identity. You become plagued by self-doubt, overthinking, and hesitation. Your confidence shrinks as you begin to echo the external narratives that have been imposed on you. You start to believe you are a burden. You start to believe you maybe aren't good enough. You start to believe you do need to just try harder. Maybe it goes so far that you start to believe that you are inherently inadequate and unworthy.

Perhaps you've heard from a young age that you would never be independent, so you believed it. Or maybe you strive to defy those assumptions and become hyper-independent. Maybe you've been pushed from a young age to be independent, so you believe that is where your worth lies. Or maybe you recognize the unnecessary external pressure and give up on trying to be independent.

Some people identify as a person with a disability, while others as a disabled person. Some people prefer to use another term altogether. While everyone has every right to use their preferred language in describing themselves, I believe it is important to examine why you use the language you use. Is it because it is the language that you deem most factually correct for you? Is it because you want to separate your personhood from the disability? Is it because you don't want to be grouped in with "real disabled people"? Is it because it is language that empowers you? Is it because you heard it and it resonated, not really thinking about why?

Two people can use the same language, one because of internalized stigma, one because it is most accurate to them. Two people can use opposing language with neither being rooted in internalized stigma. The *reason* for the language you choose is far more important than the specific words you choose.

How you talk about yourself matters. For years, I would not use the words "disability" or "disabled" to describe myself. Even right after a brain injury where I forgot everything. Even when I was having multiple seizures a week. Even when I was struggling in school because of comprehension and extreme focus limitations. I wasn't disabled. I was capable. I was intelligent. I was proving everyone wrong. I even got a job working with the disability community to prove I wasn't really disabled. A disabled person couldn't serve other disabled people. Right? Very wrong. Everything about how I described myself at that time was due to internalized stigma and at times flat-out ableism.

> *Ableism* is the discrimination of and social prejudice against people with disabilities based on the belief that typical abilities are superior. At its heart, ableism is rooted in the assumption that disabled people require "fixing" and defines people by their disability (Eisenmenger 2019).

Even when I got frustrated at the ableism my managers, coworkers, and friends would show toward the people I served, I would still not consider myself the same. I was successful because I treated those I served as if they were equals to me, and I truly believed it. But, I wouldn't consider myself disabled. Instead of fighting the stigma, I fought against being included in the stigmatized group. Because I was capable, I believed I couldn't actually be disabled. This stems from the belief that you can't be both capable and disabled. This is fundamentally untrue.

Denying that I was part of the disability community didn't make me not disabled. It just furthered my isolation by fueling my internalized stigma. It furthered my belief that I had to hide parts of who I was while working hard to highlight the acceptable parts. Decisions based in internalized stigma very rarely, if ever, serve us and most frequently actively harm us.

The experience of going through life with a disability can be an experience we don't know how to make sense of. It is much like the distortions made by funhouse mirrors where you are made to look nothing like who you actually are. Or the confusion of certain audio files that sound like a different word depending on what word you are thinking. Or the distorted perception that can occur when you are touched by ice but feel like it is burning. These are all experiences where perceived experience does not reflect reality but a distorted version of it. Because of the distorting impacts of stigma, you have flawed perceptions thrown on you your whole life, often exaggerating perceived flaws and diminishing actual strengths. This leads to a perpetual struggle to reconcile internal self-worth with external perceptions.

But what if you don't try to reconcile it at all? What if you just accept it's a skewed experience, so you give it no weight? You aren't going to argue with funhouse mirrors that distort your reflection. You aren't going to argue with a piece of ice that your senses perceived as a burning sensation. You may be confused, but you accept that it is a distortion. The same can be done reflecting on how you have been treated and who you actually are. You can accept that it is a distortion, not reality. Then you can define your identity separate from the faulty reviews of others.

Internalized stigma has a significant impact on not only who you believe yourself to be but also how you act and interact with the world. The following sections outline some of the most common ways that internalized stigma affects various aspects of your life, including decision making, performance, and health.

Impact on Decision Making

The impact of internalized stigma doesn't stop at your feelings about the world or yourself. Internalized stigma directly affects your decision making. You are likely all too familiar with the frustration and exhaustion that accompanies the perpetual cycle of others treating you less than, not understanding you, denying your needs, or demanding conformity. You learn to fight against it. Maybe you feel anger, maybe you feel bitterness, maybe you simply feel annoyance. But you naturally learn to adapt. To avoid continuing to feel negative feelings, you often adopt the very mistreatment others subject you to. You not only internalize the negative beliefs but also act out the harmful treatments on yourself as an act of self-protection. But instead of it shielding you from the pain, it only serves to perpetuate it.

You might withhold eating or drinking so others won't have to help you to the bathroom as often. You might not ask for accommodations at work because you think you should be able to figure it out without help. You might convince yourself that you are being lazy, so you don't let your body rest when needed, exacerbating your symptoms as a result. You might not want to ask for help to avoid showing weakness and potentially confirming others' view that you are weak. By doing these things, you deny your own needs because you expect others to deny or judge them.

Your choices, even seemingly mundane, become a reinforcer of stigma, or an opportunity to defy it. The choices you make, consciously or unconsciously, impact your relationships, personal development, success (whatever that means to you), even your joy and fun. The impact of self-stigma influences your present and future. It influences even the most basic decisions:

- To take medicine or not to take medicine? Do I judge myself as weak if I take it? Do I allow myself to suffer needlessly if I don't? Do I pressure myself to take it because of my doctor or peers? Or do I do what is best for me?
- To ask for accommodations or not to ask? Do I risk judgment by disclosing that I need adjustments specifically related to my disability? Do I convince myself just to push through? Do I accept that I probably won't get them anyway, so there is no point in asking? Or do I do what is right for me?
- To speak about my discomfort or just sit in it?
- To apply for a job or not?
- To set a goal or not?

While you may never be free from experiencing stigma, you can free yourself from letting external and internal stigma dictate your decisions.

As you become more aware of the choices you make and the reason behind your choices, you can start making decisions based on who you truly are, your needs and desires, and what is best for you instead of basing it on others' judgments, and expectations.

Impact on Performance

Your performance is subconsciously affected by not only your beliefs about yourself but also the awareness of certain stigmas or stereotypes and your desire to defy or disprove these stigmas and stereotypes.

When I initially met with a mediator after filing a discrimination and retaliation claim with the US Equal Employment Opportunity Commission (EEOC), the mediator made it clear that everyone thinks their case is good and that I needed to lower my expectations. His tone completely changed when he saw all the evidence I had including emails of discriminatory language and disparate treatment and positive reviews and praise before medical needs arising but negative reviews, criticism, and vague performance improvement plans afterward. He couldn't hide his surprise at some of the blatant discriminatory and retaliatory behaviors of my manager, including the email she sent to a project team I was leading directing them to halt all work while I was on medical leave. Halting all work caused a missed deadline, which was then blamed on me and used as evidence to support her previous claims that I do miss deadlines.

After months of fighting this mistreatment, I eventually did miss a deadline. When I admitted this to the EEOC mediator, he wasn't surprised at all and communicated that his only surprise was that it didn't happen sooner. He made it clear that performance issues developing in response to continued discrimination is standard and almost expected. With the increased cognitive load required by people experiencing discrimination, along with the increased pressure to prove the truth and keep their job, people make mistakes and performance suffers. It is not only normal but expected. After this experience, I found that research has been done on this for years showing that when we are at risk of confirming negative stereotypes or beliefs, heightened anxiety and decreased performance is a common response (Pennington et al. 2016). While this was first tested specific to racial stereotypes, the work was later replicated with many other groups who are the recipients of negative stereotypes, including those related to disability, gender, age, religion, sexual orientation, and immigration status (Steele and Aronson 1995).

Knowing you are being measured in situations where stigma and stereotypes are present results in elevated anxiety, hypervigilance, and stress. Managing increased stress requires a greater demand on cognitive resources, reducing availability for other tasks. Survival is priority. Your brain will naturally prioritize giving energy to anxiety, hypervigilance, stress, fear, and other survival-based responses.

Ideally, you leave the situations where discrimination and stereotype are present. But where you can't, becoming aware of this dynamic gives you the context necessary to mitigate these effects. There are professional athletes who learn how to reduce the stress and external pressure to expend more energy on their sport. There are speakers and singers who learn to use the energy from stress or anxiety to fuel their performance by cognitively interpreting the anxious energy as excitement (Brooks 2014). But without some cognitive intervention, your brain is going to give the resources to surviving, not to performing.

Not only does external and internalized stigma affect your performance in subtle subconscious ways, but it also affects your performance by hindering your drive, belief in yourself, desire to be around others or gain support from others, and your perceived self-efficacy.

In many ways, internalized stigma leads to a self-fulfilling prophecy. You prove that the internalized stigma is accurate every time your performance lacks. You give yourself more reason to doubt, more reason to lack confidence, and more reason to stop trying or to try harder in the wrong ways. It creates a feedback loop that will continue in a downward spiral until you become aware of it and do something to stop it.

Impact on Health

Perhaps most importantly of all for those of us who have disabilities of any kind is the impact of external stigmas on mental and physical health.

Along with the impacts internalized stigma can have on self-perception, it also can lead to increased stress, anxiety, and depression. This can result in avoidant coping and social avoidance leading to worsening psychiatric and physical symptoms. Increased stress and isolation have been proven to further increase the risk of other negative outcomes related to physical health (O'Connor, Thayer, and Vedhara 2021).

Beyond the mental impacts, you endanger your physical and mental health by stigma-led choices. You might delay your own access to medical care to avoid stigma, being considered an inconvenience, or because of a belief that nothing will help anyway. It is common to decrease in persistence when it comes to accessing medical care because of the increased effort required and decreased hope.

There is enough health inequity that you already have to deal with; you would do well to not add to it based on your own internalized stigma and resulting actions.

This chapter is not written to highlight the negatives, give excuses, or make you feel disheartened. It is simply to help you understand how you as a human are built to instinctively respond to external input. Just because it is instinctive doesn't mean it is inevitable. When you recognize your beliefs and actions aren't serving you the way you want and that you do have some control, you can act in ways that support you in overcoming your brain's instinctive inclinations.

You aren't wrong for feeling how you feel. You aren't alone in having the feelings you feel. You aren't wrong for having the results you've had. The following chapters will address how you can use this knowledge to empower yourself against stigmas and the judgments and expectations of others. You'll replace the distorted perspective you've been seeing yourself through with what really matters—who you actually are.

6

Shame

SHAME IS A bully that tells lies about your inherent unworthiness. It attacks by telling you that your needs are too much, your differences are wrong, your struggles are too burdensome. Shame is the invisible but insidious force that can make even the most resilient person question their inherent value and right to exist in this world. Shame is something that is deeply internal, and it perpetuates because it largely stays internal. By nature of what shame is, we don't talk about it. Stigma is shame-based, so any treatment from others that stems from stigma perpetuates shame. This makes you believe that you should feel shame for your disabilities, for your needs, for your differences, or for existing altogether. Maladaptive shame is a cycle. You feel shame for feeling shame, then act in a way that you deem deserving of shame, then hide it and feel more shame, and the cycle continues without an end in sight.

While writing this book, it became obvious that shame was going to be a prominent theme. I put out a call to discuss disability-related shame on LinkedIn and was hoping that I would get a few people willing to discuss such a vulnerable topic with me. Within an hour, all slots I had opened in my calendar had been booked. I then doubled my openings and those were quickly booked as well. What this showed me is that people want to talk about shame. People of various races, genders, religions, ethnicities, financial situations, and disabilities met with me and very openly discussed their experience and relationship with shame. A few things became apparent: regardless of specific circumstances, the experience of disability-related shame is largely universal. While specific disabilities and different cultures affected specific areas where people felt shame, shame at its root felt the same.

While it is inevitable to feel shame sometimes, especially as someone who has a stigmatized difference, it doesn't have to continue to be as prominent in your day-to-day lived experience. It doesn't have to be foundational to how you view yourself or navigate the world. It can be a fleeting emotion as it is meant to be in its healthy state.

Cause and Purpose

Shame is an innate emotion that supports maintaining social bonds by promoting moral consciousness, which serves to monitor and adjust behavior in line with social norms.

When you do something wrong or inappropriate, shame is an emotion that comes in to signal that you have violated a social norm or expectation and that you are at risk of losing the respect, trust, or affection of others. Like fear and anxiety, shame is an evolutionary tool.

Evolutionary tools help you to adapt to your environment, and ultimately, to survive. Unlike fear and anxiety, which signals are based on perceptions of the external world, shame is self-focused, signaling something that you have done that would harm reputation or relationships and therefore connection and survival. Healthy shame is a temporary source of distress. Social bonds are vital to survival, so healthy shame acts as a deterrent to behaviors that have potential to disrupt the social bond (Gausel and Leach 2011). In this way, shame promotes behavioral adaptation that leads to personal growth and increased connection with others. By feeling temporary shame, you are motivated to correct mistakes and apologize if necessary. You are also deterred from repeating the same behavior in the future as you know it will cause the discomfort of shame. Shame is a biological way to regulate impulses and actions in accordance with the values and norms of your social group.

Shame is necessarily a strong and uncomfortable emotion. If it weren't, it wouldn't effectively serve its purpose. But the very reason it is so effective is also why it can become so problematic. If shame lasts longer than necessary, it goes beyond prompting an immediate urge to stop and fix the action in question and becomes internalized as something not about the action but about you.

Maladaptive shame can stem from internal or external sources. Internally, it often starts with comparison. Recognition of differences is a normal and sometimes beneficial process that allows you to appreciate and benefit from trying to emulate others' areas of strength. However, using these differences as a basis for comparison to determine your own value or worthiness can often lead to feelings of inadequacy and shame.

Internal comparison can also include comparing yourself to past or idealized versions of yourself. Self-comparison can be healthy when used to recognize areas of past growth, as well as areas of potential growth. When those comparisons become a basis for self-judgment and shame, it hinders instead of helping self-growth. For example, it is common in education and work to force yourself to stay up all night to get things done. While that may be necessary once in a while, most things are not that urgent and do not take priority over your health. You convincing yourself that a made up deadline is a higher priority than sleep is a form of self-punishment disguised as productivity. The internal pressure to measure up to your own imagined standards can be equal to or greater than comparisons to and from others.

Alternatively, there is shame that stems from other people's judgments, expectations, and stigmas about mental and physical differences. There is shame prompted by others being uncomfortable by how you talk or look or act or exist. There is shame when you are criticized for needing help that can become shame around asking for help at all. External sources of shame are prominent and can lead to increased feelings of shame.

When you are constantly exposed to rejection or criticism, you start to believe that something is inherently wrong with you, which is internalized as shame. When you experience intense and painful experiences and are required to go through them alone, or when they are dismissed, or you otherwise aren't met with support and acceptance, the shame doesn't get to dissipate and move through you as intended. Instead, it is internalized. You believe that you are the broken one. You are what is wrong. Blaming it on yourself is a way for your body to make sense of all of the emotional overload and to move forward with bonding and belonging to the social groups you need in order to survive.

The alternative to internalizing shame is recognizing and admitting that those you rely on for support and belonging and safety are the ones not providing it. This would cause emotions that would threaten your sense of belonging in a different way. For this reason, it is more comfortable to blame yourself instead of others. The result is that you end up staying in places and around people who don't meet your needs, while convincing yourself that you are the problem. This leads to the belief that if you could just be a little more likeable, achieve more, present better, or somehow be more acceptable, then you may finally get your needs met. The problem with this mindset is that no amount of fixing yourself is going to resolve the real issue, because it was never a problem with you not being enough.

When you were a child and your caregivers didn't meet your needs, the way you made sense of that was by internalizing that something was wrong with you. It's not only easier to blame yourself; it is how your brain can make sense of the reality of something that doesn't make sense—that your caretakers aren't doing their prime job of meeting your needs. You then internalize the belief that it is your fault that your needs aren't met. This becomes part of your identity and drives other beliefs and behaviors.

There is a purpose for every feeling and psychological or physiological function. When used outside of the intended purpose, some of these necessary functions become problematic. Understanding why your mind feels shame can help you recognize it for what it is and not let it become more than what it was ever meant to be. You can allow it to serve you in the way that it was meant to and nothing more.

How It Shows Up

Shame permeates every aspect of life as it influences beliefs about yourself and the world, which then influences behavior, which influences relationships with others, and so on. Every time shame dictates your thoughts or actions, you solidify your belief that shame is right. Recognizing where shame shows itself is a key step in recognizing the harm and releasing the hold shame is able to maintain. Extreme anger, defensiveness, and avoidance are addressed specifically later in this chapter. People-pleasing, perfectionism, hyper-independence, learned helplessness, and a fear of being seen are addressed in detail in subsequent chapters. Here is a non-comprehensive list of some of the other ways shame shows up:

- Bullying or shaming others
- Devaluing what you have to say
- Struggling to speak up for yourself
- Being hypercritical of yourself and others
- Perceiving life challenges as personal flaws
- Choosing to struggle rather than show vulnerability
- Believing that everyone else is better than you in some way
- Shame-led self-awareness and hyper-intellectualization of flaws
- Acting overly confident and arrogant about your needs and value
- Feeling awkward when people compliment you or show they care
- Allowing people to treat you poorly because you think you deserve it

The line between healthy shame and maladaptive shame may differ depending on how long you hold on to it, and whether you are applying it to a specific action you took or to yourself as a whole. No matter where that line is for you, it shows when you act from a belief that you are fundamentally flawed or unworthy. For example, if you break a promise you made, even to yourself, healthy shame may encourage you to reflect on your behavior, take accountability, and take actions to regain trust. Even though you did something wrong, you know it can be repaired.

In contrast, maladaptive shame might remind you that you are unreliable, a liar, and not worthy of being trusted, leading you to retreat and further disconnect. It is then that it is no longer a healthy, and temporary, tool for improvement and connection but destructive. Internalized shame then gets integrated as a part of your identity influencing your beliefs, thoughts, interactions, and view of yourself through a distorted lens that says you are inherently defective.

Consequences

There is zero benefit to chronic shame. It harms your brain, your self-worth, your decisions, your actions, and your connection with others. It influences you to be someone you're not in the attempts to be someone you may not feel shame about. Except you will always feel shame because you know you are hiding something you feel shame about, which reinforces in your mind the belief that you have reason to feel ashamed. You can't shame yourself into someone you will accept.

Impact on Identity   Shame resides at the identity level. It makes you believe that you inherently are not worthy of safety, love, and connection. Even if you logically believe that you are worthy, shame keeps questioning that belief and tries to convince you it isn't true.

Chronic shame convinces you that you are struggling to change your life because you aren't trying hard enough, you aren't good enough, you aren't smart enough, you aren't capable. That is all lies. Change is hard for all humans. You aren't uniquely bad; you are just human.

Shame is not only effective at convincing you that you aren't enough. Shame can also convince you that you are too much—too needy, too intense, too particular. It tells you that you need to dilute who you are—downplaying your experiences, emotions, and needs—if you are ever going to be loved or belong. Shame may tell you that you are simultaneously too much and not enough, leading you to constantly strive to balance being more of who you think you should be, while being less of who you really are.

Shame convinces you that you don't deserve good things because you are inherently undeserving. You fear being more of you, even the best of you, because that would result in you becoming more of all the things you've been taught to feel shame around. You may believe that you don't deserve to succeed or belong. Shame makes you believe that you have to heal or change before you can truly be accepted.

It is all lies. You deserve good things. You deserve peace. You don't deserve conflict, pain, and loneliness. And you deserve good things even with all of your complexities and uniqueness. Shame is lying to you.

Impact on Physical Health   Emotions directly influence the physiological state and physical health of the body. Shame tells you that your needs aren't met because of you, which means they can't be met as long as you are you. Despite the egregious inaccuracy, the body believes it to be real, which requires the body to act accordingly. Believing that your survival is in constant threat puts an extreme amount of stress on the body as it attempts to deal with the survival threat it perceives from feelings of shame.

Prolonged or chronic shame causes an increased level of stress on the body, even more so than anxiety and fear (Dickerson et al. 2004). Cortisol and inflammation increase as a result of chronic shame as part of the coordinated psychobiological response to social threats (Dickerson, Gruenewald, and Kemeny 2004). Cortisol affects many physiological systems including glucose and metabolism, immune function, and sympathetic nervous system functioning. Increased inflammation also affects many functions in the body, and among other results can lead to lower levels of good cholesterol and higher blood pressure, both of which have adverse effects on your heart.

Impact on Mental Health   The most significant commonality in all of my interviews about disability-related shame is that nearly everyone I spoke with said some variation of that shame was their biggest bully. Shame leads you to talk to yourself and about yourself in a way that you would never find acceptable from others.

High levels of shame correlate with low self-esteem, negative self-evaluation, and feelings of worthlessness (Gross and Hansen 2000). This makes sense considering that shame is also strongly associated with depression, anxiety disorders, PTSD, and other distressing mental states (Pineles, Street, and Koenen 2006). Depression often accompanies shame because shame has such a significant impact on self-perception. Shame is also highly correlated with addiction, suicide, and eating disorders (Schaefer et al. 2018).

Simple and neutral thoughts viewed through the lens of shame become evidence of doing wrong or being wrong. Instead of simply remembering that you broke your phone because you dropped it, you blame yourself for it and wonder how you can be such a clumsy idiot. Instead of "I have a deadline on Tuesday" it turns into "I'm probably not going to meet the deadline; I never do. Why am I so bad at this?" Instead of handling a missed flight because of a wreck that closed down the highway or another external factor, you blame yourself for not planning better and see it as more evidence that you are a screw-up.

Shame shapes every thought you have and changes factual observations to further evidence of reason to feel shame. It could be the most neutral experience—saying a simple greeting while you're passing someone on the street—that becomes "Why did I say that; why can't I ever act normally. They probably think I am stupid, too." Even though you did not act abnormally to others, shame adds unwarranted opinion, judgment, and resistance to every situation.

Impact on Connection and Belonging   If you don't feel positively about yourself, it becomes more likely that you will withdraw socially, treat others poorly, or both. Shame can lead to social withdrawal, avoidance, and difficulties with interpersonal functioning (Lutwak, Panish, and Ferrari 2003). Shame is highly correlated with anger issues and aggression that can present as violence and bullying.

Shame may make you self-absorbed, believing that you are the only one to experience certain challenges. If you believed others existed with your same challenges that you feel shame about, it would threaten the existence of the shame as it wouldn't be shameful if it is common for other people to experience it, too. So your brain convinces you that you must be the only person with your certain set of shameful challenges. Except you aren't. Ever. Even if you are the only person on the planet with a specific disability, there are others who understand what it is like to not be able to find doctors who know how to treat you. Others know what it is like to have family, friends, coworkers, and acquaintances who have no idea how to treat you. Others don't need to have your exact diagnosis to experience what you experience, especially as it relates to shame.

Rejecting positive interactions such as compliments or someone being kind to you teaches those people to not behave that way in the future , which in turn reinforces your belief that you aren't deserving of the positive treatment. It also pushes the other person away.

Shame may also make you isolate yourself as you believe that is the safest option to mitigate the risk of rejection. Isolation causes an obvious barrier to connection—you can't possibly connect if you never give yourself the opportunity to connect in the first place. This will only further your belief that you don't belong anywhere.

Because you hide parts of yourself that you are ashamed of, you deny the opportunity for support and acceptance.

Fight, Flight, or Freeze Because shame poses a threat to survival by making you believe you may never belong, it initiates the fight-or-flight response. Living in a chronic state of shame means living in a chronic state of fight or flight. Fight-or-flight responses are meant to be temporary as they are hard on the body. No living thing was designed to sustain that long-term. Certain parts of the body that aren't necessary for survival start limiting functioning, while other parts of the body increase their functioning with the goal of optimizing your body to survive the threat.

In addition to the well-known fight-or-flight responses, another survival response is the freeze response—a state of physiological shutdown in response to an overwhelming and inescapable threat (Volchan et al. 2011). The freeze response is activated as a last defense effort when fight and flight haven't worked or aren't feasible. Shame keeps your body in a dysregulated state that was never meant to last long-term. Chapter 12 goes more into the impacts on the body and how you can work with your nervous system to better manage and mitigate prolonged survival responses. Here we will focus on three common external impacts of a prolonged fight-or-flight response.

Extreme Anger or Defensiveness (Fight) Anger is a common physiological and emotional response to pain, including the pain of shame. Shame is not just emotionally painful but physically, as well (Dickerson,

Gruenewald, and Kemeny 2009). Whether it is due to insecurity, a threat of bullying or exclusion, or being embarrassed, aggression is a common response. This is rooted in our most basic functioning as a fight response to real or perceived threat. When you accidentally stub your toe on a table, it is common to yell as a way to let out the aggression that came as an immediate subconscious response to the pain. Anger and aggression are tools to respond to the threat, even when there is nothing to actually fight. In these cases, anger may be directed at any available target. The primitive brain takes over ready to fight any threat to the self or self-worth.

The fight response can also manifest as extreme defensiveness to any perceived slight or critiques as a way to preemptively shield against shame. Extreme defensiveness, especially unwarranted, is ineffective and perpetuates the cycle of feeling shame for behaving in a shameful way. Instead of the ineffective reactive response, you can learn to be proactive about recognizing the fight response for what it is and, by doing so, releasing its control over you.

Extreme Avoidance (Flight)   Other times, shame triggers a flight response or an overwhelming urge to escape, withdraw, or otherwise avoid any situation that risks exposing parts of yourself that you deem unworthy. Instead of fighting the threat, you attempt to avoid it altogether in hopes of staying protected.

This can manifest as social isolation in general or avoidance of specific social activities. It isn't just people you avoid but trying new things, having new experiences, or presenting your work to others. Eventually, who you see, where you go, and what you do is reduced to the very few situations where you feel safe. But instead of being freeing, that version of safety is isolating and suffocating. Avoidance in this way stifles connection, ambitions, and potential, which further reinforces shame.

Avoidance of shame can also manifest as not taking accountability for something you actually did do wrong. No matter how (in)significant the wrong really is, any wrong prompts shame, and your mind believes addressing it will intensify the shame, so you avoid it. But that avoidance of a hard conversation only avoids a temporary perceived threat while intensifying the belief that you are worthy of shame. The shame around your wrongdoing will only dissipate if you allow for the discomfort of taking accountability and addressing it and then move forward.

Shame avoidance never successfully avoids shame but instead perpetuates and intensifies it.

Functional Freeze (Freeze)   As a result of prolonged shame that hasn't been mediated by fighting or fleeing, the body may attempt to avoid drawing attention to itself by involuntarily freezing. This reaction is known as "functional freeze" and is a psychological response like fight or flight. It can be crucial in situations where fight or flight are not possible or not advantageous. Some animals have this instinct built in, for instance, opossums, who go so far as to play dead. When the predator thinks the opossum is dead, they eventually lose interest. When the predator gets bored and leaves, the opossum has effectively survived the threat. In other situations, an animal may play dead because it is too tired to fight or isn't strong or fast enough to fight or flee. In these cases, freezing conserves the body's energy so that if the situation arises to fight or flee, the animal has conserved the energy to do so. While long-term freezing isn't a feasible reality in today's society, the body may enact an internal state of freeze that allows the body to go through day-to-day life doing only the bare minimum necessary to function.

In all of these cases—extreme anger or defensiveness, extreme isolation, and functional freeze—the very behaviors that are subconscious attempts to stave off shame end up instead compounding it. While you aren't to blame for your primitive subconscious response, you can take steps to respond more constructively. Even when it isn't a conscious choice, you can take steps to improve your response to shame. By doing so, your body won't see it as such a serious threat to survival, and the damaging impacts will be mitigated.

Stop the Cycle

You can move from internalized shame to compassionate self-awareness. Start recognizing actions, traits, or thoughts where you shame yourself. Signs of shame-rooted thoughts or judgments are "I should," self-criticisms, and comparisons. "Should" comes with inherent judgment and comparison. If it is a good thing to do, then do it because it's a good thing, not because you "should." If it is something that others think you "should" do, then ask yourself if you really want to do it. If so, do it because you want to, not because you "should." Doing it because it is a good thing or because you want to has no inherent shame. Removing "should" from your vocabulary when referring to yourself and others necessitates that you find more accurate language. That more accurate language will remove the judgment and comparison, which is a step toward removing the shame.

Recognizing when you act or think from the basis of shame is enough to inhibit the cycle from continuing. Even if shame won't allow you to do more than develop awareness, this is a significant step. And needing to focus on this step does not signify any decrease in your capability or value. There are leaders of large organizations and experts in their field, as well as recent high school graduates or entry-level employees, all whose brains require they focus on this step alone. It doesn't matter how educated you are. It doesn't matter how much money you have. A brain is a brain, and a threat is threat. If your brain perceives a threat, it will do everything it can to avoid moving toward it. Moving too fast too soon will inhibit progress instead of help it. Do what you can without judgment. Mastering awareness is enough.

If you are ready to go further than awareness, you can start developing acceptance. There will always be stigma, and there will always be an inclination to compare. If you put too much weight in external perspectives or your own judgments, you are setting yourself up to have chronic shame. Accepting that stigmas exist, that judgments are going to come from other people and yourself, and that those stigmas and judgments are not truth allows you to detach from them. Remind yourself that there is no reason to feel shame about needing or about being different or about failing. While failing may feel inherently shameful, it is not. Babies fail to walk many times when they are starting and fall over and over. When I was in rehab after my brain injury and relearning to walk, my balance was nearly as bad. We know not to judge either of those situations as a true failure but as progress to learning and growth. Every step is celebrated. Also reject the inclination to feel shame for feeling shame. Shame is a natural human emotion. Accept it as it is in order to not feed the cycle.

Recognize chronic shame for what it is—a bully. Bullies can be ignored. Bullies can be dismissed as irrelevant. You can feel compassion for the bully, knowing that they may have some shame, too. That compassion doesn't allow it to continue but maybe will stop you from being a bully in return. After you develop awareness around where shame shows up for you, accept it—both the shame and the thing that prompted the shame. Breathe. Reach out to someone if you need to. Start to recognize any patterns of what initiates feelings of shame and accept those patterns.

Meet yourself where you are, accept that you feel shame, and allow self-awareness, self-acceptance, and self-compassion. If you resist that belief that you are deserving of self-acceptance and self-compassion, recognize and accept that it is shame that says you don't deserve it. Recognize and accept that your feelings are a natural reaction, and remind yourself of this as many times as you need.

Whatever feelings you have, there are biological reasons for them. That they are a natural reaction does not mean you have to act on them, but it isn't helpful or accurate to judge feelings as good or bad when feelings are the brain's response to input. Initial feelings are outside of your control. It is what you do with those feelings and how you respond after the fact that you can aim to improve.

As you develop awareness and acceptance around when you are acting or thinking through the lens of shame, you can start to differentiate between where you are shaming yourself because you want to do better and where you are shaming yourself because of external input. You can start to differentiate between where you are shaming yourself for things that really don't matter and where you are shaming yourself for things that do have an impact on your life and those around you. If the things you are shaming yourself for don't really matter, or if it is because of others' input, you can stop putting so much weight on those things. If the things you are shaming yourself for do matter or you want to improve upon, ask yourself if you can change them. If not, your goal is to accept them. If you can change them, your goal is to start as small as necessary to make change. These changes are not because of shame; they are simply taking action on the areas that you want to improve and dismissing the areas that don't matter, while accepting the things you can't change.

You can start to give your brain a new truth. Having needs is not anything to be ashamed of. Others' inability to meet your needs is not evidence that you are undeserving of getting your needs met. It may be because others don't know how to act, which can be resolved by you advocating clearly for what you need. It may be because of others' bias, which reflects a flaw of theirs, not yours. It could be because the person doesn't like you. Whether it is due to preference or prejudice, their dislike shows an incompatibility rather than anything inherently undeserving about you. While it isn't your fault that your needs weren't met as a child, and it isn't your differences that are at fault now, there are things that you can do. Recognize it isn't your fault. Recognize when there is something you can do to make the moment better and times when the best thing to do is leave. Recognize where there is a shame-inducing pattern that you can eliminate from your life. If it is a pattern of behaviors, stopping shame about the behavior will go a long way to allowing you to stop the behavior. If it is another person or environment that you can't eliminate, look at what you can eliminate. Can you eliminate the topic that sparks shame? Can you eliminate in-person interaction and utilize email or another form of communication instead? Does having someone else present reduce the feelings of shame? What can you eliminate and what can you do to accommodate those situations that you can't eliminate?

Some other actions you can take to reduce shame and its influence in your life:

- Shame will persist if it is kept internal, so finding somewhere to share it is important in releasing the shame and freeing you from it.
- Address maladaptive shame regulation: isolation, anger, drugs, alcohol, shaming others, etc.
- Remind yourself that you aren't morally or humanly inferior because of differences.
- Practice the things that bring you shame related to your disability:
  - Do nothing for periods of time intentionally if you have shame around needing rest.

- o Ask for your needs to be met if you have shame around needing.
- o Use your mobility device if you have shame around needing something that others don't.
- Be prepared to stand up for yourself to others and yourself when someone attempts to shame you. Like anything learned, it is a process that becomes easier the more it is done.

Stop being your own biggest bully. What are the things bullies do to you that impact you the most? Don't do those things to yourself. How would you prefer others to treat you? Give that to yourself.

Do you tell yourself, "Just get over it" or "Stop being so stupid"? Do you constantly ask yourself why you are such a screw up or why you can't get anything right? You aren't alone. People at every stage of life talk to themselves like this. People who you'd think of as successful, kind, and intelligent talk to themselves like this. You aren't alone in battling with yourself. Thoughts are not facts. You don't have to believe them. The difference between confidence and self-perception isn't your achievements, intelligence, or appearance but how you view, talk to, and treat yourself.

The best long-term solution to free yourself from the confines of shame is to know who you are free of shame and then to be who you are. The biggest shame is the shame in not being who you truly are— the pain of hiding your true self. Alternatively, when you know who you are and intentionally live as who you are, you are less able to be manipulated by shame and are no longer going to use shame as a primary driver of your actions.

You may not remember who you were before shame. That is okay. You are still you. Removing the shame will allow all the shame-based pieces posing as you to fall away. Part I is all about deconstructing faulty beliefs so that in Parts III and IV you can reconstruct your identity free of the detrimental impacts of shame. You are worthy of connection, you do not need to be someone else to be worthy of connection, and you are not deficient because you are different. As pervasive as shame can be, it is not an inevitable companion. Because you, with all your complexities and uniqueness, deserve to, and can, belong.

7

People-Pleasing

PEOPLE-PLEASING STEMS FROM a belief that your sense of safety and security is dependent on pleasing those around you. It is linked to sociotropy, a personality trait defined by a strong need for social acceptance to the point of forgoing your own desires to do what pleases others (Satô and Gonzalez 2009). At a surface level, people-pleasing manifests as prioritizing others' comfort, preferences, and expectations at the expense of your own needs or desires. The choices you make are dependent not on what is best for you but what will get the most acceptance from those whose opinions you prioritize over your own.

At a deeper level, people-pleasing is externally sourcing your sense of self and self-worth. Instead of cultivating internal acceptance and validation, you subconsciously make your value and identity dependent on the acceptance and validation of others. It is seeking approval for your permission to exist. Except it isn't seeking for permission *to exist as you are*. Instead, it is asking if you give enough, if you change enough, are you then acceptable? You end up looking externally to learn how acceptable you are and, therefore, how to exist at all.

People-pleasing behavior results in hypervigilance around others' needs, preferences, and feelings. This requires that you neglect meeting or even being aware of your own needs, preferences, and feelings. To avoid abandonment, you end up rejecting and abandoning yourself. In doing so, you suppress who you are to become what will be accepted by others, even if that means sacrificing a better version of you. While you may gain a false sense of acceptance, you eventually lose your sense of self.

Cause and Purpose

People-pleasing is one of the many survival skills that has its roots in shame. It is often the result of learning that it isn't okay for you to be you and that you can make up for who you are by focusing on making others happy or comfortable. It's learning that others' comfort around your disability or differences is more important than you and your needs. It's learning that if you give above and beyond to others, they won't feel as inconvenienced when you need their help. It's learning that it is your job as the disabled person to adapt to the world and the people around you instead of the other way around. It's learning that it's the appropriate response as the one who is different to be gracious when people's intentions are good even when their actions are not.

It's not just recognizing that these are real patterns in life but internalizing those patterns as evidence that you are fundamentally unacceptable as you are. It is internalizing that you are the problem or the thing that needs to change for others. As a result, you consciously or subconsciously believe that the only way to be accepted is by people-pleasing.

Everything you do is to seek reward and pleasure and to avoid pain. This includes pleasing others, which is an automatic animalistic behavior. When your brain detects that someone else is happy from an action that you took, it encodes their happiness as a social reward that motivates you to keep doing that behavior. On the other hand, when your brain detects someone's unhappiness or disapproval with you or your actions, that response acts as a deterrent. Social rewards are a fundamental and necessary biological process that teaches you what actions help you stay an accepted member of the group. Pleasing others is a good thing and necessary for inclusion, connection, and survival.

However, acting out pleasing behaviors beyond what is necessary for genuine connection often comes into play as a result of low self-esteem, extreme fear of rejection, and a lack of internal validation. This is often the result of dismissed needs, lack of acceptance, and at times real threats to safety. This combination creates the insatiable desire for external validation. The belief that being accepted is dependent on pleasing others is solidified every time you receive external validation as a result of people-pleasing (or rejection for a lack of people-pleasing).

Another reason for pleasing behaviors beyond what is necessary for genuine connection is a desire to avoid the unexpected, unknown, or uncomfortable. This is often the result of chaotic environments and unpleasant and unexpected responses to you being you. This combination can lead to a subconscious need to control the situation, including others' emotions. The comfort that comes from a sense of control solidifies your desire to control every time someone is happy instead of annoyed, or complimentary instead of judgmental. While this is a less obvious reason, it is just as common as people-pleasing for validation. Most often, the two go together. Even if you don't outwardly seem controlling, attempts to manipulate someone's feelings by people-pleasing is an attempt to control, even subconsciously.

People-pleasing, even to the point of self-destruction, wouldn't exist if it didn't serve you somehow. It provides a sense of safety and security when you feel needed, useful, and validated by others. It gives comfort when you avoid rejection, disappointment, or other negative feelings from others. It gives feelings of peace, acceptance, and validation, even if temporary.

It becomes problematic, however, when pleasing others takes priority over your own basic needs. At this point, people-pleasing becomes a counterproductive survival skill. It is now serving as your go-to response not just to build long-term connection and to get your needs met but to avoid any short-term pain and discomfort that may arise from others' unhappiness, disappointment, or rejection.

How It Shows Up

People-pleasing isn't only saying yes when you want to say no or always doing what others ask of you. It can present itself as a myriad of behaviors, many appearing admirable. The individual actions on their own are not a problem. The problem arises when it comes at the expense of your own needs, goals, and desires. Even the seemingly admirable traits will eventually erode your identity and self-worth when used primarily to gain acceptance and validation.

Here is a non-comprehensive list of the various ways people-pleasing shows up in our actions:

- Validation seeking
- Lack of boundaries
- Control seeking
- Constant need for approval
- Overcommitting
- Telling others it's okay when they mistreat you
- Valuing others' opinions over your own beliefs and knowledge
- Difficulty saying no
- Blaming yourself for everything
- Emotionally suppressing to protect others' comfort
- Giving into social pressure when you know you don't want to
- Feeling responsible to keep those around you happy
- Making jokes to make someone else feel okay about how they treated you
- Staying in a job you don't want because it's what your parents expect
- Neglecting personal needs but constantly giving to others
- Shifting your schedule to accommodate others despite your own needs
- Not communicating your needs in order to avoid being an inconvenience
- Feeling responsible to resolve awkward situations created by someone else
- Diminishing where you did well so as not to make others feel bad

For some, people-pleasing guides every decision of every day. For others, it may be limited to certain people, certain situations, or certain moods. What makes a people-pleasing action destructive is when it is done at the expense of yourself solely to gain acceptance or positive feelings from others. While short-term acceptance may occur, it will disintegrate when you can't keep it up long term or become bitter about the relationships you have built around people-pleasing. That is what makes even good actions nonviable in fostering connection and only ensures your continued lack of acceptance.

Consequences

Despite being rooted in survival, people-pleasing to the extreme is self-destructive. In trying to please everyone, you deny others and yourself the chance to understand, accept, and appreciate who you genuinely are. While aiming to please may initially seem like the right move, its long-term effects are detrimental to self-worth, authenticity, physical and mental health, and genuine connection with others.

Impact on Identity   People-pleasing requires you to morph yourself depending on what you believe others want you to be instead of who you are. This requires convincing yourself that you aren't valuable enough on your own. It further ensures that you are never recognized for who you are, only who you believe others want you to be. The opinions of others will change person-to-person, day-to-day, mood-to-mood—they are irrelevant and fleeting metrics. Using the opinions of others as the scale to judge yourself is a recipe for low self-confidence and never being who you actually are.

The more you prioritize others over yourself, the more natural it becomes to suppress and abandon who you are. Eventually, it is more natural to be one of the many curated versions of you, depending on any given situation. These curated versions further confuse your identity. You may not know your likes, your dislikes, you needs, or what brings you joy. Who you are is so dictated by others that you lose your sense of self.

People-pleasing requires you to pay more attention to the cues of others than the cues given by your own body. Consistently neglecting your own needs shows yourself that even you aren't a safe person for you (Wouters-Soomers et al. 2022). When you change your opinions dependent on others, you confirm to yourself that you can't be trusted and must look to external sources for answers. This directly leads to a lack of self-trust (McLeod and Sherwin 2000).

When you always are the one to change, you first look to yourself as what is wrong in any situation. Instead of looking at the external changes that may be necessary, you primarily look at where you may be at fault. When it is an external change that is required, you are unlikely to see it because you are too busy blaming yourself. Then the problem doesn't get fixed, reinforcing your belief that you are at fault.

Impact on Physical Health   Neglecting basic needs such as sleep, food, exercise, and rest very obviously impacts physical health, yet when done in the name of serving others it somehow gets confused for a positive thing. (Hint: it's not.) Eventually, neglecting your physical needs leads to not recognizing your physical needs, requiring your body to have more extreme warning cues. For example, when you don't listen to hunger pangs long enough, you will eventually get dizzy, then nauseous, and if you still don't eat, you will pass out. Do this consistently, and the stress on your body increases further, leading to more severe ailments.

Beyond neglecting physical needs, suppressing your own feelings while taking on the responsibility of others' emotions adds a less obvious impact on your physical health. Suppressing your own feelings keeps your body in a state of chronic stress making your body systems more vulnerable to flares or relapses (Richards and Gross 1999). Taking on the stresses and feelings of others adds to what your already maxed-out systems are attempting to handle. These factors add to the reasons that many people-pleasing behaviors have been proven to negatively affect heart disease, autoimmune disorders, gastrointestinal issues, memory, focus, headaches, and so much more (Booth-Kewley and Friedman 1987).

Impact on Mental Health   By pushing yourself to be someone you're not, you cultivate feelings of internal conflict, self-resentment, inadequacy, and a lack of confidence. You set others up to have unrealistic beliefs and expectations about you that they believe are perfectly realistic. This creates self-induced stress as you constantly strive to live up to those unrealistically high views of you. How can you not be worried or anxious when using others' feelings and expectations to dictate your own? Even subconsciously, there is a constant anxiousness and worry about rejection, about misunderstanding or being misunderstood, or about not being enough. There is anxiousness and guilt when you can't help or fix someone else. The more energy you prioritize on making others happy, the less energy you have to spend on yourself. It is no wonder that depression is highly linked to sociotropy (Lester and Dadfar 2022). Burnout becomes inevitable. Guilt just for being yourself is common. Happiness (or any other positive emotion) becomes nearly impossible. Even if you do manage to feel happiness, it is dependent on others remaining happy or being okay with your happiness.

The solution is letting go of others' judgments, but you can't because people-pleasing is dependent on being hyperaware of others' judgments. It is a cycle that keeps feeding itself. (See Chapter 20 for more on how to tune out others' judgments.)

Impact on Connection and Belonging   Beyond making it impossible for others to know or accept the real you, people-pleasing further complicates connection and belonging. People-pleasing often results in breaking trust with others and yourself. For example, when you over-promise and underdeliver you are seen as unreliable. When you don't speak your thoughts or opinions, others eventually realize they don't know when your compliments or critiques or anything that you say is sincere. It is a recipe for not being trusted and further adds to the lack of trust in yourself (Smith 2023).

People-pleasing directly impedes communication. By not wanting to offend, many requests end up being so convoluted that they are confusing for all. As part of my disability accommodation consultations, I offer to review and provide feedback on clients' written accommodation requests. Most often, they are trying to soften and justify their request so much that it isn't clear what they are asking, what they need, or why. This communication leads to results that are less than ideal, leaving you to wonder what you did wrong when you tried so hard to do it right. You are asking for subpar results by focusing on how to make the other person comfortable instead of how to most effectively communicate your need. (See Chapter 18 for tips on how to effectively self-advocate.)

A consistent habit of people-pleasing sets you up to be seen as rude when you do finally speak your mind, stand up for yourself, or simply assert a preference or question that you have. When people aren't used to that style of communication from you, they may be startled. This can be especially problematic in a new workplace or in a new relationship when the tone you originally set is one of acquiescence. The other party may not take you seriously when you voice a concern or disagreement because it isn't the "you" they've known. Or they may think you've changed and judge this new you.

When you wait too long to set boundaries in the name of people-pleasing, standing up for yourself in any way often comes off as too extreme after days or weeks or years of pent-up frustrations. Bottling up emotions makes them stronger (Chervonsky and Hunt 2017). Bitterness and resentment build because you know you aren't being accepted despite all you are doing and giving up for others. The problem is, they don't have a chance to accept you or to appreciate all you are giving up because there is no way for them to know.

Overall, relationships become one-sided, and you feel used and taken advantage of. The other person doesn't know if they can trust you, you can't trust yourself, and it sets up all parties to experience disappointment, confusion, or anger. This only reinforces your beliefs that you can't receive care and love unless you engage in people-pleasing more effectively next time.

By constantly seeking to please, you erode your own sense of belonging. Even when you seem to belong, the question lingers if that would still be true if they knew the real you.

Stop the Cycle

The first step to breaking the cycle, and the whole point of this chapter, is to bring a deeper awareness. Awareness includes what people-pleasing is and what it looks like for you, as well as where pleasing is a healthy connection tool in your life and where it is harmful. As you determine whether and when pleasing is maladaptive, it is also important to develop awareness around the impacts it is having on you. Developing awareness does not mean developing shame or blame for acting in people-pleasing ways. Even when pleasing is harmful, it stems from a natural biological process to survive based on what you experience and understand. You aren't to blame, yet you can still improve.

The second step is acceptance with self-compassion. Even if you don't feel deserving of compassion, you are. You have just been doing what you know to do to exist and survive.

Practice compassion on yourself every time you become more aware. Practice kindness and celebration of growth and learning. When you recognize guilt, blame, and shame as they arise, you can practice kindness and celebration of growth and learning instead of sitting in it. You have reason to be proud of yourself for every moment of awareness. Awareness is change. Even with no other change, awareness is enough to celebrate. Even without any outward action, awareness is action enough to catalyze change.

Then when you decide to start taking different actions, you can address the inevitable fear that comes with letting go of a survival skill. Breaking free from the cycle of people-pleasing requires breaking away from dependency on others' judgments for safety. It involves embracing and expressing your true self, even if it means risking initial discomfort or surprise from those accustomed to your people-pleasing behavior. This will threaten your perception and feeling of safety. Luckily, your brain is adaptable, and you can retrain it to feel safe working toward connection and belonging in a more effective way. The rest of the book shows you how.

With awareness and compassionate self-acceptance, you will begin to take action. You can start discovering and asserting your personal needs and preferences. You can start setting boundaries and saying no. You can start prioritizing your well-being despite guilt and eventually without guilt. There are going to be people who are uncomfortable or upset, but you can practice letting them have their emotions without taking it on as your responsibility to fix. It is going to be uncomfortable. But it is uncomfortable now, anyway. Every time you push through the discomfort of choosing to not do people-pleasing, you increase your ability to withstand that discomfort for a greater goal.

Thought or Journal Exercises

- What does helpful pleasing vs. harmful people-pleasing look like for you?
- When do you prioritize people-pleasing at the expense of your own needs?
- How can you have compassion for yourself as you gain awareness?

8

Perfectionism

PERFECTIONISM STEMS FROM a belief that you can minimize inadequacy and harsh judgment, therefore qualifying for safety and security, if you are perfect. It is a belief that your value, and therefore your acceptance, is conditional on your output or appearance. This includes the belief that failure, lack of quality, and anything less than perfect reduces your value.

It may seem on the outside like you are striving for excellence or pushing yourself to be your best, but it is more accurately described as avoiding looking weak, flawed, or imperfect. Like people-pleasing, the action on its own isn't inherently damaging and can be beneficial. People who hold themselves to a high standard regardless of external rejection or approval typically have positive emotions around high achievement and hold themselves to high personal standards, pushing themselves to be their best. This is self-oriented perfectionism and is less harmful. Then there is socially prescribed perfectionism, which completely revolves around meeting your own or external standards with the goal of gaining acceptance or avoiding negative judgment from others. It is perfectionism based on what others think. Like people-pleasing, it becomes more problematic when others' perceptions are the motivating factor at the risk of neglecting yourself. Most people who are different, especially due to disability, have learned some level of socially prescribed perfectionism.

Like people-pleasing, perfectionism is externally sourcing your sense of self and self-worth in a way that is unattainable. Being perfect according to others' judgments is impossible. Avoiding failure is impossible. You aren't perfect on day one of anything, and it takes imperfection to get to be the best. Even then, the best of any field aren't perfect at their craft. It is seeking to attain perfection to prove to yourself and others that you have value. It is seeking to be perfect to avoid failure. It sets you up to never believe you have value because you will never be, and can never be, perfect. You never will, and never can, avoid failure.

Cause and Purpose

Perfectionism is another defensive mechanism rooted in shame. It is often the result of learning that you aren't enough but that you can receive acceptance when you achieve enough. It's learning that others' acceptance of your disability is dependent on what you can offer them. It's learning that if you appear perfect enough, they won't see you as less than for your disabilities. It's learning that it is your job as the disabled person to prove your worth instead of just being accepted as a human worthy of existing.

People with certain disabilities, especially mental differences, are especially likely to be perfectionists. You're likely told to try harder, do more, stop complaining, don't quit. You likely learned from an early age to value perfection and to hide weakness. Maybe you found success in working harder, but maybe you didn't, so you found that if you were perfect in in a different area, you would be less criticized for your mental differences.

Perfectionism is another result of our brain seeking reward and pleasure and avoiding pain. It is painful to be told that you didn't try hard enough, that you need to be more like your sibling, that if you just stopped making excuses, you would succeed. It is rewarding to get good grades, a promotion, a medal, or even nice words.

Perfectionism, even to the point of self-destruction, also wouldn't exist if it didn't serve you. Whether pain or pleasure, our brain records it as such so you know what to avoid doing and what to keep doing. Being motivated by good performance is a good thing and necessary for survival.

Perfectionism is a hope-based mindset that you can do better and that if you do better, you will finally be enough. It gives a reason to keep moving forward. It provides a sense of acceptance when you excel instead of being viewed as less than. It provides validation and comfort when you do perform well enough.

It becomes harmful when perfectionism sets you up to never view yourself as successful. It becomes harmful when you deny and neglect your needs because you can't admit to or accommodate perceived weakness. Perfectionism is a counterproductive defense mechanism that increases your belief of not being enough instead of ameliorating it.

How It Shows Up

Perfectionism can look like someone who has no obvious flaws physically, professionally, or socially. Or it can look like someone who never looks put together physically, professionally, or socially. It can be someone whose house is always perfectly clean with the smell of fresh flowers and perfect vacuum lines, or it can be someone who doesn't clean at all because there is no point when it can't be done perfectly. It can be someone who stays up all night perfecting their project and then still apologizes for it, or it can be someone who doesn't get it perfect so doesn't submit it at all. Both can be equally problematic on the psyche. Even the seemingly admirable traits associated with perfectionism undermine your happiness, as the pursuit of perfection is impossible and inevitably leads to stress, burnout, and dissatisfaction.

Below is a non-comprehensive list of various ways perfectionism shows up in our actions:

- Inability to delegate to others
- Not admitting that you are struggling
- Trying to excel to an unrealistic degree
- Not trying at all if you can't do it perfectly
- Never being happy with what you produce
- Not asking for help when you are struggling
- Not admitting that you need accommodations
- Judging yourself against impossible standards
- Being hard on yourself for being hard on yourself
- Saying you completed something when you didn't

- Not using noticeable assistive devices when needed
- Hiding your weaknesses, imperfections, or mistakes
- Not learning new skills because you can't do it perfectly
- Being equally perfectionistic regardless of whether the situation requires it
- Not learning new skills (such as sign language or assistive tech)
- Avoiding self-care tasks because they can't be done perfectly
- Giving up on the whole day because you were late waking up
- Apologizing for imperfections no one noticed or commented on
- Not applying to a job because you don't have the perfect résumé
- Judging yourself according to what you can do on your best days
- Avoiding social situations where you fear interacting imperfectly
- Feeling embarrassed of anything that isn't perfect or high enough quality
- Canceling on an event because you don't look or feel perfect enough
- Calling in sick to work or school when you don't have a project perfect yet
- Submitting something late or not at all rather than something imperfect but on time
- Avoiding new experiences or opportunities (such as a job or a relationship)
- Prioritizing getting something perfect over basic needs such as sleep and food
- Avoiding necessary medical care or therapy because you see them as admission of imperfection

The individual actions on their own are not always perfectionism and not always problematic but become damaging when done with a perfectionistic mindset at the detriment of one's own well-being, self-esteem, and personal fulfillment.

Consequences

Despite being a defense mechanism, perfectionism can be self-destructive and has long-term impacts on self-worth, physical and mental health, and connection with others.

Impact on Identity   Perfectionism continues to perpetuate the belief that you aren't good enough as you are. It requires you to give more than you have to give. Perfectionism requires convincing yourself that you aren't valuable enough as the imperfect and flawed human you are. It further ensures that you are never recognized for who you are, only for what you do and who you believe others want you to be. What is viewed as perfect will change person to person, situation to situation, and trend to trend—they are irrelevant and fleeting metrics. Using the opinions of others as the scale to judge yourself is a recipe for low self-confidence and never reaching your potential.

Impact on Physical Health   Physical health is directly affected by perfectionism, and the effect only increases if you have a disability, including neurodivergence. Because perfectionism results in extra stress on the body, it increases the risk for any stress-related diseases including certain cardiovascular and immune system disorders. Stress as a result of perfectionism also increases the risk for flare-ups. It increases the likelihood of seizures if you have them. It decreases the level of stimulation you can tolerate.

Perfectionism often means avoiding doctors or being dishonest with doctors about your lifestyle and ailments to avoid showing imperfections. It often means being oblivious to or lying to yourself about certain behaviors and the impact you are having on your own health. It may result in not wanting to take certain medications, especially those prescribed to support mental functioning, because you have excessively high standards for yourself. Perfectionism makes you more susceptible to substance abuse as a means to achieve the excessively high standards you set for yourself, or as a means to cope with the inability to meet those excessively high standards.

Social disconnection is a common result of perfectionism, which has further adverse impacts on your health, including increased blood pressure, increased stress and stress hormones, and impaired immune function. Social isolation compounds the effects that come from perfectionism alone.

By striving to be perfect, you end up impeding your ability to thrive at all.

Impact on Mental Health Perfectionism has strong links to pathological worry, anxiety, and extreme self-criticism, leading to low self-confidence and self-efficacy. Anyone living it knows this to be true, but multiple studies show that perfectionism and disability together predict depression. It doesn't just have a higher correlation but actually predicts depression, especially at high levels of disability (Smith and Arnett 2013). Perfectionism is linked as an antecedent to some personality disorders and has strong links to eating disorders and substance abuse disorders. Perfectionists have a decreased ability to effectively cope with even basic life inconveniences.

Perfectionism leads to both objective and subjective social disconnection. Objective social disconnection is an absence of social interactions, often by choice to avoid rejection and criticism from self or others. Subjective social disconnection is feelings of loneliness and isolation. It arises from a hyperawareness and hypersensitivity to other people's reactions, reading innocuous comments and actions as critical or rejections. The feelings of loneliness and isolation lead to feelings of social rejection and exclusion even when it isn't the reality. Regardless of the feeling being based in truth, they are equally consequential. Both objective and subjective social disconnection negatively affect our mental health, but subjective social disconnection is a significantly stronger predictor of negative health.

Impact on Connection and Belonging Perfectionism makes it nearly impossible to connect with others because you are constantly judging yourself, and possibly others, on what you could be doing better. You also are likely hypersensitive to others' judgments or perceived judgments of you, causing a distorted belief around others' perceptions of you. As an example, while writing this book, my editor told me my writing was great after I sent chapters I thought were horrible (only because they weren't perfect). Despite him never having been anything but factual and direct, I didn't believe his words. It had nothing to do with his perception but mine. And nothing that he said could have made me believe he thought those chapters were good, because I myself didn't believe the chapters were good.

Perfectionism makes it nearly impossible to be present in the moment or feel as if you belong because you don't even feel like you belong yourself. If you can't be open about your failures, inadequacies, and insecurities, you keep a wall up that doesn't allow for connection. It also makes you unrelatable to others who don't see their humanity reflected in you. It also makes it difficult for others to support you when you won't show that you need help because it means showing your imperfections. This not only hurts you and your perception of the support and connection you have from others, but it also makes you a frustrating, sometimes impossible, person to work with. You won't believe the positive feedback when it doesn't match your perception but you are often overly sensitive to the negative feedback. It is a lose-lose for people who want to be there to support you as it impedes or even blocks their ability to support. The perfectionism is a stronger driver of your beliefs about others' perceptions of you than their words, actions, or actual perceptions of you.

Stop the Cycle

As you develop awareness of what perfectionism is, where it originates, and what it looks like for you, it is also important to be able to distinguish between where perfectionism is a healthy tool in your life and where it is harmful. Where it is helpful or harmful depends on the motive as well as the impacts it is having on you. Having perfectionist tendencies does not mean that you are wrong or to blame, yet you can still improve.

After developing awareness around how perfectionism presents for you specifically, the second step is compassionate self-acceptance. It is going to be really easy to judge yourself as "wrong" from a perfectionistic mentality every time you recognize yourself engaging in it. Instead, aim to practice compassion with yourself every time you become more aware. Practice kindness and celebration of growth and learning. Recognize feelings of failure, inadequacy, and shame as they arise, but don't sit in it. Be proud of yourself for every moment of awareness. Even with no other change, awareness is enough to celebrate.

As you start to move through awareness and acceptance, you will naturally start to choose different actions. You will experience inevitable fear and discomfort that comes with letting go of a survival skill. Breaking free from the cycle of perfectionism requires breaking away from the fear of being rejected for imperfection, as well as the fear of not achieving what you believe you are capable of. It involves embracing and expressing your humanity—flaws, mistakes, and failures included. The discomfort will threaten your perception and feeling of safety. But your brain is adaptable, and you can retrain your brain to feel safe working toward your goals in a more effective way.

As you want to take different actions, start first in your mind by thinking what you care to do when it isn't about output or appearance. You can start trying and improving in (and failing at) new activities and skills. You can start prioritizing your joy and value. Start submitting things you know are imperfect. Start trying new things to fail on purpose. Realize that not everything is there to be perfected, but some things are there simply to experience joy, connection, and humanity. Prioritizing perfection removes much of the fun, joy, and peace that life can have, while releasing perfectionism as a maladaptive survival skill allows you to garner more joy and connection.

Thought or Journal Exercises

- What does self-oriented perfectionism vs. socially prescribed perfectionism look like for you?
- When do you prioritize perfectionism at the expense of your own needs or wants?
- How can you have compassion for yourself as you gain awareness?

9

Learned Helplessness

LEARNED HELPLESSNESS STEMS from a belief that nothing you do will change the outcome, so there is no point in taking any action. It occurs when a traumatic event or persistent failure to succeed results in a sense of powerlessness. It is a belief that the state of your life is inevitable, and any effort is a waste. It's a belief that no matter what you do, positive change won't happen and negative things will continue. It is summed up by the belief that there is no point in trying.

There is objective and subjective helplessness. Objective helplessness is when regardless of your action, the circumstance is truly unaffected. Subjective helplessness is the belief that you have no control over the outcome even when there is something you could do. In a world that has barriers, inaccessibility, and ableism, it is easy to believe there is nothing you can do to improve your outcome. While there are some things you really can't control, the problem arises when you believe that to be true for areas that are within your control.

Learned helplessness isn't just outsourcing your power; it is completely giving it up altogether. It is not hoping for or believing in better. It is believing that better might be possible for others but not for you or your situation. It is believing that where you are in life is because of ableism, inaccessibility, or disability, and there is nothing you can do to change your life until those things change.

Learned helplessness results in a lack of recognition of and belief in your own capabilities. It is surrendering to the belief that you lack control over your circumstances. This surrender leads to a continual disregard for your own skills, growth, and strengths. It leads you to disregard your ability to learn and grow and improve as you have all of your life. In seeking to avoid repeated disappointments or setbacks, you internalize a sense of powerlessness and stop recognizing your own ability to affect change. This directly impedes your ability to grow and improve in the ways you've decided are impossible. Giving into the belief that change is impossible leads to a lack of self-efficacy and stymied potential for growth.

It is a fact that inaccessibility exists—in buildings, websites, and processes. It is a fact that ableism exists—in school, health care, work, society, and within your own mind. It is very easy to believe that regardless of what you do, these things control your outcome. While these factors affect how you achieve, they don't dictate what you can achieve.

Cause and Purpose

A common anecdote told to explain learned helplessness is that of circus elephants. As babies, circus elephants are tied to a pole with a metal chain. When the elephant tries to break free, it is unable to do so. No matter how hard the elephant tries, it can't get free from the chain and pole. Eventually it learns to stop trying. That is when the heavy chain can be replaced by a thin rope. As the elephant grows, it doesn't realize that its size and strength is more than enough to break free from the measly rope, so it stays as controlled as it was when it was a baby with a chain. Despite the ability to change its circumstance, the elephant never even thinks to try.

When learned helplessness was originally theorized and tested in the 1960s, the belief was that after continued exposure to an inescapable negative stimuli, helplessness was learned (Seligman and Maier 1967). It was tested in various animals and humans with the same results showing that after consistent exposure to a negative, unpredictable, and uncontrollable stimuli, eventually efforts to escape ceased.

In other experiments, humans were given mental tasks to complete in order to escape a negative stimulus in the form of a loud sound (Hiroto and Seligman 1975). One group was given tasks impossible to solve. The other group was given solvable tasks. Then both groups were given solvable tasks. The individuals in the group who were initially given impossible tasks were less likely to solve solvable tasks. Even when the problem becomes solvable, your brain has started to believe that it isn't possible, so you stop trying.

Over time, a new hypothesis was developed and tested eventually showing that becoming passive and increasing in anxiety is the normal state when experiencing uncontrollable stressors (Maier and Seligman 2016). This occurs due to a biological reaction in the brain.

The first and most natural reflex is to get defensive in the presence of threat, thus producing fear or discomfort. However, when that defensiveness does nothing to change the outcome, our brains switch to conserving energy (freeze response) and devoting it to physiological adjustments. Not trying is actually adaptive in order to use our energy the best way possible.

The problem is that we apply this to situations where it may not be accurate. When our teachers or parents don't provide for our needs, we learn to not even ask. We then apply that to others who maybe would help, but we don't even try. Then we don't ask for accommodation in the workplace. Then we don't apply to jobs at all because we can't work without the accommodations. All because of a belief we learned years ago that there is nothing we can do to get our needs met.

How It Shows Up

Here is a non-comprehensive list of various ways learned helplessness shows up in our actions:

- Giving up easily
- Decreased motivation
- Not applying for jobs
- Perpetual pessimistic outlook
- Not asking for accommodations
- Self-eliminating from opportunities
- Give up trying to connect with friends
- Believing nothing good will happen
- Dismissing others' suggestions to improve
- Always blaming external factors for your situation
- Not trying to make new relationships or friendships

- Avoiding going to the doctor because you believe it won't help
- Self-imposed restrictions assuming incapability or inaccessibility

Consequences

Learned helplessness is one of the most consequential learned survival tactics that has significant impacts on all areas of your life. When you have internalized a belief that you actions have absolutely no impact on outcomes, it shapes your identity, mental and physical well-being, and social connection. The repercussions of maintaining this belief end up being far more significant than the situation(s) that served as the catalyst for the belief originally.

Impact on Identity   Learned helplessness affects your view of everything, including your view of yourself. You might focus on the negative aspects of yourself and believe you are always going to be like this. When you see external influences as the reason for you being the way you are, you don't look at where you can improve. You don't look at who you are. You lose a sense of who you are and your power because the external influences seemed more powerful.

Learned helplessness destroys your beliefs about your intelligence, strength, and abilities as far it relates to affecting your controlling outcomes. This leads to beliefs of ineffectiveness that turn into beliefs of uselessness. Left to fester long enough, this eventually morphs from a belief about your abilities into a belief that you are useless as a person, and you don't add benefit to others or the world.

Impact on Physical Health   Learned helplessness, like previous factors we have considered, affects physical health by elevating stress and leading to all the downstream effects that elevated stress has on the body and health. Learned helplessness leads to a lack of taking care of your body in basic ways to support your basic functioning. It leads to lack of care about being consistent with medicine, vitamins, physical activity, or socializing. It leads to a lack of initiating medical care when necessary because you don't see a point if it's not going to get better anyway. It also leads to increased isolation and loneliness, real and perceived, and all the related negative impacts on your cardiovascular and immune systems.

Impact on Mental Health Learned helplessness is strongly associated with depression and a desire to not be alive (Smith and Arnett 2013). After all, if there is nothing you can do to make your life any better, what is the point of living? That is what our distorted view very convincingly tells us. But like an adult elephant being controlled by a thin rope, the control we think someone has on us is perceived from previous events and misapplied to current events. Learned helplessness is very convincing as it stems from very real life events that you had no power to stop or change. Having it backed by fact can make us absolutely certain in our related beliefs, including hopelessness and the conviction that there is no point in trying. Learned helplessness results in very deeply held phobias, general anxiety, and low self-esteem. And there is very little others can do to change your perception, beliefs, or feelings until you see a new way yourself.

Impact on Connection and Belonging Learned helplessness affects connection and belonging most significantly by removing the hope for connection and belonging. The desire and need is still there, but if it takes effort, the hope is often not. A common belief that accompanies learned helplessness is that there is no point in connecting when it probably won't work anyway, and you're not worth it even if it did work out.

When connection does happen, there is often a lack of self-accountability for your own life that affects how open you are to accepting your part in relationships, which can negatively influence how you treat others.

The smallest sign of something not working acts as a deterrent to building connection. This can keep you from seeking or accepting support or friendship. Learned helplessness can cause you to believe you can't possibly be accepted, so you don't see it even when it is there.

Depending on what you specifically have learned helplessness around, you likely believe the very thing you want and need most is impossible whether it is being understood, being accommodated, being supported, being accepted, having a successful relationship, having someone you can trust, having coworkers who respect you, etc. If you think it is impossible, you don't seek it out and don't recognize it when it is there. If you do recognize what you believe to be impossible, you likely question its legitimacy. Your brain doesn't like conflicting beliefs, so it will either keep you from seeing evidence that you are wrong or it will make up lies that the situation isn't really what it seems to be. You have to believe in the possibility of connection and whatever else it is that you need and want so that you allow your brain to see it when it is there.

Stop the Cycle

The first step is deeper awareness around what learned helplessness is, what it looks like for you, and awareness of where retreating or accepting defeat is a healthy energy conservation tool in your life and where it is harmful—awareness of the impacts it is having on you, awareness that even when it is harmful, it stems from a natural biological process, and awareness that you aren't wrong, yet you can still improve.

The second step is acceptance with self-compassion. As you accept that you have been acting from a state of learned helplessness, you also accept that there is change that can occur. Acceptance is not to place blame but to recognize what is so that you can move toward what you desire. As you accept, practice compassion on yourself every time you become more aware. Practice kindness and celebration of growth and learning at every stage, regardless of how small or insignificant you may judge it to be. No amount of awareness or acceptance is insignificant. Recognize feelings of hopelessness as they arise, but don't sit in it. Be proud of yourself for every moment of awareness. Even with no other change, awareness is enough to celebrate.

There is going to be some fear that comes with letting go of a survival skill, the beliefs that led to it, and the actions that stem from it. Breaking free from the cycle of learned helplessness requires differentiating between a real lack of control over the outcome and a perceived lack of control over the outcome. It involves taking accountability for your own part in your suffering, even when it means discomfort. This will threaten your perception and feeling of safety. Your brain is adaptable, and you can retrain your brain to feel safe working toward connection and belonging in a more effective way.

As you move from awareness and acceptance to taking action, the first and most powerful actions are going to be in your own mind. You can start recognizing where you place blame fully on external circumstances, and instead recognize that external circumstances have an impact *and* that you also have some influence. It is true that at some point in your life, maybe even in your present, there were significant external factors that contributed to your circumstances. That is not to be denied. It just isn't fully true when applied beyond that circumstance and maybe not to the degree it was in that circumstance. Like the grown elephant who is strong enough to break free from what kept it chained as a juvenile, there are some situations where you are a different person with different strengths and more power than you were made to believe in your past. Just because it was true once doesn't mean it is true now. And just because it is true now doesn't mean it is the only truth. You have some control somewhere.

Thought or Journal Exercises

- In what situations do you recognize you have no control and stop trying as an effective energy conservation tool versus when you stop trying because you believe there is no point, even if there is?
- When do you give up meeting your own needs because you believe there is no point?
- How can you have compassion for yourself as you gain awareness?

10

Hyper-Independence

HYPER-INDEPENDENCE IS THE constant attempt to do things alone even if others could help. Whether it's to prove that you can, to protect yourself from being let down by others, or because you believe you are undeserving of help, it leaves you disconnected from yourself and others.

Relying on yourself alone requires you to disregard some of your own needs. It requires you to decide which of your needs can be delayed, which of your needs can be ignored completely, and how you can do it all anyway. Sure, hyper-independence might lead to some great creativity and problem solving, but taken to the extreme it leads to loneliness, worsened health, and an inability to feel like you belong.

There are certainly times where you have to figure something out on your own. Hyper-independence does not refer to those times— that is self-sufficiency. Hyper-independence is when you convince yourself to do it alone to prove something, to protect yourself, or to avoid showing vulnerability. That is when the behavior goes beyond beneficial self-sufficiency and becomes harmful hyper-independence. It is when you have the access and ability to seek help whether it's in person, over the phone, or via computer, but you still don't. It may be driven by feelings of pride or fear or unworthiness, but the end result is the same. You use more mental and physical energy than necessary and often for a lower quality result.

Dependence on yourself alone requires you to be highly critical of your capabilities. You justify continuing to do it alone by continuing the stories that your worth is tied to your ability to be independent, that others can't be trusted or relied on, or that vulnerability is a weakness. It requires that you continue to trust faulty beliefs of yourself, others, and society as a whole. Even if your beliefs are rooted in some truth, they have to be taken to the extreme to reasonably justify hyper-independence long-term. And any belief that can do that is faulty.

Beyond an unwillingness to ask others for help, hyper-independence also tends to include emotional detachment and avoidance of close relationships. You can't show that you need, and you can't show any situation that may even remotely give the perception of needing, so you limit sharing a significant portion of your life with even those close to you. If you are willing to share anything related to your needs, the needs are likely downplayed and dismissed to ensure the other person doesn't perceive it as needy. Hyper-independence often gives the appearance of a capable and competent person but actually is hiding an insecure and lonely person, at least in part.

Cause and Purpose

Hyper-independence for people who are disabled often comes from a necessity at some point when needs weren't met by others no matter what you did, so you developed the skills necessary to do it all yourself. In this case, it stems from learning that you are the only one you can rely on to meet your needs, so you don't ask anyone else for help to avoid being let down again.

The desire to prove that independence is not only possible but achievable to a degree that surpasses even standard independence is another cause of hyper-independence. It may stem from parents, teachers, or others telling you that you would never be independent, so you pushed to prove them wrong. It may stem from parents, teachers, or others telling you the opposite, that you can't use your disability as an excuse, and that you can do anything, even if means risking your health.

Regardless of its origin, hyper-independence is another maladaptive survival skill. It is unnecessarily attempting to prove your worth to those who underestimated you or to avoid others underestimating you in the first place. It is protecting yourself from being let down, abandoned, or hurt by not showing the vulnerability of having needs at all.

Hyper-independence on its own is one of the lesser damaging survival skills. Except it rarely, if ever, happens on its own. It almost certainly is accompanied by perfectionism, fear of being perceived, or shame. In situations where shame isn't the driving force of hyper-independence, it often is a result. If shame is a driving force, it is further exacerbated the longer hyper-independence is practiced. This is because relying on yourself beyond what is necessary to survive leads to heightened expectations and judgments of self. You start to feel weak asking for help even in areas you wouldn't have previously cared. You judge yourself as incapable if you have an off day. Instead of asking for help, maybe you suffer on those days and believe you deserve it. These beliefs aren't true. You aren't weak for asking for help. Off days aren't evidence of incapability, and you don't deserve to suffer.

How It Shows Up

Regardless of the reason, hyper-independence shows up as not asking for help or actively turning down help. This can be for both physical tasks or emotional support.

Below is a non-comprehensive list of various ways hyper-independence shows up in our actions:

- Inability to collaborate
- Not asking for accommodations
- Giving up on a task if you can't do it on your own
- Overexerting yourself to the point of medical issues
- Willing to risk physical pain over the discomfort of vulnerability
- Reluctance to share emotions, fears, struggles, and other vulnerabilities
- Impeding necessary connection in relationships by attempting to avoid dependency
- Spending extra time finding a solution that somebody else already has instead of asking them to share it
- Lost interest in partnership
- Heightened stress when depending on someone else

The line between healthy independence and hyper-independence may differ depending on your cultural norms. No matter where that line is, hyper-independence shows when you avoid asking for help as a response to ego, pride, or fear. It is then that it is no longer healthy but destructive. While it may not start out obviously harmful, it grows until you don't know how to ask for help at all, and your health and relationships suffer as a result.

Consequences

In a backward way, your motivation to be hyper-independent was originally to avoid losing connection. But humans were not meant to be independent. Your inherent need for belonging is necessary to survival. You need others. You need others to help provide sustenance and safety, to learn and improve, as well as to connect. While you may be able to live off the land alone for a period of time, the lack of connection alone will eventually negatively affect you. Humans are social animals and we gain significant benefit from connecting with others. Hyper-independence directly inhibits your ability to connect, while also affecting the other main components of health and survival.

Impact on Identity   No matter where or how it started, hyper-independence often starts out as a mere reluctance to ask for help. Left unchecked, this reluctance can evolve into a full-fledged identity where you believe you can or have to do things entirely on your own. Whether it originated from self-perception or self-protection, it was (or will be if left to continue) internalized as a fundamental belief about who you are. Maybe it is a source of pride that you are independent, or maybe the belief is that you aren't worthy of help. Both are equally destructive as they prime your brain to avoid any contradicting evidence. If you believe doing everything on your own is prime confirmation that you are independent and capable, asking for help or allowing help doesn't just feel like a weakness but it becomes a threat to your independence and capability. If doing everything alone is to protect yourself from being let down by others, your brain won't see accepting help as disproving that belief but evidence that you are about to be let down. Even if someone follows through with helping you, your brain will convince you it was a one-time event, an outlier, or luck. It won't see it for what it is.

The beliefs tied to your identity around hyper-independence will continue to ensure you stay hyper-independent, until you decide that independence can be defined by something different, something more balanced and accurate. Independence isn't the ability to do it all alone; it is the ability to ask for help when doing it alone isn't possible or isn't the best option.

Impact on Physical Health   The most obvious impact on physical health is not asking for help when your body needs it. This imposes physical risks on the body when you push your body to extremes or contort it in ways not intended that could cause injury. Not getting support also results in allowing initially insignificant issues to grow into harmful issues. For example, a mere muscle strain can turn into weeks of decreased mobility simply because you didn't ask for help doing heavy lifting.

Even when it seems only physical, the mental beliefs that lead you to being hyper-independent place undue stress on all body systems, exacerbating existing disabilities or causing new issues. Stress weakens all bodily systems making you more susceptible to disease.

Excessive reliance on self leads to burnout and stress that affect sleep, energy levels, and immune function.

Impact on Mental Health   Social support has long been proven to have a positive impact on social satisfaction in general and this effect is even stronger for people who have disabilities (Fisher et al. 2022). Positive social support improves every area of mental health, whereas a lack of social support negatively affects every aspect of mental health. While experiencing a lack of social support can be outside of your control in some ways, the lack of social support caused by hyper-independence is completely within your control.

By acting hyper-independently, you are reinforcing your belief that you don't have any support, that you can't trust others, or that you don't belong. In addition to continuing to curate false views of yourself and your world, the continued decision to act hyper-independently depletes mental capacity, leading to feeling overwhelmed and burned out.

(Burnout is often blamed on external factors even when it is a result of your own doing.)

Being hyper-independent now doesn't mean you have to stay that way moving forward. The benefits of asking for help can quickly outweigh the benefits of doing it alone. Seeking and allowing support from others after traumatic events significantly improves the recovery from the stress of that event (Calhoun et al. 2022). These are the moments that depending on the support of others would be most beneficial yet is the time it is most likely to be dealt with alone when you tend to act hyper-independently.

Impact on Connection and Belonging   While hyper-independence isn't as immediately damaging as some of the other maladaptive survival skills addressed elsewhere in this book, it can be the most detrimental of all to belonging. Some of the most effective ways to improve connection and feel that you belong are to support others and to be supported by others.

Hyper-independence isn't only outward actions but emotional hyper-independence, which means emotional distance. Denying others the opportunity to be there for you in your times of need denies them the opportunity to develop deeper connections with you. Denying yourself the opportunity to be supported by others denies yourself the opportunity to develop trust and connection with others. Being cared for and supported are two key components to social connectedness. Whether you consciously know it or not, being cared for is what you crave when you crave connection. Being cared for can start with care of your words, care of your feelings, or care of your experience. Being cared for can start with someone respecting your desire for autonomy instead of you just taking it without discussion by acting hyper-independently. You can start small and still gain significant improvement in connection. Relationships that show respect for autonomy and support of each other's needs are the relationships that have the most positive outcomes (Deci and Ryan 2014).

Stop the Cycle

Developing awareness around the fact that you may be hyper-independent is the first step to change. Start recognizing when you avoid asking for help or sharing vulnerabilities and start calling it what it is. At first, it may be very simple recognition in the moment that "I am avoiding asking for help," "I am avoiding sharing my needs," "I am choosing to do it all alone." This is enough and a good start whether the recognition stays internal or is shared.

After general awareness, you may be inclined to jump straight to changing the behaviors, but moving too fast too soon will result in resistance in the form of extreme discomfort. This extreme discomfort will be perceived by your brain as a threat, which will lead you to revert back to your old beliefs that hyper-independence is the solution. Going slow and steady will be much more effective and long-lasting.

Beyond general awareness, you will benefit by developing awareness around how hyper-independence appears in your behavior, what purpose it is serving, and how it is harming you. In the moment, awareness may advance to realizations that "I am avoiding asking for help because I don't trust people will follow through," "I am avoiding sharing my needs because I fear I will be judged as weak," or "I am choosing to do it all alone because I think I will be seen as incapable if I don't." These sources of additional awareness will build a stronger foundation to support long-term change, even when encountering inevitable resistance.

While incorporating self-compassion, you can then use the awareness you have gained to develop new and more effective ways of providing for yourself by allowing the support of others. When you start enacting these new and improved skills, you can continue applying compassion as self-judgments, fear, and insecurities arise.

If you find that a specific belief consistently arises, you can start challenging it and eventually recognizing that there is a more accurate belief. There are going to be some times where the old belief isn't necessarily wrong, so it will be accepting what is true and adding nuance that makes it even more true. For example, it is true that people can and will let you down sometimes, just as you can and will let others down sometimes. But that isn't the only truth. Table 10.1 shows other examples of faulty versus accurate beliefs.

After awareness and acceptance comes action. Practice asking for support, even if you may be seen as needy or if you may be let down. Start first with people, environments, and situations where you are safe

Table 10.1   Faulty versus Accurate Beliefs

Faulty Belief	More Accurate Belief
People will let me down if I ask for help.	People are fallible and may let me down, but I can find who is willing and reliable by asking.
Doing it alone proves my capability.	Knowing when to get outside help improves my capability.
I should be able to handle this on my own.	Seeking and allowing support from others enhances my ability to handle challenges.
Showing I need help is showing I am weak.	Everybody needs help. Admitting it and allowing it improves relatability, connection, and belonging.

whether your request is rejected or not. If you find that it is a specific situation in which you are most hyper-independent, you can identify a new action to implement next time you find yourself in that situation. Instead of taking the lead on every project at work, and doing it all alone, you can engage other people, even if it is just informing them of your plan. Then maybe you can ask them to support you in a way that recognizes and utilizes their strengths. Every step you take to be a little less hyper-independent is also a step to more acceptance of yourself and more support and connection with others.

11

Fear of Being Perceived

THE FEAR OF being perceived stems from a belief that being who you are in the proximity of others results in criticism, judgment, and eventually a lack of acceptance. At its most basic level, the fear of being perceived is a fear of being judged. It is protecting yourself from the possibility of judgment by avoiding situations where you may be criticized, misunderstood, or rejected. This may mean avoiding showing up at all, or it may mean avoiding showing up as you truly are. Any choice that may result in judgment is decided by what will be the most likely way to avoid being seen, either at all or for who you are.

At a deeper level, the fear of being perceived leads to hiding who you are by completely disconnecting from who you are. It is avoiding success to avoid being seen by more people. A fear of being seen often accompanies a fear of success. A fear of success leads to self-sabotage. The very actions that could make you more fulfilled, more understood, or more successful are the very actions that open you up to being perceived and judged on a larger scale.

Seeking to stay safe by staying limited is the common solution. Except staying protected by being limited doesn't ensure not being judged (that will happen no matter what); it just limits being judged for who you truly are. Which also means you limit being truly yourself.

Cause and Purpose

Lack of acceptance is one of the oldest signals to the brain of a lack of safety. Survival in most species says being part of the group is the key to survival. When you are laughed at, judged, and ignored, you learn to not engage in the behaviors that lead to judgment, which leads to rejection, which leads to exclusion. When you are laughed at, judged, and ignored for simply existing, you learn that not being perceived as you are is the safest way to avoid rejection.

Fearing being perceived can be learned by experiencing others doubting you so frequently that you learn to hide certain parts of yourself. It can be learned by being constantly misunderstood so you're made to feel that your natural way of being is somehow wrong. It can be learned when you attempt to mimic the seemingly acceptable behaviors of others yet still aren't accepted. It can be learned by being shamed for simply existing differently. Your brain then learns that it isn't safe to be seen at all. It may even be learned by being subjected to abuse for being who you are. This directly threatens your safety and quickly teaches you it is necessary to hide who you are to remain safe. The fear of being perceived and inevitably rejected is a result of very real threats to your acceptance and safety. The original reason for your fear is legitimate. However, the legitimacy of applying that fear generally is questionable.

Just like wild animals who hide when they are vulnerable to protect themselves from predators, there is legitimate reason for us to hide or disguise ourselves from danger at times. Some animals have built-in camouflage capabilities or other reflexes to more effectively hide. There is no shortage of evidence that hiding or disguising can be a natural and effective survival tactic. While there are times that hiding or disguising who you are is beneficial to survival, it was never meant to be applied generally. In fact, it is harmful when applied generally.

Of course, there are situations you don't know are unsafe to show who you are until you already have encountered the danger. It is this realization that leads to being hypervigilant about hiding or camouflaging due to a possible threat, no matter how unlikely. Being judged on its own is not a real threat. It may be a threat to our comfort and ego, but judgments alone aren't a threat to our safety. People will judge you in life, guaranteed. There is no way around that. No amount of hiding, no amount of success, no amount of molding yourself to fit others' expectations will protect you from being judged. Not even death will stop people from judging you. Trying to avoid this is futile and will only lead to your own unhappiness and isolation.

How It Shows Up

The fear of being perceived can show up by physically avoiding any opportunity to be perceived in the world, or it can show up by diminishing who you are with the hopes of not being noticed.

Below is a non-comprehensive list of various ways a fear of being seen shows up in our actions:

- Being extremely non-confrontational
- Self-sabotage to avoid success
- Not trying new things around others
- Not attending events you would enjoy
- Diminishing or hiding accomplishments
- Avoiding growth to avoid bringing attention to yourself
- Staying with the same "safe" environments and people, limiting growth
- Wearing more muted clothes instead of the clothes you want to wear

Hiding at times is necessary for survival. Altering presentation at times is necessary for connection, survival, and acceptance. Altering your appearance or how you interact with others may show respect for the situation or improve the likelihood of outcomes aligned with your goals. Altering your appearance or interactions, even in ways that aren't natural to you, can be beneficial. It is when you change to stay hidden out of fear when no threat is present that it becomes problematic.

Consequences

Success of any kind requires allowing yourself to be seen. Success in health requires allowing yourself and your ailments or weaknesses to be seen by experts, both to diagnose and to support healing or growth. Success in the professional world requires you to be seen in your strengths so you can be recognized, as well as in your weaknesses so you can either improve or so others can accommodate. Success and belonging in relationships is impossible without allowing yourself to be perceived by others. Being perceived comes with some valid fears, but those fears lead to what you are most afraid of—not being accepted at all.

Impact on Identity   To have a fear of being perceived means that you have internalized some variation of the belief that it is unsafe or unacceptable to be who you are. This means that you don't feel safe or accepted inside of yourself. This means that you will do everything possible to disconnect from who you are. This results in rejecting your identity. You adopt identities that are more acceptable, eventually disconnecting from your core identity entirely. It removes your ability to know and understand yourself.

Acting out of the fear of being perceived doesn't just result in not being perceived by others—it also results in not being truly perceived by yourself.

Impact on Physical Health   Like all of these survival skills, the fear of being seen requires extra energy spent on every decision, including hiding. It adds a level of stress on the body that is constant and unnatural. It likely results in you being extremely tired after any social interaction because of the energy required to constantly assess for threat. It requires you to reevaluate who you are moment-to-moment to avoid judgment and rejection.

The extra stress doesn't just show in mental and physical fatigue but also in stress on all of your systems. This means exacerbated symptoms for existing medical conditions, as well as a heightened risk for any stress-related medical condition.

If you already see yourself as being inherently defective, it is unlikely that you will be very accepting of other vulnerabilities or perceived weaknesses. This will lead to avoiding health care, pushing through physical pain and discomfort until it's so bad it can't be ignored, or dismissing your own symptoms before those who can actually help even have a chance.

Impact on Mental Health   A lack of self-acceptance accompanies a fear of being perceived and judged. This lack of self-acceptance intensifies as you continue reinforcing the belief that you aren't acceptable every time you act as if you must hide who you are. It reinforces the belief that you don't belong, that you won't be accepted, and that you are alone. These feelings are likely to result in depression or exacerbate existing depression. The act of avoiding being seen often leads to anxiety and various phobias that involve being in public or being around others. Because the fear of being perceived requires hypervigilance, you may experience a constant state of anxiety concerning potential judgments and a heightened threat response when judgments inevitably occur.

Impact on Connection and Belonging In order to meet and connect with others, you must be perceived. An obvious result of a fear of being perceived is that it keeps you from being in situations to connect with others. If you do put yourself in situations to meet and connect, you may be so hypervigilant of potential threats that your brain is primed to focus on judgments, real or perceived, while ignoring moments of acceptance. You may even feel uncomfortable when you do receive displays of acceptance or compliments because it goes against your core belief. This results in believing that you aren't accepted even when you are. It results in you not recognizing people who are showing their acceptance, interest, or admiration of you. By not wanting to be seen, you set yourself up to believe you are not accepted and don't belong.

Stop the Cycle

Increasing basic awareness of what the fear of being perceived is, where it stems from, and how it presents for you are the first and most important steps to facilitate change.

In what situations are you most afraid of being perceived? In what situations are you most likely to hide or diminish yourself to avoid discomfort? When do you alter your presentations in ways that aren't aligned with your goals or values? When do you avoid doing something because you wonder if it might be "too much"? When do you avoid going somewhere just in case someone sees you? Becoming aware that it happens and when it happens is the first step to change.

Hiding is a natural response when you have been taught that judgment and rejection are likely. Compassion and understanding for this response are necessary to move forward and change without further self-judgment. Identify the situations in which you are afraid of being perceived and what staying hidden is doing to protect you. This will help you identify more effective solutions. Are you afraid of being perceived as failing? Instead of not trying at all, you can try in private. Even better, you can practice failing in public and teaching your brain that it is okay. People may laugh, people may judge, but most likely nobody cares or even notices. Even if they did, trying and improving while being judged is better than not trying at all and still being judged.

Focus on yourself. People will judge you. It's a fact. But they are almost always projecting their own insecurities onto you. Judging you, discriminating against you, telling stories about you help others to feel safe themselves. If they are strangers who don't have an impact on you, you can freely dismiss their judgments as irrelevant. If they aren't strangers, their judgments are still likely irrelevant. Are you safe? Are you acting in line with your values and goals? Dismiss the judgments as irrelevant if you are acting in line with who you are. If you aren't act-ing in line with who you truly are, it isn't the judgment but your own behavior that you are unhappy with.

Once you have become aware of how the fear of being perceived shows up in your daily life, practice being perceived in ways that you know are safe. Cross the road at a regular walking pace instead of rush-ing across the road even if it means cars have to wait a few seconds. Post online. Raise your hand in class. Submit a suggestion to your supervisor. Disagree with someone. Sit on the ground in public. Do it confidently.

Whether or not you feel ready to be perceived by others, you can practice letting yourself be perceived by yourself. Record yourself—on camera, recordings, written works, anything. Then read it, listen to it, or watch it back. Whether it is quality work or not doesn't matter. What matters is that you are practicing allowing yourself to be per-ceived by the person who matters most—you.

The more you let yourself see who you are, the more you know who you are, and the less valid criticisms become. Then maybe you'll share your work with someone else. Not because you want their approval but simply to practice the vulnerability that you have been hiding from by not letting yourself be perceived. This is the same vulnerability that is required for real connection and belonging. If being judged is the biggest fear, then you can take actions to actively solicit judgments from others. Then feel whatever feelings arise. Let it be. Realize it doesn't change anything about you, your worth, or the joy you can feel in being who you are.

The more you strengthen the skill of being judged and moving through it comfortably, the more you aren't afraid of being judged. Being who you are will make people uncomfortable even when you do nothing to provoke it. It's most often going to be the people who were told they can't do what you are doing and who are afraid of being judged for doing exactly what you are doing. For those people, if they didn't judge themselves so much, they would recognize what they feel for you is actually admiration. For some people who are judging you for other reasons, the reasons are always their own. If their reasons don't also support your own values and goals, their judgments are just as irrelevant.

12

Strategies to Question and Reframe

Now THAT WE have developed awareness of various faulty belief systems and taken steps to deconstruct them, what do we do next?

First, accept that the way you perceive the world is not as it really is but how you *experience* what is. Then accept that your perception can be flawed. Because your brain doesn't like conflicting beliefs, it is only by introducing the belief that you could be wrong that you give permission to your brain to recognize where you are wrong. Whether you can see, hear, feel, taste, or smell, or you have diagnoses of dyslexia, schizophrenia, anxiety, or you've developed survival skills of perfectionism, people-pleasing, or anything else, you have a unique filter through which you experience the world. It is a combination of beliefs, neurochemistry, neuroanatomy, genetics, environment, experiences, disabilities, sensory experiences, motivations, expectations, and more. It is this combination that creates your default state of existing, experiencing, and perceiving.

Second, become aware of your faulty belief systems. Not just faulty belief systems in general but specifically the faulty beliefs systems you hold that guide your actions. We all have more than we know. You may be surprised at the sheer volume of faulty beliefs that come to light once you start examining your belief systems more purposefully. If you aren't sure what faulty belief systems you have, try something new, and they will show themselves.

For example, as someone brand new to the writing and publishing industry, I identified more faulty belief systems while writing this book than I have in the past five years combined, and I practice these exercises regularly. I believed I had to write the book completely independently and have it perfectly publishing-ready on my own. This led to hyper-independence, perfectionism, and a fear of being seen. This showed up for me as overthinking, being uncomfortable sharing my work before it was perfect, not asking for help made available to me by the publisher, and not believing compliments when I received them. This came to light when my editor called me out for overthinking and told me that it is my job to get my ideas clearly on paper and then the editors' jobs to turn it into publishing-ready. Doing something you have never done before will bring faulty belief systems to light. Following through with the thing you've never done before will also challenge and diminish those faulty belief systems that arise.

Third, question your faulty belief systems, especially those that are deeply ingrained. Question if they ever serve you or if they only cause harm. Question what truth they hold, if any, and whether that truth is still relevant today. Question whether they have power over you. Question whether they are belief systems that you want to keep holding.

Fourth, develop a replacement belief system. Just as you have, even subconsciously, created them up to this point, you can revise them or replace them with something more true that better serves you, your values, and your goals. You can develop belief systems that support you rather than hinder you in navigating life. Others do enough to oppress you—you don't have to oppress yourself.

Fifth, implement the new belief systems. Even after you logically know something to be more true, change takes time. This is the case for everyone, especially when emotions and long-held beliefs are involved. Give yourself compassion.

Your Perception of the World

Everyone's perception of the world is shaped by the context of the priorities, thoughts, and beliefs they hold at any given time. A certain name, location, or song may mean something to you because of what it reminds you of, not because of what it actually is. It may bring you joyful and pleasant feelings or feelings of fear and distress even though it is just a name, location, or song that is neutral on its own.

When your attention is on a specific task, you notice different things than you may otherwise. One of the best examples of this is when a group of people watching a video of people tossing a basketball were told to count the number of times a basketball was passed between players. While they were counting, a man in a gorilla suit walked through the gym, yet few of the people assigned to count passes noticed it. This is now known as the invisible gorilla effect (Simons and Chabris 1999). It shows that when you tell your brain to focus in one area, it is incredibly effective at blocking out other stimuli it considers irrelevant to the task at hand and other factors, no matter how significant.

If you expect to experience something in a certain way, you are likely to perceive the experience according to your expectations. For example, if someone tells you that you are about to feel something burning and they put a piece of ice on the back of your neck, you will immediately perceive a burning sensation. But, if they told you that you were about to experience something freezing, you would perceive the touch of the ice cube as a freezing sensation. Another example is a group who was shown non-words such as "sael." People who were told they were looking at boat-related words read the word as "sail," while people who were told they were looking at animal-related words read the word as "seal."

Another factor that significantly affects how you perceive and therefore interact with the world is confidence. Inflated confidence changes your experiences and can be both a benefit and a detriment depending on the context. Inflated confidence can be a benefit when it leads to taking bold actions that open opportunities you wouldn't otherwise have had (Barron and Gravert 2018). But, inflated confidence can also cause you to ignore new information on a subject you are an expert in because you subconsciously rely more on data from past experiences (Zhang, Harrington, and Sherf 2021). You may have experienced this in doctor's offices where you are disbelieved, or are given a solution that doesn't address all relevant factors. It's not just doctors, though. You and I do it, too.

Even hunger can drastically affect how you experience the world. If you are ever around a child (or even an adult) who is hungry, they become increasingly irritable, see everything as distressing, annoying, and wrong, and don't even know why. They don't know they are being irrational, because according to their current feelings and mental capacity, it seems completely rational. When the body needs food, blood sugar and blood pressure may drop, both affecting internal sensations in the body, as well as cognitive function. There is a rational explanation to the behavior, but it is a lack of food, not the external factors that seem to be the issue. This can be applied to all unmet needs. When the body has needs that aren't met, bodily functions change, leading to more irritability, less ability to handle other stressors, and worsened judgment and decision making.

Memories, focus, expectations, motivations, self-perception, unmet needs, emotions, prejudice, and stigma all affect how you experience and perceive the world around you in any given moment. You might believe that you experience what really is, that you remember what really was, that you understand what will come, and that you know who really you are. Yet, every human is far less accurate in perceptions, memories, and assumptions than they believe themselves to be. In fact, the more certain you are about your existing beliefs, the less open you are to taking in information that conflicts with those beliefs, and the less likely you are to act in ways that conflict with those beliefs. This is true even when you are wrong or act in ways that are harmful. You are unable to recognize where you are wrong or hurting yourself when your beliefs have convinced you that you are right.

By accepting that you don't experience the world as it truly is and that your perceptions can be flawed, you introduce a new belief system that allows your brain to question your current perception-based beliefs.

Now, decide whether you want better. Decide whether you want to no longer feel how you feel, think how you think, or have the results you have. Decide that you want better, even if that means letting go of things you have believed up to this point.

You don't have to believe you deserve it. You don't even have to believe it is possible yet. You can just believe that you want to see whether it is possible. And that is enough for your brain to start allowing new data in. Even if you don't feel great, doubt yourself, and have had a lot of bad things happen, you can decide that you want to feel happy. You can have regrets or feelings of failure and still decide that with the time you have left in life you want to enjoy yourself.

Understanding Your Default State

You have a default state based on your belief systems (Li, Mai, and Liu 2014). It is in this default state that you are least likely to recognize your faulty thoughts and are much more likely to defend and continue them. This default state causes you to ignore even the most obvious errors, solutions, or realities. This is especially applicable when survival or survival skills are a significant factor.

I was once driving during the winter on a highway in a remote area after a snow storm the previous day. At one point of the drive, I was forced to choose between being hit by a semitruck that was coming into the lane I was in, slamming on the breaks to avoid the semi but causing a wreck with the cars and people behind me, or driving off the edge of a road, over a few foot drop, and into feet of snow. I chose to drive off the edge. After I drove off, I immediately came to a stop in the snow without even using my brakes. My heart was racing as I was thinking about who I could possibly call for help and how long it would likely take because of the remote location, when a kind driver who saw it all showed up at my passenger door. They asked if I was okay, checked the car for damage, and told me they were there to help. Another kind person showed up a few moments later who said they had a truck and straps to pull me out, and if that didn't work they knew someone who lived about 30 minutes away with an actual tow truck.

The first person seemed to primarily be focused on ensuring that I was okay. The second seemed to be primarily focused on figuring out a way to get the car out. It wasn't until after a few calls were made and we were brainstorming the best way to tow me out that the first person asked, "Can you go forward or reverse at all?" I thought for a minute and realized I didn't even try. I didn't consciously know it, but I had assumed I was stuck because of how deep the snow was. I chuckled sheepishly and responded that I just realized I didn't try. I then drove forward with ease, and with just a little bit of help getting up the steep, snow-covered incline, I was able to continue my drive on the highway as normal.

Obviously, the three of us each had different experiences of the event, different past experiences and knowledge, as well as different emotions, thoughts, and goals that affected how we acted in the moment. When you are so enmeshed in a particular way of thinking, you largely ignore context that doesn't support what you already believe. This is your default state. You organize your experiences in the world according to your default even when it may not apply to the present situation or when it applies in a different way. I had strong feelings of fear and stress while making a split-second decision to stay physically safe in a remote area during winter. Stress and fear only increased as I willfully drove myself over the drop-off. When I finally stopped, I was totally enmeshed in the feeling of shock and the belief that I was stuck in snow. The kind drivers who stopped to help had their own experiences of watching me drive off the road, as well as their own past experiences, related feelings, views, and means to help. The first helper had subconsciously assumed that I would have already tried to move and so believed I was stuck in the snow. The second helper also believed that I was stuck based on the depth of snow and size of my car and tires but had a means and experience to pull my car out, so he was enmeshed in thoughts of the best way to do so. We were all focused on what mattered most according to our own perception, only to later realize that all of us had overlooked the easiest possible solution.

Seeing situations incorrectly is not unique, and it does not speak to your intelligence, value, or capabilities. There are billions of ways to see a situation incorrectly and only one way to see it correctly. The odds are you are going to have some flawed understanding of your current state. Knowing and accepting this allows you to have some compassion for yourself as you accept where you were wrong.

Assessing Your Default State

Another example of how easy it is to stay in your default state is how it took almost a century for people to accept the heliocentric model of the universe after it was first postulated by Copernicus. The prominent belief of the time was that the Earth was the center of the universe and everything revolved around it. When Copernicus suggested that the Sun was the center and that the Earth and other celestial bodies moved around it, it was considered inconceivable and incongruent to the long-held beliefs of the time. For the next 100 years, more and more scientific evidence gave reason to doubt the geocentric model that the Earth was the center of the universe. The heliocentric model of the Earth revolving around the Sun was only accepted scientifically after there was too much scientific evidence to continue denying its validity. Even then, it was another century before the heliocentric view of the solar system was universally accepted by scientists and the greater population.

While most of us wouldn't be largely affected by holding the false belief that the Earth is the center of the universe, most of us have stayed stuck in a situation longer than we needed to because of other faulty belief systems. Whether it is finding the best solution for a given problem, or improving understanding of how the world works, we must be able to reassess our existing beliefs for assumptions, stigma, and inaccuracy while considering new information that might challenge our beliefs. Relying on established belief systems for every new situation will lead to continued suffering, disengagement, and staying stuck, whether literally like me in the snow or figuratively in our minds. It's the staying stuck in our minds that can be the most damaging and keep us in suffering and limitation, even when there is a way out.

Once you start challenging existing beliefs, you will more naturally continue to notice established patterns of thought that may or may not be true. Even when the patterns of thought and belief systems are true, you will learn to better assess their relevance to a situation based on current context.

The goal isn't to deny past experiences and understanding, nor past or present feelings. The goal is to ensure accuracy and utilize all of your knowledge, present and past, to ensure that you are the one deciding how to act in any given situation instead of giving control to your faulty belief systems and default state.

Identify Your Faulty Belief Systems

Looking inward and accepting where you are causing or exacerbating or prolonging your own suffering is important for growth. Accepting where you may be causing or adding to your own suffering can be the hardest part, but once accomplished, the rest gets to be easy, perhaps even fun.

To identify your faulty belief systems requires being honest with yourself about what you believe. This step will be much easier if you have compassion for yourself and separate your beliefs from who you are. Yes, they may affect how you see who you are, how you see the world, and how you act, but they do not define you. And they do not need to diminish you.

If you are having trouble disconnecting your beliefs from who you are, it may help to redefine this step in a way that makes the disconnection more possible. This is an example of when you can use the stories you tell yourself for your benefit. You can tell yourself this is just data collection, clearing out the old and making room for the new, or freeing yourself from untruths. If you believe your beliefs are who you are, you can tell yourself that those beliefs helped make who you were in your past, but you can choose new beliefs to influence who you will become in the future. You can tell yourself these beliefs were never really yours anyway, and you are identifying those that you don't want to keep. Use whatever perspective helps you disconnect from the beliefs.

Did any of the beliefs covered in the previous chapters resonate with you, how you see the world, how you see yourself, or how you make decisions?

What beliefs, if any, do you have about yourself regarding the following topics:

- **Ability or likelihood to:** Succeed, have friendships, be in a relationship, get reasonable accommodations, be accepted, feel a sense of belonging, obtain a job that meets your needs, be happy, travel, be active, participate in the activity you want, do the job you want, be independent, relax, or experience less pain—physical, mental, or emotional.
- **Likelihood to experience:** Discrimination, retaliation, rejection of reasonable accommodations, disbelief of your disability, disbelief of your experience of disability, disbelief of your abilities, disbelief of your needs, people being annoyed by you, inaccessible environments, losing a job due to disclosing, being taken advantage of.

- **Likelihood to experience:** Success, a promotion, recognition for your skills, acceptance, approval of your accommodation request, a smooth travel experience, and so forth.

Go back and ask what beliefs, if any, you have about disabled people in general about the ability and likelihood regarding the previously listed topics. What about others with your specific or other disability? Does your view differ depending on the group? Are your beliefs different than the beliefs you have about yourself? If so, are they better or worse?

Do you have beliefs about the reasons for the following situations?

- Why your living state is what it is.
- Why your mental state is what it is.
- Why your physical state is what it is.
- Why your financial state is what it is.
- Why you are treated the way you are.
- Why your professional state is what it is.
- Why your relationships are the way they are.

What do you believe regarding what would be necessary for the current state to improve?

Are there any recurring beliefs or themes? Is there a main underlying root belief?

Do you blame yourself most often? Do you blame external circumstances most often? Is it your lack of acceptance from others? Is it your lack of acceptance or belief in yourself? Is it rooted in past traumas? Are hopelessness, anxiety, shame, or fear prominent themes? Is lack of getting your needs met a prominent theme? Is it the disabling effects of stigma and inaccessibility?

You may have one overarching theme or many. Either way, once you have identified faulty beliefs or common themes, you can then assess them for truth. Some are going to be factually untrue. Some may be technically true but incorrect in how you are applying them. Some beliefs may be true in fact and application, except that you are applying them broadly to everything you do or that happens to you.

Question Your Faulty Belief Systems

Now that you have identified (or you at least know how to identify) your belief systems, you can question them. You wouldn't have any belief if it didn't serve you somehow. So first identify how a given belief attempts to keep your brain feeling safe.

- Does it provide perceived clarity to the unknown?
- Does it provide a perceived sense of control?
- Does it provide a sense of safety from a perceived threat?
- Does it provide a sense of safety by avoiding possible rejection or criticism?
- Does it provide temporary comfort by ignoring or denying uncomfortable truths?
- Does it provide temporary comfort by keeping you in a known discomfort rather than risking a new type of discomfort?

If none of the above, how does this belief provide you a sense of safety and comfort?

Now that you have identified the purpose of maintaining the belief, let's identify the errors and harms.

- Is this belief true?
- What truth, if any, does this belief hold?
- Is this belief rooted in truth?
- What truth, if any, is this belief based on?
- Is this belief rooted in stigma, bias, or shame?
- Does this belief put others over myself?
- Is this belief rooted in the present or the past?
- If rooted in the past, does it still apply to the present?
- Does this belief support me or harm me?
- Is this belief causing me to self-sabotage?
- Does this belief protect me from real harm?
- Do I want to keep acting the way this belief leads me to act?
- Would I apply this belief to someone else the way I do myself?
- Does this belief control me more than I control it?

Are you ready to let go of and replace this belief? If yes, do it. If no, ask the following questions:

- Does it feel hard to let go of this belief?
- Is it scary to consider letting go of this belief?
- Does it feel unsafe to consider letting go of this belief?
- Do I want to hold on to this belief even though I know it harms me?
- Does letting go of this belief feel as if I am letting go of or losing part of my identity?

If you answered yes to any of the above questions, can you identify why? If yes, is there a way you can resolve the why? If not, can you move forward despite the discomfort?

Repeat this as many times as necessary. When you can, go to the next step and develop a replacement belief. If you can't, believe you can't, or simply don't want to, that's okay too. There is no requirement to replace your faulty beliefs. A conscious choice to keep it is still better than unconsciously being controlled by it. The awareness alone allows your brain to be receptive to alternatives, even before you are ready to consciously change.

Develop New Belief Systems

Some beliefs will be effectively diffused by identifying the flaws and irrelevance of the belief itself. For example, if someone tells you that your pink hair is ugly, but you know you don't have pink hair, their insult means very little, if anything at all. Even if you do wonder if they're right and your hair somehow turned pink spontaneously, you can easily confirm this isn't true, and the attempted insult will mean nothing. It works this easily for other egregiously incorrect beliefs, too.

Other beliefs may have the effective replacement belief become obvious from the flaws, irrelevance, or harm of the faulty belief. Other beliefs may be more effectively diffused by a replacement belief that directly replaces the flaws and harm of the faulty belief with truth and support. Other beliefs may be most effectively diffused by a replacement belief that isn't directly related to your faulty belief yet calls into question the veracity of the faulty belief with a direct contradiction.

To identify the most effective replacement belief, identify what you want to believe. Don't think about reality, possibility, need, or how others may judge you; just think about what you want to believe. What goals do you want to meet? Who do you want to be? How would you prefer this belief support you? This not only helps you identify what you want, but it also gives your mind permission to see beyond the constraints that the current belief mandates.

After you've identified what you want to believe, can you believe it? Does it effectively replace your related faulty belief? If so, choose to believe what you want to believe. It can be that simple to get it started. Then the more you think it and act from the new belief, the more the brain cements it and weakens the old belief.

If not, keep going.

Referencing how the faulty belief serves you as identified in the previous step, identify a new and more effective way to give your brain the safety it is attempting to get from the faulty belief:

- What is more true than your faulty belief?
- What does the belief look like if it is based on your goal instead of stigma, bias, and shame?
- What does the belief look like if you apply what you know to be true in your present more than past experiences or fears?
- What does the belief look like if it is designed from confidence, not fear?

For example, my belief that I can't send chapters to my editor until they are perfect is faulty. It exists to protect me from experiencing perceived failure and being judged according to work that is less than what I am capable of. It is not true nor is it based in truth. Acting accordingly to this belief causes me to self-sabotage, keeps me feeling overwhelmed and unsupported, while perpetuating the belief that my writing is not, and never will be, good enough. Acting accordingly to this belief denies myself the support I could have from an expert and denies myself the opportunity to make my book the best it can be. Effective replacement beliefs could be "My book will be better with the help of an editor than it could possibly be on its own" or "The sooner I deliver chapters to my editor, the sooner I get feedback to make the chapters as good as they can be" or "The editor is here to support me, and I will reduce stress by utilizing him" or "Perfection is not possible, and the pursuit of it perpetuates insecurity and overthinking instead of protecting me." Any of these beliefs could effectively replace my current belief. And then it is time to act.

Implement New Belief Systems

Implementing new belief systems involves both taking action according to new beliefs, as well as ceasing giving attention and validation to the old beliefs. To do this, it means cementing the new thought as a belief and releasing the old belief as simply a thought.

Having a thought does not mean it is true. It doesn't even mean that you believe it. It simply means you are having that thought. It could be a thought that originated from something you read or heard even years before. Just because the thought is occurring in your mind does not mean it is yours to keep or believe or act on.

When you believe a thought is when it takes root in your brain. Once it has taken root, it can continue to be maintained in the mind as long as it continues to be fed. It can and will continue to regenerate more of the same or similar thoughts, even leading to more extreme versions of the thought (Connors and Halligan 2022). You can choose to stop feeding it, and like a plant that doesn't receive light and water, it will naturally die.

Now, when you feel your faulty belief systems present themselves, remind yourself of your new beliefs. Remind yourself that the old belief system is flawed and harmful. Remind yourself that the old beliefs can just be thoughts that do not control you or guide your actions anymore. Then keep moving forward in acting from the new belief. You aren't fighting against it, just letting it exist while you choose to act on a different thought or belief.

Remind yourself that change takes time and effort for all humans. You are not a computer that can be reprogrammed with a new operating system and automatically perfectly implements the new system. You are human.

Remind yourself of the new belief systems or the flaws in your old belief systems as many times as you need to get your body to feel safe believing it, too. The more you choose to act according to the new belief, the more you internalize it and diffuse the old belief.

PART

III

Self-Acceptance
and Self-Confidence

Now THAT FAULTY belief systems have been effectively deconstructed, you have room to identify who you are free of stigma and shame.

This section starts with how to reduce stress and increase feelings of safety in your body through nervous system regulation. You will learn what it is, why it matters, and how you can take action to implement it in your life. The goal is to remind your body that it is safe to be your true self regardless of previous rejection and threat that you have experienced just for existing differently.

After you learn to bring safety back to your body, you can start to dive into who you truly are. You will be guided through identifying your values, goals, and needs. Combined, these will effectively serve as a guidance system in every decision you make and every action you take. Instead of acting to meet others' expectations or avoid others' judgments, you can start making decisions based on *you*. Instead of making decisions based in fear or a deficit-based identity, you can start to make decisions based on what you want while taking into account your needs, preferences, strengths, and limitations to decide the how.

Identifying who you are provides a more accurate way to judge yourself and a more fact-based way to accept yourself. You don't need to reframe yourself or certain traits into something extremely positive, because who you are is enough as is. In addition to learning to accept yourself as you are, you will also learn to accept others as they are. Increasing your ability to accept others directly enhances self-acceptance, while also increasing your ability to separate others' judgments and treatment of you from the truth about you.

You will then learn how to put it all in action and really start living as you are, or living more as you are. You'll learn to develop trust in your body and in yourself and how to be who you are through small and consistent actions. Confidence is gained by action, and you will learn to take actions that will increase self-confidence, becoming easier and easier the more you do it. Eventually, living your life according to who you are will become more natural than living life trying to avoid others' judgments.

13

Nervous System Regulation

THE BODY HAS many systems that all work together to maintain your overall health. When one system doesn't function as expected, other systems often compensate. When multiple systems are worked simultaneously, it is necessary to have one directing the others to ensure all work together in harmony. The nervous system is that command center of the body that sends, receives, interprets, and responds to the body's sensory signals. Dysregulation (an abnormality or impairment in function) of the command center affects all other systems including the immune, endocrine, cardiovascular, and digestive systems.

Sensory processing by the nervous system happens both inside and outside of your awareness. What happens within your awareness is managed by the *somatic* branch of the nervous system. This is what enables you to move willfully or reflexively. When you choose to move any body part, it is your somatic nervous system at work, sending signals from the brain to the muscles. The somatic system also processes four of the senses—smell, sight, touch, and taste.

> The *somatic* nervous system is a component of the peripheral nervous system associated with the voluntary control of body movements via the use of skeletal muscles (Akinrodoye and Lui 2022).

The sensory processing that happens outside of your awareness is managed by the autonomic nervous system, which works by sending signals from the brain to your organs. It is responsible for regulating your heartbeat, blood flow, digestion, breathing, and all other involuntary processes. It is the autonomic nervous system that tells the body how to compensate when either internal or external stimuli signal the need for a change. It tells your body when to increase heart rate, reduce blood flow to one area and increase it to another area, or otherwise ensure the most efficient support for your body's needs at any given time.

The autonomic nervous system is also what regulates the stress response. The autonomic branch of the nervous system is further divided into two separate branches—the sympathetic and parasympathetic nervous systems. The *sympathetic* nervous system is what kicks in when threat is perceived. It is the system that controls the fight-or-flight response and prepares you to respond to threats. The *parasympathetic* nervous system, also referred to as the "rest and digest" system, is what calms the body when the threat is gone. It is the system that slows breathing, relaxes your muscles, and otherwise returns you to a sustainable baseline state by increasing processes that aid in relaxation. The parasympathetic nervous system is also what controls energy conservation when rest and healing are necessary.

Autonomic Nervous System

Before you get into identifying, accepting, and being who you are, your body needs to feel safe to do so. That means calming the stress, fear, and anxiety that signals a lack of safety. You don't have to get rid of those feelings completely, just neutralize them enough that they aren't in control. This can be done most effectively by strengthening your stress response.

Stressors and the stress response are necessary for growth and an optimal human experience. Living a stress-free life does result in better moods and decreased likelihood of chronic health conditions, but it also results in lower cognition and less joy (Charles et al. 2021). People with stress-free lives have no negative experiences but also are less likely to have positive daily experiences. People who report no stress are those who don't have significant social interactions, if any, and are likely single, don't work, and mostly stay isolated. Never being around people is a great way to reduce stress, but it is also a great way to not have any connection or real joy.

Better than aiming to avoid all stress is aiming to find your ideal balance. You can limit avoidable stress and strengthen your stress response to better deal with unavoidable stressors. This way you can maximize connection, joy, and cognitive functioning while limiting the maladaptive effects of stress on your mental and physical health.

Stress, fear, and anxiety are all natural responses. Hopelessness, avoidance, and anger are all natural responses. Even when you may label it overreacting or unnatural, it is natural in the sense your brain deemed that response appropriate based on what it perceived at the time. Every response you have ever had is your brain's natural response from the experiences it has had and what has helped you through similar situations in the past. Seeing these responses for what they are—natural—is imperative to removal of judgment, which is vital to feeling safe in your own body.

Recognizing responses as natural does not mean you are accepting them as inevitable. If you let the natural fear-based protective state of your brain drive, it will eventually begin to control who you are. Unchecked fear, anxiety, and stress become invasive and oppressive. Unchecked hopelessness, avoidance, and anger become controlling and destructive. They are still natural, but natural doesn't mean not harmful. Natural means you shouldn't shame yourself for it, but it does not mean you shouldn't seek to guard against it.

When responding to shame or attempting to avoid the discomfort of fear, stress, and other emotions, humans often turn to behaviors that give immediate but temporary relief and end up causing long-term harm. It may be some of the survival skills addressed in previous chapters, or it may be other obviously harmful actions such as relying on mind-altering substances, harming yourself, or harming others. By understanding your brain, why you do what you do, and how the harmful coping skills provide relief, you can identify more effective ways to achieve the same goals, except better. You can replace the harmful coping skills with beneficial skills that achieve long-term support, not just the appearance of relief in the short term.

The most effective way to keep stress and fear from taking over is acceptance, but that isn't possible if your body already doesn't feel safe.

Brains are so adaptable they can handle nearly anything. Should you have to? No. But if you have to, you can. The way to keep your body feeling safe despite the external happenings is intentional nervous system regulation. You can train your body to respond to stress in ways that are more beneficial not just to your survival but also to your long-term comfort and health.

Certain stressors are inherent to being alive. They are necessary for survival and growth. It is far more effective to accept this and prepare yourself to handle hard things than try to avoid hard things. We all have a window of tolerance—a level of intensity and duration of stressors we can handle before crossing into overload. The window of tolerance is not static and can be increased or decreased. The way to increase your window of tolerance is by learning about and working with your natural stress responses. Your body's response to stress is managed by the nervous system, so this means learning about and working with your nervous system. When you understand your tolerance thresholds and have tools to actively regulate distress, you will increase your capacity to navigate periods of stress while reducing negative effects.

Responding to Stress

The body has a masterfully designed stress response. When your body perceives danger, hormones are released that communicate to the body to make certain changes that will support you in fighting or escaping the danger. The fight-or-flight response includes increased heart rate and breathing, increased adrenaline production, dilated pupils, tensed muscles, and suppressed pain. These are all necessary responses to support surviving real threats. Once the threat is gone, it only takes about 20–60 minutes for the parasympathetic system to kick in and calm the body again. When working as designed, the balance of sympathetic and parasympathetic responses keeps the body safe and functioning at its optimal level.

While the natural stress response is subconscious, humans have learned how to consciously work with the stress response to promote growth. You can intentionally put stress on the body to increase muscles mass, intelligence, and resilience. The stress response is the sympathetic and parasympathetic nervous systems working in tandem. The body systems that are necessary to survival are prioritized, while energy is reduced to the body systems that are not necessary to survive the threat. Every time you successfully navigate a stressor, your body becomes more efficient in whatever manner you navigated the stress. If you avoided the stressor, took drugs to deal with the stressor, fought the stressor, or froze, the body remembers that response as being successful at surviving the threat. The next time you experience the same or similar stressors, you will have the urge to do the same thing you did last time to mitigate the stressor in the short term, regardless of how unhealthy it may be for the long term.

When the body is under prolonged states of stress, recurring states of stress, or extreme levels of stress, the stress response becomes compromised. However, the body doesn't know the difference between perceived and real threat. Learning to regulate the nervous system builds your ability to navigate threats and trust in your body's ability to handle it.

Heightened energy states are your body supporting you in responding to stress, just as decreased energy states are your body conserving energy. Your body is only trying to support you, nothing more. It is common to make a value judgment about yourself or others based on someone's energy level, but having energy or not having energy is not a personal or moral indicator. Energy is an indicator of what your body thinks it needs at that time.

Autonomic Nervous System Dysregulation

Autonomic nervous system *dysregulation* occurs when your nervous system is under real or perceived stress *without time to recover*. This can occur due to prolonged stress, extreme stressors without support, or avoidance of stressors. It leads to perceiving danger even when there isn't any and continues the stress response long after the stressor has passed.

An important distinction: There are disabilities related to autonomic nervous system dysfunction, which is different from dysregulation. Dysfunction typically includes damage to nerves while dysregulation is simply overactive or underactive sympathetic and parasympathetic responses from a misinterpretation of stimuli.

While most nervous system inputs happen subconsciously, the stress can be made worse by the stories you tell yourself about what that stress means or how you believe you should act in a certain situation. While there are times that you can be under very real stress for extended amounts of time, many times it isn't the external situation that is the stressor but your thought and interpretation around it.

I once heard the saying that anxiety is an overestimation of a problem with an underestimation of your ability to overcome it. I think that applies beyond anxiety alone and can be applied to emotional overload, stress, and hopelessness. It is increased stress, or energy, with added mental judgment. Other animals react to threat by how their brain prompts them to react, and then they shake it off. I don't mean that figuratively; many animals actually shake their body once the threat has passed and get back to life as normal within minutes. They could have just been in a fight where their life was in danger and still shake their body and then return to normal. The shake is a response to the threat being over and marks a completion of the stress response. Recommended reading to learn more: *Why Zebras Don't Get Ulcers* by Robert M. Sapolsky (2004).

Humans don't have an instinctive response to the end of a threat. What we do have is a brain that can interpret feelings, tie meaning to an experience, and start judging ourselves for our response. We can use our thoughts to perpetuate the feelings of threat longer than the threat actually lasts. We can use our thoughts to suppress the feelings and ignore that the threat existed at all. Either way, perpetuating or suppressing feelings doesn't allow an end to the threat. Not allowing an end to a threat means not allowing an end to the threat response.

Dysregulation and Disability

Most people who are disabled are likely to have some level of nervous system dysregulation. The more marginalized communities you are part of, the more this likelihood increases. Discrimination, stigma, and abuse along with isolation and lack of accessibility are all significant causes of stress and as a result, a significant cause of nervous system dysregulation. Even when the threat isn't present, the fear and potential of the threat are perceived as a threat, which ensures the brain and body are always ready to respond. In societies where discrimination, stigma, abuse, isolation, and lack of accessibility are common, that pretty much ensures you are always ready to fight, have accepted your fate and become hopeless, or some mix of the two.

Shame is another significant factor and almost always present in nervous system dysregulation. Within the disability community, shame is likely the root cause of nervous system dysregulation. Shame leads you to believe that you are in danger by simply existing. If existing is perceived to be dangerous and threatening, your nervous system is going to constantly act to protect you. It doesn't matter what the threat is, just that your body believes the perceived threat to be real.

Depending on your experiences and what has successfully kept you safe up to this point, nervous system dysregulation can present in different ways. The sympathetic nervous system can become hyper-vigilant in assessing for and responding to perceived threats and protect you by increasing energy. This often presents as anxiety, perfectionism, and overworking. Alternatively, if a threat is deemed to be inevitable and you start to feel hopeless, the body decides to protect you by conserving energy. Conserving energy is managed by the parasympathetic system, which when overactive results in the person being unreactive, hopeless, and emotionally numb. This often presents as burnout, depression, and reclusiveness.

Because the nervous system tells the rest of the body how to use energy, where to send blood, or how to digest food, a dysregulated nervous system directly affects health. Stress-related illnesses can be caused or exacerbated by the dysregulated nervous system. It exacerbates or predisposes you to asthma, anxiety, allergies, depression, diabetes, rheumatoid arthritis, and even cancer (Salleh 2008). This isn't theory but well proven that stress directly exacerbates and causes many illnesses or creates the perfect environment for stress-related illnesses to thrive (Russell et al. 2018). When one or more systems do not function well at the same time, our bodies lose overall resiliency.

When you are in a heightened alert state or a state of hopelessness, every piece of information the brain processes is filtered through that lens. This causes heightened sensitivity to even the smallest perceived threats. It results in perceiving threats even where none exist. It causes you to interpret actions as discrimination or rejection even when they aren't. It reduces your ability to receive constructive criticism, and instead you see it as a personal attack on you or a community you are part of. This directly diminishes your ability to accept areas of growth and take actions to improve. It causes you to not see possible solutions and accept defeat prematurely. The stories your brain tells you in a heightened or hopeless state are almost certainly not based on facts but on cognitive biases that support the beliefs behind the heightened or hopeless states.

Then there are the diagnoses that can also cause stress themselves and are exacerbated by stress, ensuring the cycle continues. You have anxiety over asthma, and then asthma attacks are triggered by anxiety. You have anxiety over seizures, and then seizures are triggered by anxiety. You stress over not performing well enough, and then your performance suffers because you are stressed. You feel depressed because you lost hope and then you take actions that reinforce the belief that you have reason to lack hope. The longer this goes on, the more negative the impacts are. And the longer this goes on, the more your brain gets accustomed to the cycle, and the more likely the cycle is to continue.

But there is good news. While most of the functions of the autonomic nervous system are completely independent of your thought, there are many ways you can support your nervous system and improve its regulation.

How to Regulate the Nervous System

The entire body, including the nervous system, requires hydration, nutrients, and sleep to function at its best. Prioritizing hydration, nutrition, and sleep as you are able is the easiest way to reduce stress on the body. Lack in any of these areas reduces the efficacy of every body system. The body will still function but is less able to handle additional stressors. If you have disabilities that impact any of the basic body functions, do what you can in the affected areas, and then turn your focus to the areas not directly affected by your disability. Your body will adjust accordingly. If you have a sleep disorder, do what you can to support quality sleep, and then accept it is what it is and shift your focus to nutrition and hydration. Improving any of the base needs will improve your overall health, so focus where you can.

You can also make constructive changes to your environment. Light, sound, and smells are all inputs your body has to process. This means music, conversations, flashing lights, and strong smells. The level of sensory stimulation that amounts to stress on your body will be different for everyone. Someone with sensory sensitivities may experience heightened stress at lower levels of sensory input. Someone who requires increased attention while lip reading may experience heightened stress at lower levels of conversation. Someone who requires increased levels of rest may experience heightened stress at lower levels of physical exertion. Anyone in the process of healing will experience heightened stress at lower levels of any sensory input or demands on the body as the body prioritizes returning to a healthy state. It is recognizing what things add stress to your body and brain specifically, at what level that input becomes stress, and then accommodating for those needs. You can judge yourself for not being able to handle as much as the person next to you, a past version of you, or an idealized version of you, or you can accept it and act accordingly. Only one option serves your body.

Additional basic body support is meeting disability-specific needs. Take your medicine regularly. Use your assistive devices as needed. Ask for accommodations. Do the exercises recommended by your doctor. Provide the structure or spontaneity your brain needs. Communicate to others what you need from them. Leave situations that you can that are adding more stress than benefit. This decreases stress on your body by not only meeting your needs but showing your body that it can trust that your present and future needs will be met.

Of course, reducing all stress you can control won't reduce all past stress, future stress, or external circumstances that you can't control. Nervous system regulation is what helps protect yourself against the negative impacts of external stressors on your body.

While the sympathetic nervous system naturally causes an increase in respiratory rate when it perceives a threat, you can consciously choose to slow it down. Slowing your breathing sends a signal to the brain that you are safe, which then causes the brain to send signals to the rest of the body that it can relax. While the sympathetic nervous system naturally heightens your focus on perceived threats, you can consciously choose to focus elsewhere which signals to the brain that your present reality is not a threat, prompting the brain to signal the rest of the body to stop the stress response. It's by knowing why the brain is doing what it is doing that you can communicate to the brain that it no longer needs to respond as if there were a threat.

No matter what state of nervous system dysregulation you experience, there is something you can do to improve regulation. Slowing breathing may not work when hyperventilating during a panic attack, but engaging your senses by identifying five red things, or five sounds, or five textures may help. Slow movement and intentional breathing may work for some, but others may laugh at the suggestion and think there is no way your brain or body can calm down enough to be calm or still. For you, it may be running, jumping, or screaming that helps to regulate. No matter the situation, there is something that can be done to calm the brain. You can learn to better regulate your nervous system.

If you are in such a heightened parasympathetic state that movement doesn't seem possible, or such a heightened sympathetic state that slowing down seems impossible, be especially compassionate with yourself. Accept where you are without judgment, and do whatever you can do. There is no wrong way to start, and there is always somewhere you can start. Even if you can't muster the energy or desire to make any other change, intentional breathing is an effective start.

Breath work can seem unrelated to reducing anxiety, enhancing the immune system, decreasing levels of adrenaline, and lowering heart rate. What does breathing have to do with the immune system or adrenaline? Breathing is a means to voluntarily influence the nervous system, which affects all body functions including the immune response, inflammation, and heart function.

A study was done where a group of people were intentionally given food poisoning (Kox et al. 2014). The group had some individuals who had been trained in specific breath work techniques and exposed themselves to a short-term stressor in the form of immersion in ice cold water. After they received the relevant training, they engaged in the breath work techniques on a daily basis for about a week until they were willfully injected with bacteria. Those who had practiced breath work and cold exposure had less flu-like symptoms and a quicker recovery. There were increased epinephrine levels, which is an anti-inflammatory produced by the body that is also used in medicine to treat severe allergic reactions. Strengthening and regulating your nervous system doesn't just improve your mental ability to navigate external stressors, but it also supports your overall body functioning and reduces anxiety while increasing the immune response. If your nervous system is better prepared to respond to stress, the rest of your body is better prepared to respond to stress, as well. Physical movement is one of the most accepted manners to decrease the stress response. Animals in the wild typically use movement to regulate their nervous system once a threat is gone. Some animals kick, others shake, others run. It is especially useful if you feel angry, annoyed, or extremely stressed but don't feel that you can calm enough to focus on breath. It is equally useful on the opposite end when you are in burnout or shutdown and can hardly get out of bed even to use the bathroom. Movement can be done anywhere.

Nervous System Regulation Exercises

There is no shortage of ways to regulate your nervous system. The best way is what you are able and willing to do in any moment. Over time, you may be able and willing to try alternative methods. As you consistently engage in any of these methods, you will learn what your body responds to best and what methods work best for various situations. Whether you are in a room full of people in a professional setting or alone in your living space, whether you have a lot of energy or very little, whether you are terrified or angry, there is a technique that you can try.

Breathing Techniques (Balban et al. 2023)

- **Box breathing:** Breathe in for a count of four, hold for a count of four, breathe out for a count of four, hold for a count of four. Repeat as necessary.
- **Cyclic sighing:** Breathe in through your nose followed by another short breathe in, and then breathe out through your mouth until there is no air left to breathe out. Repeat as necessary.
- **Cyclic hyperventilation with retention:** Breathe in for two counts, breath out for one, and repeat 30 times; then hold your breath for 15 counts. Repeat as necessary.

Sensory Exposure

- **Cold:** You can stand in a cold shower, jump in a cold body of water, lay in the snow, or you can dunk your face in a bowl of ice cold water. You can start with a few seconds and slowly increase the duration every time you do it.
- **Nature:** Whether being out in nature or using virtual videos and sounds of nature, the body responds to nature with decreased heart rate (Gaertner et al. 2023).
- **Binaural beats:** Listening to binaural beats through headphones supports the reduction of heart rate, further regulating the stress response, inducing effects similar to meditation (Bakaeva et al. 2022).

Physical Movement (Salmon 2001)

- Dance
- Shake your whole body or part of your body
- Lift heavy weights
- Walk or roll outside
- Body weight exercises such as squats
- Simple movement such as shoulder rolls or head turns

Mindfulness

- **Progressive muscle relaxation:** Flex and relax muscles one muscle at a time (Li et al. 2020).
- **Tapping:** Recognizing in your body where you feel. Even if you aren't able to identify what you are feeling, you can identify where you are feeling a sensation. Tap on that body part.
- **5, 4, 3, 2, 1:** Focusing on your present environment, identify five things in one category, four in another category, and so on (Shukla 2020). Some examples of categories are a specific color, anything you can smell, hear, or sense, or the names of people, cereals, or businesses around you.

Self-Expression   Artistic expression in the form of artwork, writing, and singing has shown a great reduction in anxiety, depression, and nervous system dysregulation (Sandmire et al. 2012).

Co-regulation   Hugs, talking, or existing in the same room safely with someone: the impact of having someone with you after a traumatic event reduces the likelihood of lasting trauma. There is a lot you can do on your own, but sometimes having someone be with you is what helps close out the threat, stop the shame spiral, or otherwise bring your body back to feeling safe (Sippel et al. 2015).

Petting a dog or cat (Beetz et al. 2012). Or getting a service animal if your disability warrants it.

Service   When you serve with no expectations of anything in return, you receive more dopamine to your system than when someone else does something for you. Supporting others reduces the stress response (Inagaki and Eisenberger 2016).

After you've done something to regulate, then take an action. It solidifies that you are safe, that you can act, and that you have returned to a regulated state. Also, the ability to take action increases your self-efficacy (belief in yourself to get through). When you feel dysregulated, regulate—and then act. If you are in an unsafe situation, nervous system regulation can help you withstand the situation, but getting out is ideal if possible.

Nervous System Regulation Indicators

Even when you don't feel that nervous system regulation is working, it is. Some signs that it is working are as follows:

- You are able to move through feelings more quickly without avoidance
- You feel stress when a threat arises, recognize that the threat isn't real, and let it pass
- Reduced emotional reactivity
- Quicker return to a regulated state
- Expanded window of tolerance
- Lower resting heart rate
- Decreased headaches, panic attacks, or other physical symptoms
- Executive functioning (cognitive processes that help you navigate daily life including memory, organization, problem solving, planning, focus, and emotional regulation) increases
- Increased awareness of somatic cues

Nervous system regulation is not a one-time thing, nor is it something only to be used in times of stress or stress recovery. Taking part in activities that support your nervous system when it isn't under stress will increase your ability to more effectively manage stressors when they do arise. It will bring an increased level of calm in your body as you navigate everyday life.

14

Know Yourself

ACCEPTING YOURSELF REGARDLESS of others' acceptance of you is a bold act. Accepting yourself when others actively *don't* accept you is an especially bold, even defiant, act.

Humanity has been judging differences, including disabilities, unfairly since the beginning of time. Others' input, your own survival systems, and shame lead to judging yourself unfairly, as well. This almost certainly has led to an inaccurate perception of your self-identity. Because disability is primarily viewed through a deficit-based lens rather than a strengths-based or a more neutral difference-based lens, mental and physical differences are often viewed with an emphasis on limitations and challenges. This limited perspective perpetuates stereotypes and undermines an accurate perception of yourself.

It is in the moments when you feel that the deficit-based identity is most true that you are most likely to act out of people-pleasing, perfectionism, learned helplessness, hyper-independence, or a fear of being seen. This isn't completely erased when you see yourself more accurately, but shame and stigma lose their power, which naturally increases your own power. When you see yourself more accurately, the moments of acting out of shame, fear, and survival only last moments instead of months, years, or an entire lifetime.

The antidote to navigating a stigma and shame-filled world is knowing who you are without stigma and shame. It will take intentional effort to change this mindset and replace it with the truth about who you are. It's going to take some level of objectivity to identify the truth from the fallacy. When identified, you can use the newfound truths to drive your decisions and actions instead of being driven by your fears or external judgments.

In this chapter you will be guided to look at yourself objectively to identify who you are at your core without stigma and fear. You'll be able to identify your needs, values, personality, likes and dislikes, and strengths and weaknesses. This sets the foundation to replace fears and external judgments as the key drivers of your decisions, actions, and self-perception. Knowing who you are provides an internal guidance system that can be stronger than any external guidance system if you let it. You will enable yourself to more confidently say no, ask for what you need, and know that you have the justification for it regardless of others' responses. You'll be equipped to adapt to various situations without giving up who you are. This doesn't mean that it will always be easy or successful, but it will be much easier than trying and failing to be someone you're not. It will also give you a realistic possibility to experience acceptance and belonging for who you are. Most importantly, it will help you know yourself free of stigmas. It will help you build or improve acceptance in all of who you are, disability and limitations included.

You Are Enough

Before we get into the core of it, I want to spend some time reminding you that you are enough. The way you experience the world, the way you learn, the way you communicate, your skills, and what you care about—all of it is enough. That doesn't mean you are perfect, never need to improve, or don't need help from anyone else. It simply means you don't need to be anyone other than yourself to navigate this life and to find belonging. Who you are is enough.

Knowing you are enough means being aware of what is and isn't you. It's not only knowing what is natural to you and what you can control but also knowing what is not natural to you and what is outside of your control. It's knowing that you are enough even if you can't function in a certain environment the same way as someone else, or perhaps even the same way as you previously did.

Nothing functions in every environment, and that is not a bad thing. It is by design. Asking a boat to move on a roadway is pointless. It would get nowhere. A boat requires complete support to even exist on a road, but even with complete support it isn't functional on a road. A boat only ever exists on a road to be transported to an environment where it can function. A boat's value isn't based on its functionality on a road. A boat's value is based on what it can do in the right environment.

While it is easy and natural to account for the right environment when judging a boat, environment is rarely considered when judging yourself or others. When being judged, others also rarely take into account the environment you need. Unlike boats and other inanimate objects that come with defined specifications, humans don't come with defined specifications. That leaves it up to you to identify and define your own specifications and then to educate others on your environmental needs.

Can it get annoying when you're consistently in environments not built for you? Absolutely. But it doesn't change the fact that only you know the environment where you thrive. And if you don't, you are the one best equipped to figure it out, whether alone or with the support of parents, friends, or support workers.

There are many times that acceptance means accepting that what you need is not being provided, and that is why the results aren't what is desired. Wanting a boat to be a car because it's in an environment meant for cars is a lack of acceptance of what the boat is. But wanting a boat to move as fast as a car on a road is lack of acceptance for what a boat needs to function, let alone thrive. Some boats can move as fast as cars. But not in the same environment. Acceptance of both what something is and what it needs is necessary. We can and must both accept what we are *and* what we need. This also results in knowing when to accept that we can't do something versus when we can't do something in a specific environment or without specific support.

A boat is enough for what it is. A car is enough for what it is. It is only when comparing to something that is functionally different that it seems that it isn't enough. Even among different boats, there are certain boats meant to do certain things. Some are small and fast. Others are sturdy and built to transport or tow. Others are meant to hold thousands of people on board. You can't have a speed boat that also carries thousands of people. Comparing an old boat to a new boat is an unfair comparison. Comparing a boat used in the ocean compared to a boat used on a lake is an unfair comparison. I could use animals, flowers, or people to make the same point. Comparing two things that have fundamentally different capabilities, purposes, and environmental and functional needs is irrelevant and pointless. Yet, it is what we do all day every day when we judge ourselves and others against equally irrelevant factors. And it is what we allow to influence us when we take into account irrelevant external judgments.

As you move toward identifying who you are, remember that you don't have to be everything to everyone—you can't be. Remember that others' judgments (in many cases) are as irrelevant as comparing a boat to a car in the same race. Remember that you are enough, and the way you will see that is by identifying *all* of who you are and what you are not.

Identifying Who You Are

You are always changing, growing, and learning, so knowing who you are is a lifelong endeavor. This is not something that will be done in one sitting and then never thought about again. This is not something that you need to feel pressured to get perfectly right immediately or ever, for that matter. All you need is to know enough to make your own choices, to advocate for your needs and desires, and to be able to effectively identify where you belong. Knowing those things will lead to increased confidence, so when you do need to ask for help or you find yourself in an environment where you don't belong, you don't take it as a personal failing. Because it's not.

Values

Values aren't just a buzzword. They drive how you do anything in life, whether you realize it or not. They are reminders of what matters to you in the moments of greatest stress. They are signposts of when you are acting aligned with who you are and want to be—and when you're not. When somebody treats you poorly, values remind you to not act like they did or how you may want to in the moment, but in a way that is true to who you are at your core.

Values also explain why doing something you don't believe in results in low self-confidence. They explain why you don't feel good in certain relationships when the other party doesn't value the same things and may even do things that directly conflict with your values.

Values can be used as a guidance system not only in how you act in any given situation but also a guidance system for which situations, jobs, and relationships you allow yourself to be in in the first place. Acting out of survival may lead you to lie, cheat, steal, or to be in otherwise compromising situations, but acting in line with your values keeps you true to who you are. Remembering your values guides you to solutions that won't make you hate yourself, lose yourself, or be ashamed of yourself.

Table 14.1 is a list of example values you may hold. Following the list are questions for a thought exercise. The goal is to identify three to five values that encapsulate what matters most to you.

Table 14.1 Core Human Values

Value	Value	Value
Acceptance	Accessibility	Accountability
Accuracy	Adaptability	Adventure
Appearance	Authenticity	Autonomy
Balance	Belonging	Challenge
Community	Compassion	Confidence
Connection	Courage	Creativity
Determination	Empathy	Faith
Family	Forgiveness	Freedom
Generosity	Gratitude	Growth Mindset
Hard Work	Honesty	Honor
Hope	Humility	Humor
Inclusion	Integrity	Joy
Justice	Kindness	Learning
Loyalty	Optimism	Peace
Politeness	Presentation	Purpose
Recognition	Reflection	Resilience
Resourcefulness	Respect	Security
Self-Discipline	Self-Expression	Self-Respect
Service	Simplicity	Spirituality
Status	Teamwork	Teamwork
Tolerance	Trust	Understanding

Why three to five? Less than three leaves room for your own questioning or others' input when the one or two chosen values don't perfectly apply to a given situation. More than five values adds complexity rather than simple guidance. Three to five is ideal to provide adequate guidance without becoming overwhelming or confusing in application.

Exercise 14.1: Identify Your Values

If you aren't sure what matters most to you, use Table 14.1 and also consider the following questions. While the answer will likely not be in value form, it will pinpoint the topics, feelings, and actions you care about the most, guiding you to a corresponding value.

- What makes you most mad when you do it?
- What makes you most proud when you do it?
- What makes you happiest when others do it?
- What are you most likely to fight for or about?
- What gets you most frustrated when others do it?
- What do you find yourself being offended by the most?
- What is most important in how you want to feel about yourself?
- What do you find yourself giving unsolicited advice on the most?
- What is most important in how you want people to feel around you?

After you've identified your values, ask yourself whether they are what matters most to you, or whether they are what you think should matter most. If it's rooted in "shoulds" or others' input, reevaluate to identify what matters most to *you*.

When you're satisfied that you've chosen the values that matter most to you, define them. Values mean different things to different people, so it's important to define what each means for you. For example, integrity to one person might mean never lying. For another, it might mean acting true to yourself. For another, it may mean doing what is right even when no one is looking. It doesn't matter what it means to other people or what the dictionary says—it matters what it means to you.

Lastly, it's okay to change your values as you learn more about yourself, especially if this is your first time considering personal values. It is also okay to recognize your values change as you go through different stages of life and as you learn. There are some values that will stick with you throughout your life, while other values may ebb and flow in priority.

Goals

While goals don't define who you are, they are a big driver in really being who you are. Goals are a reminder of what matters to you when you start to be influenced by others' input. As opposed to values, which define what you most prioritize in how you act, goals are something you are working toward. Goals can be whatever you want them to be and can change as often as you want them to change, but having goals is important so you have something to guide where you're going and who you're becoming. Goals are a guidance system for you decided by you.

Depending on where you are in life, you may have multiple goals in multiple areas in life—health, relationships, finance, career. At times, you may just have one main goal that drives everything. There is no right or wrong way to set goals, but there is a way that will work best for you at any given time. Trust yourself to know what that is for you.

I once had no specific goals in life except creating peace. I was so overwhelmed and sick of the chaos in my life that all I wanted was to experience peace. I wasn't sure it was possible, but I hoped for it. I kept working and living, but every decision I made was decided by asking myself whether any given action would add peace or hinder peace. It felt as if I was making no progress until a few years later somebody asked how I was able to keep peace in the middle of being laid off. It wasn't until then that I realized I had done it; I had reached my goal a while before without even realizing it. Since then, I have largely sustained a peaceful life. Stressful things still happen, and I still have hard days, but I have cultivated a life where peace is the foundation and is easy to return to. That one goal has had more impact and lasting power in my life than any other individual goal I have ever made. Don't doubt the power of one quality goal. Sometimes, if you want to change health, relationships, purpose, and finance, one quality goal will have a more positive impact than several individual goals. Sometimes one high-priority goal takes care of them all.

You could have multiple goals in one area of your life, or specific health, professional, and social goals all at one time. If you are going to judge yourself for not reaching your goals, start with fewer. If you aren't motivated unless you have specific goals, start with more. Either way, don't believe that you have to take big action. Consistently doing the best you can, no matter how small, is enough. Small does not mean insignificant. Even 1% improvement every day for a year will lead to you being 37 times better by the end of the year (Clear 2022). Making a 1% improvement is barely different than making no change at all in the moment, yet it results in a significant change over time. Making no improvement one day won't ruin the improvement that is accumulating. Even taking a few steps back isn't going to ruin consistently doing the best you can.

Pick goals that you care about, not what others think you should care about. Pick goals that are going to enhance your life, not make your life appear better in the eyes of others. Pick goals that are helping you be more you, not the version of you that you think will be more acceptable.

Once you pick your goal(s), run any decisions through the question "Does this action support my goal or hinder my goal?" Then choose the one that supports your goal more often than not. If you realize in the middle of something that it isn't supporting your goal, you can stop. You can turn off the TV, end the conversation, start looking for another job, choose another thought, call someone for support.

Beliefs

While social identity is made up of social characteristics, self-identity is mostly made up of beliefs. It isn't made up by how others see you, your accomplishments, or your job. It is how you see yourself. It is who you believe yourself to be. It is what you believe to be true for you.

Your beliefs dictate how your brain interprets other people's treatment of you. Your beliefs about yourself dictate the opportunities and possibilities your brain will allow you to see. Your brain will confirm what you believe to be true about the world and your identity (Connors and Halligan 2022). Knowing your core beliefs around your identity and the world helps you to recognize when they are inhibiting you, which then enables you to replace them with something better.

What you believe about your identity affects how you perceive others' treatment of you far more than how people actually treat you. Somebody can compliment you, and you interpret it as a sarcastic insult because you don't believe it to be true about yourself. The same thing can happen the other way around where someone can insult you sarcastically, and you can interpret it as a serious compliment if you believe the statement to be true.

Beliefs also shape how you view opportunities that are available to you. If you don't believe you can get a six-figure job until you get certain certifications, you won't look for or notice job postings that don't require the certifications and for which you are already fully qualified. If you'd like to surf but don't believe you can because you are blind, you will never look for or notice the many organizations around the world that support adaptive surfing. If you believe that people suck and never understand you, you will notice all the ways you aren't understood instead of seeing the times that you are.

How you view others is influenced more by your beliefs and interpretations of their actions than their actions themselves. I once had a teenager live with me temporarily because their home was unsafe. Within a few days I learned that they thought I was either a thief or sold my body for money. Nothing that I said changed their mind. As I tried to identify the reason for this belief, it eventually came out that it was because I had a fridge full of food. While they acted as if it was the most obvious thing that a fridge full of food meant the fridge's owner was a thief or a sex worker, I was incredibly confused. Because they already believed me to be a thief, they interpreted my confusion as denial and further dishonesty. When I told them they could have whatever food they wanted whenever they wanted, it just reinforced their belief that I was a horrible person. The more I learned, the more confused I was. What did a fridge full of food and not rationing that food have to do with me being a thief or a sex worker? Because the teenager didn't exactly have the highest perception of me, it took a lot of time to get to the bottom of it. Eventually I understood that in their experience, a fridge full of food only happened when their mom stole it or slept with somebody. Even when there was a full fridge, it had to be rationed because who knew when it would be full again. Their entire lived experience as well as the beliefs passed on by their mother led to the root beliefs that jobs don't pay enough to provide for food, jobs aren't consistent, and women can't work and support children simultaneously. Therefore, any woman who is single and has a fridge full of food is getting it unethically, the same way this teenager had seen their entire life.

This example very clearly shows how beliefs can affect perception and experience more than the actual facts of a situation. It also shows how beliefs can prohibit you from recognizing or taking advantage of all that is around you. You may starve yourself because of your beliefs even though there is more food available to you than you've ever previously had.

This example may seem extreme, but you and I and everyone else has equally extreme and illogical beliefs that seem completely logical to us given our experiences. It is a fact that the teen had never experienced someone making consistent money or having consistent food. It is a fact that the only way they knew female adults to get food was from stealing or selling their body. It is a fact that they had never encountered a woman who both worked and cared for kids. The beliefs were rooted in facts, but it didn't mean they were true.

The teen started to replace the existing beliefs with more correct beliefs that people can work for honest money. They learned that they too could earn money and be respected. They learned that they could hope for something better than the only reality they previously knew. They learned they could be both honest *and* have a fridge full of food. There was a visible and audible sigh of relief when they learned that they didn't have to choose between integrity and food.

To improve your view of yourself, your acceptance of yourself, and your outlook on life, you must challenge your beliefs. Even if your entire existence has supported one truth, you must look for what else is true and what is more true. You must look outside of your experience for different truths if you want to have a new experience.

There are some questions you can ask to identify core beliefs, but most beliefs are going to show themselves spontaneously. Pay attention to how you talk about yourself, your disability, and the life you can have. Pay attention to any time you say, "I should" or "That's not possible" or "I know what will happen." Pay attention to any time you make one action mean something completely unrelated, even if it seems related to you. When you identify a belief that isn't helpful, immediately ask if it is true. If it isn't, look for what is true. If the belief is true, ask whether there is something else that is just as or even more true. Get in the habit of questioning your beliefs, especially your longest-held beliefs about yourself.

To determine your self-identity, consider the following questions:

- Why do you love who you are? Why don't you like who you are?
- What parts of you are you proud of? What are you ashamed of?
- What do you believe you have to change or achieve before you can be happy, accepted, or loved?
- Why do you believe you have had the success you have had? Why do you believe you haven't reached some of the goals you have?

Needs

As someone who is disabled or functions a bit differently, you're often told to try harder, do more, or pretend to be someone you're not—essentially, be less disabled, less different. Because of this, it's common to look at yourself as a problem to fix instead of seeing the environment as inadequate in meeting your needs. I see so many people dismissing their own needs because they believe what they've been told their whole life that *they* are the one who needs to change. I am telling you now, you do not need to change. Can you improve as a human? Absolutely. But do you need to change your differences to find success? No. Do you need to dismiss your own needs so as not to be "needy"? No. You deserve to get your needs met. Your needs do not make you less than. Your needs do not make you too much. Asking for your needs to be met does not make you difficult. While you are responsible for communicating your needs, you are not to blame when your needs aren't met.

Some needs are obvious and constant. Some needs differ depending on environment, health, what day it is, and other factors. Regardless of the need, identifying where it is a deficit in the environment versus a disability-related limitation helps you to assign the solution to the right place. To identify needs, we are going to look at basic needs, limitations specific to you, and external barriers you commonly experience. Then we will compile effective accommodations for each.

Basic Needs   First let's make clear that disability needs are human needs, not special needs. Human needs include nutrients, hydration, and sleep. You further need safety, connection, mental stimulation, purpose, and a sense of self. How these needs are met depends on multiple factors including availability, culture, preference, and finances. Disability is only one of many factors that influence how needs are met. Unfortunately disability-related needs carry the stigma that accompanies anything tied to disability (as we covered in depth in Part II). But because the stigma exists doesn't make the stigma true, no matter how many people believe it to be.

What are your basic needs to maintain functioning? Consider the following categories and related factors.

Sleep is one of the most vital needs of every human. It is also one of the things that can easily be disrupted by any bodily stress including pain, emotional stress, overthinking, and medication changes. Knowing sleep-related needs enables prioritizing those needs. What is the minimum sleep necessary versus the ideal amount? Do you find yourself frequently prioritizing deadlines or other external pressures over sleep? While it may be necessary once in a while, it is not necessary as often as we make ourselves believe. Even in the short term, risking sleep is not sustainable or supportive of your overall life and well-being. Do you need a nap, or do naps negatively interfere with your sleep? Are there certain factors that improve sleep such as temperature, weighted blankets or certain textures, sound, light, or medications? Are there actions that inhibit good sleep such as somebody else's snores, blue light, or caffeine within a certain amount of hours? Is there a certain bedtime routine or morning routine that supports easier waking up?

Providing adequate amounts and types of nutrients are vital to body functioning. Not eating because you don't want to be an inconvenience, embarrassment, or because your boss won't let you use the bathroom as much as you need isn't helping anybody. There may be some periods where temporarily not eating is the best choice, but making it a habit is putting strain on your body that will exacerbate existing symptoms or cause new ones. It is not worth it. Do you do best with three meals a day or small snacks all day long? Do you have allergies or certain foods that your body doesn't process well? Do you need extra salt to keep you from passing out, or do you need less salt to aid your heart? Do you need more food or different foods on days you are exercising, traveling, or interacting with a lot of people? Do you need less food on those days? Do you decide what to eat based on others? How can you decide what you eat based on what is best for you?

Medication and supplements, mobility aids, exercise, sunlight, sensory needs, and human connection are the other basic needs. Consider what is necessary to meet your bare minimum needs and what it would look like to meet your needs at an ideal level. Aim to never go below the bare minimum and to meet the ideal level as frequently as possible.

If you don't know your needs, track all of the above factors along with corresponding mood and physical symptoms. You probably already know the obvious ones, but hidden, yet relevant, patterns can reveal themselves if you track them even for a week.

Limitations, Barriers, and Accommodations I use the word "limitations" intentionally. Limitations are a neutral fact that every human has. Limitations related to disability are not any more telling of a person or their value than any other human limitations. Limitations may limit what you can achieve in some ways, but most often they limit not what you can achieve but how you can achieve it. Limitations are parameters to work within to decide how to move forward, not factors that inevitably hold you back.

Height can be a limitation. Someone who is five feet tall is going to interact with the world differently than someone who is six feet three. Both can drive but may require different cars, or at the very least different seat positions. Both can walk the same distance, but one would take more steps while the other takes longer steps. Both can have equally supportive and comfortable sneakers but might require different sizes. The person who is six feet three is limited in shoe styles and sizes they can choose, doorways they can fit through, and cars they can drive. Once limitations are accepted as a normal function of differences, they cease to have a negative connotation. Limitations are not inherently negative. They are neutral results of differences.

Someone who is blind will navigate the world differently than someone who is sighted. Someone who is depressed will navigate the world differently than someone who isn't. Someone who uses a wheelchair will navigate the world differently than someone who walks. And someone who communicates via tablet will navigate the world differently than someone who communicates verbally. These all come with their own limitations. Limitations are not a bad thing. They can be frustrating, they can be exhausting, and it can be hard to be different, but limitations are not inherently bad or defining.

Barriers are different from limitations in that they are external. Barriers are blockades that you encounter along your path whether they are nature- or human-caused. It could be inaccessibility, discriminatory policies, or ableist views. Like limitations, barriers also don't have to be defining. They can also be frustrating and exhausting to navigate, especially when human-caused, but building them into your considerations and then preparing the best ways to navigate around them enables you to progress forward and still achieve what you want.

To identify your needs, look at your own personal limitations, as well as environmental barriers. I suggest comparing situations where you are successful to situations regarding the same task where you struggle. Consider all factors, even ones that seem irrelevant. Consider the time of day, day of the week, what you have eaten and when. Consider the people present and the technology being used. Consider the task type and communication type. Consider your stress levels and whether you did anything to mitigate the stress. Did you have clear directions and expectations? Did you receive training? Were you surprised?

Compare the differences between the situations where you are more successful and those when you aren't, and look for patterns or obvious differences. Therein often lies the need and an effective solution to mitigate the limitations and barriers.

Sometimes the need and solution are directly related to your body and something you can provide for yourself. If you struggle when you haven't eaten for four hours but excel when you've eaten within two hours, you know your need is to eat every two hours, and the solution is something like more frequent breaks or portable snacks in your bag. If you struggle with creative tasks in the morning and systematic tasks in the evening but excel when switched, the need is to complete systematic tasks first thing, and work on creative tasks in the evening.

If you struggle when you are in a new room or when the room has been reorganized, but you excel when you know where the light switches, doors, exits, and bathrooms are, then a need is to know the specifics of any new room, and the solution is to get a tour of any new room to identify the important parts.

Other times you are going to require external accommodations to meet your needs. You learn that you need speech-to-text software, or quiet while working, or the ability to switch desks day-to-day. You might recognize that you do better when you receive an agenda with meeting requests, time to process changes, or a desk that faces away from the window.

Some of your needs are constant, and some are dynamic. You may realize that some needs only come into play when you are overstimulated, didn't sleep well the night before, or are having a flare-up causing increased pain. You may recognize the tasks that increase cognitive load and learn to limit those tasks to certain duration or frequency per day.

Limitations, barriers, and solutions often become obvious when you stop believing that you are too much and instead let yourself recognize and accept your needs. Even when you think you know your needs well, stay open to seeing where you may be denying yourself of your needs or where there may be a better solution to meet that need. There is always room for improvement.

Energy Drains and Sources   The thoughts, actions, people, and environments that deplete you of energy and those that give you energy are important factors when identifying needs. Your body needs energy to keep you alive and to best manage your mental and physical functioning. When dealing with disabilities, energy drains and sources become even more important so you don't unknowingly waste energy and miss out on opportunities to replenish your energy.

To identify energy sources and drains is fairly simple on the surface—what gives you energy, and what depletes you of energy? Going deeper, it is identifying what are effective energy sources to follow energy drains. What are effective energy drains when you have heightened energy? What are energy drains you have to deal with, and how can you plan for them? What are energy drains that you don't have to deal with and can eliminate from your life?

Energy drains are those activities, people, and environments that deplete you of energy. Energy drains aren't necessarily bad but could be. There are energy drains that aren't necessary or enjoyable, such as trolls on social media. Engaging with them is draining energy for no benefit. Those are situations you want to avoid at all costs. Then there are energy drains that aren't enjoyable but are necessary such as job interviews or dentist appointments. There is benefit, but it requires planning and recovery. You want to limit these to when they are truly necessary, and adequately plan around them. There are energy drains that aren't necessary but are enjoyable. These may be concerts, dinners with friends, or watching movies. These are energy drains that you can do as often as you have the energy for it because enjoying yourself is of immense benefit in life, but you want to plan accordingly to be able to handle the event and the aftermath.

You may even use some of these energy drains, such as intense exercise, when you have so much energy that you need to release it. Then there are energy drains that are both necessary and enjoyable. These you plan for, ask for accommodations if necessary, and give yourself enough recovery time so that you don't eventually stop getting enjoyment from it.

Knowing how to manage your energy is especially important to avoid burnout, manage burnout if you're already there, and to ensure you aren't unintentionally putting more stress on the body while negatively affecting your physical or mental health. Knowing how to manage your energy will help with emotional regulation, cognitive load, and healing. It will also directly influence general happiness and life fulfillment. And if you have a disability that leaves you constantly lethargic, these are especially key factors to consider consciously instead of just going through life miserably tired—a shell of who you wish you could be.

Correctly categorizing energy drains requires objective assessment of what is actually necessary. Many things you think are necessary are rooted in "should." "Should" does not mean necessary. Necessary to avoid judgment does not mean necessary. Necessary means truly necessary for survival, to reach your goals, meet your needs, or to stay aligned with your values. If it isn't any of these, then it is *optional*. And accept the energy leak for what it is so you can appropriately get rid of it or accommodate for it.

Energy sources are those activities, people, and environments that fill you with energy. While these are likely to be beneficial, there could be times that additional energy is not ideal, or even harmful. Calories and caffeine are literal energy sources that could be harmful in excess. There are environments where you come alive, people who are motivating and energizing, as well as activities that you can seemingly keep going on forever. These are the things that you want to fill most of your life with. These are the things that most people replace with what they convince themselves they *should* be doing, what is responsible to do, or what others expect you to do. This is a recipe for burnout, depression, and an overall miserable, unhappy, and draining life.

There are times energy sources require energy to initiate. If you are already drained of energy, initiating can be hard. These are the things that you want to remind yourself that you will feel better after you do them. Or you may want to prioritize these activities when you do have energy knowing that it will only result in more energy. These are the things that will keep you from burnout, help you get out of burnout, and bring enjoyment back to your life. These are the things that you want to do even if you get judged (as long as they don't harm yourself or others).

Some activities are simultaneously a drain and a source of energy and require accommodating. Baseball games are an example in my life. While I am at a game, I am excited, focused, and have a lot of energy. They invigorate and motivate me. They also take a lot out of me mentally and require that I prepare to withstand all the noise, sound, and action, while also requiring a plan to rest and rejuvenate after.

There are also activities, environments, and people who are neither drains nor sources of energy. These don't require preparation or recovery. These are most likely unconscious habits, or things you can do without much thought.

Now that you know how to identify energy drains and sources, look at what most fills your life. Notice where you can rid yourself of drains or reorganize and better plan to recover after drains. Notice where you can utilize energy sources to get through necessary energy drains. Notice where you have convinced yourself that you should do something, but it actually isn't necessary at all, and replace those activities with those that you find energizing.

Personality

Up to this point we haven't addressed what you may have thought is what makes you unique, such as your personality traits, likes and dislikes, and strengths and weaknesses. You find who you are in these ways by living. You find who you are by making choices that are true to you instead of others. You try and fail. You find where you excel, what you like, and what you don't like by trying new things. You may know who you are to some extent depending on how accepting people in your life have been and how much you've been allowed to explore who you are. Either way, you will find out more of who you are by consistently trying new things.

There are strong opinions on how you should apply to jobs, seek new opportunities, or create change in your life. But there is no one right way. And thinking that there is either leads you to be judgmental of those who aren't doing it your way or it leads you to believe you are the one doing it the wrong way. But what if people can do things differently, and it is right for them? What if you can do things differently, and it is right for you? The fact that you are reading this book says you likely are already different in some way, so you know this to be true. Whether it is you or others who are different, being different does not mean being less or wrong.

How do you best make decisions? Are you someone who instinctively knows and decides in the moment? Do you take some time to make sure you're in an emotionally neutral state before deciding anything? Do you need to talk it out before coming to a decision?

Are you someone who has always known their purpose and has consistently had the same interests? Or are you someone who changes interests and life purpose every year? Are you the same person no matter who you are around or do you naturally shift in the environment?

There is no one right way. The only right way is being you.

It is constant stress to not know who you are, to not know how to act, to always figure out how to act based on external factors. It requires more mental pressure than just being. This chapter, hopefully, has helped you know even a little bit more of who you are to relieve the mental labor of trying to be someone you're not.

15

Accept Yourself

Now THAT YOU know who you are, or at least how to identify who you are, acceptance becomes more feasible. Stigma taught you to reject, hide, and fight against who you are. But it is when you stop fighting, denying, or attempting to change what is that allows you to realize what can be. Acceptance reduces suffering and stress. Acceptance allows change with ease and peace instead of force and discomfort. Acceptance fosters self-empowerment, confidence, and freedom. Most significantly, self-acceptance allows you to believe that it's true when others accept you, too.

Self-acceptance isn't just accepting who you inherently are but also who you aren't. It is accepting what you can do and what you can't. It is accepting that you can't be everything to everyone, and that you can be more to yourself. It is accepting that you can be a better version of you and that you can't be someone other than you. It is accepting the parts of you that don't work the same way as others. It is accepting the parts of you that are better when compared to others. It is accepting the parts of you that are self-sabotaging and accepting that even the self-sabotaging is out of survival. It is accepting that you have more control than you think internally and have more responsibility for where you are in life. It is accepting that you have less control than you think externally, and less responsibility for how others act, perceive you, or treat you. It is accepting that you will benefit from enacting more self-control while letting go of what you can't control.

Accepting who you are, especially your legitimate limitations, isn't a one-time or linear process. It has different stages. It requires leaving behind judgment and resistance. Luckily, acceptance is the antidote to both. Where judgment and resistance deny more possibility than nearly any other mindset, acceptance creates more possibility than nearly any other mindset.

Acceptance requires embracing self-compassion, self-awareness, and self-prioritization. Compassion, awareness, and prioritization of your needs and humanity are the traits most missing in the ways society views and treats disability and those who are disabled. It is that mistreatment and the resulting shame that strongly influences a lack of self-acceptance. Acceptance also includes accepting that even when stigma, inaccessibility, and discrimination still exist externally, you don't have to wait for others to change before you can cultivate and provide acceptance for yourself.

Non-Judgment

Acceptance does not entail adding positive or negative values to a neutral fact. In fact, that isn't acceptance at all. Negative definitions of any aspect of yourself increase the likelihood of stress, low self-confidence, increased depressive symptoms, and hopelessness. Adding positive definitions to neutral aspects of yourself increases the likelihood of not being open to correction, not questioning your assumptions, or overestimating your abilities. Toxic positivity also requires denying reality and results in additional stress.

Examples of neutral facts without positive or negative emotional attribution:

- You have an overdrawn account.
- You just received a promotion.
- You experience chronic pain.
- You are an award-winning singer.

You may have read these and attributed seemingly obvious positives or negatives. You may have even thought, "An overdrawn account is literally in the negative." The overdrawn account may be because rent just got paid and went out on time despite not being enough money in the account. It may have kept you from being evicted. Or maybe you just didn't pay attention to what you had and spent more than you realized before rent was due. Depending on which relevant facts you focus on, you could redefine the overdrawn account as a positive or negative. It is the story you attach to a fact that makes it emotionally positive or negative.

Adding either positive or negative definitions to who you are increases resistance and suffering. Believing positive or negative versions of the truth require you to fight against what *is* while not seeing what is *possible*. Viewing all aspects of yourself as the neutral facts they are is true acceptance. Accepting who you are also means accepting actions you take and mistakes you make.

Perhaps you received a promotion but may have just been offered a job somewhere else for more pay and were planning on quitting. Now you feel stress and overwhelmed with the decision. It's only a hard decision because both options could be great options. Depending on which relevant facts you use to attach meaning, you could redefine the promotion as a positive or a negative.

Being an award-winning singer may seem to many an obvious positive, but even it is also a neutral fact. Winning the award may have been a joyous moment and perceived as evidence that all the hard work paid off. Winning the award could also be a moment of pain and regret if the award was a result of work that required the person to give up part of who they are, their values, or relationships to fit in to industry standards and meet external expectations. Depending on how the award was achieved, the winner's beliefs about the award, and the relevant state of mind at the time, even winning an award and being an award-winning singer can be experienced and perceived as a positive or negative.

Accepting what is doesn't mean you don't celebrate parts of yourself and your life or desire to improve other parts of yourself and your life. Non-judgment ensures these views are based on what really is, not what you are resisting, not compared to what you desire it to be, and not a story that you are telling yourself based on flawed perceptions. I believe that chronic pain is one of the most miserable experiences a person can have. Pain hurts. That is fact. Pain doesn't just affect physical sensation but also the ability to function physically, mentally, and emotionally. Pain can cause irritability, anger, and decrease the will to live. These are all facts. Acceptance of these as facts and not tying meaning to it will help keep the suffering from being more than it needs to be. It doesn't have to mean God hates you, nothing ever works out for you, or that your life is a series of unfortunate events. It doesn't have to mean you are destined to pain for the rest of your life. It might, but you don't know the future. Chronic pain and other disabilities are already miserable enough; the stories just add to the existing misery.

Trying to act in non-judgment doesn't mean you don't have feelings. Feelings are natural reactions to input our brain receives. You might experience feelings of joy, safety, and gratitude; or fear, anger, and despair. True acceptance is having all those feelings, and experiencing the experience, without making the feelings mean anything. Feelings are neutral, too. They don't define your circumstance, and your circumstance does not need to define your feelings. Let them be what they are without adding elaborate stories.

Non-judgment applies to even the uncomfortable emotions. It's letting yourself grieve what once was or what you wish could be. It's feeling anger. It is fear of the unknown and fear that you won't be accepted. It is jealousy and resentment. It is letting yourself feel what you feel without suppressing it and without perpetuating it. The chemicals in your brain are what make you have certain emotions. If you just let the chemicals do their thing, the feelings can shift. If you suppress it or hold on to it, the feelings become more than they need to be. If you shame it or judge it, you are enabling the cycle to continue. If you shame or judge yourself, apply non-judgment to that, too. Judging yourself for judging will lead to more judgment and a never-ending cycle. The same with shame. But, no matter how long the cycle has gone on, applying non-judgment will allow momentum to wane and the emotion to eventually stop.

Non-Resistance

Resisting what is causes more suffering than the original cause of suffering itself. Resistance in this sense refers to denial, blame, and trying to change what you can't control. Resistance in this sense refers to the act of trying to avoid the pain of a situation, inadvertently causing more and longer-lasting pain.

Denying the progression of a disability and not using mobility devices is one example. Accepting the diagnosis or the disability progression will open you up to feel the pain that comes along with it and will open you up to potential judgment from others. So you choose to deny it or hide it as long as you can. Resisting what is causes the pain and judgment to last longer than necessary. Even if you are able to temporarily avoid external judgment, you are judging yourself, so you aren't avoiding judgment at all. The fastest and most effective way through it is acceptance.

When you have thoughts such as, "I shouldn't feel these feelings," "Others have it harder than me," "Other people have 'real' disabilities; I shouldn't complain," it's accepting these thoughts without resistance, too. It isn't accepting the thoughts as truth but accepting that they are a thought you are experiencing. Resisting it or telling a story to explain it will cement the thought more. But simply accepting it as a thought allows the thought to change to a different thought.

It means, for example, not fighting against the fact that you don't have motivation. Trying to motivate yourself when you lack motivation is fighting against what is. Resisting your lack of motivation typically results in shame, guilt, or feelings of inadequacy. Then it leads to frustration and annoyance at yourself for not being motivated to do even a basic task. But what if you just accepted that you weren't motivated? What if you didn't resist it? It doesn't speak to your morals, value, or identity—it simply speaks to your state of being in the moment. When you stop resisting that you aren't motivated and that the specific task still needs to be done, you then can identify an effective solution that uses both facts as parameters to work within. How can you do the thing without any motivation? How can you make it so simple that it would be harder to not do it? How can you take the first action? If you really can't take any action right now, how can you mitigate any potential issues? Can you ask someone else for help? Does it need to get done? Can you accept that it's not getting done and stop caring? Reducing the resistance reduces the mental load and allows you to focus on the solution forward.

Even if you self-sabotage, it is okay and doesn't need to be resisted. Maybe you waited until the last minute to complete something and now are rushed to get it done at all, let alone well. Acceptance of the fact that it happened and that you now are on a new timeline allows you to shift mental energy to where it will actually help. You can shift from resistance in the form of judgment and shame to using your cognitive capacity to find the best solution forward given the new parameters. No matter what you've done or how long you've been in the cycle, you can stop it by not resisting what is. The continuous judgment and resistance of what is enables the cycle to continue.

Self-Compassion

No matter what your goal is, being compassionate is going to be beneficial. Do you want to change a behavior completely? Move through a hard emotion or situation? Find a way to be happy or reduce emotional overload? All of it is made more possible by kindness and understanding of where you currently are.

Compassion reminds you that you aren't broken, you aren't deficient, and you aren't hopeless. Whether it's regarding your disability, habits, or how you treat others, this is true. Even the unacceptable actions. Compassion stops the shame. Stopping the shame stops the shame-led actions, which are often the worst actions.

Without compassion, you see things through judgment, good or bad. Labeling your actions good or bad often results in discomfort. The brain wants to avoid discomfort so will then keep you from accepting yourself or even seeing yourself. Compassion is the opposite of what you are given by others and yourself. Holding yourself to impossibly high standards, pushing for better or more, judging yourself harshly, comparing yourself to others or what you "should" be is all the opposite of compassion. Compassion is being kind, understanding, and supportive. If treating yourself with kindness, understanding, and support feels wrong, imagine someone you respect or love doing what you did, and ask yourself whether you would judge them as harshly. Aim to give yourself the same compassion that you do for others.

Give yourself compassion as you start to recognize the parts of you that were developed in survival. Give yourself compassion for isolating, anger, people-pleasing, helplessness, lack of connection, even harming yourself or others. You brain was protecting you. It did what it knew to do in the moment. You can't remove shame while continuing to shame yourself. Practice compassion instead. And practice compassion when you inevitably fail to give yourself compassion.

Self-Awareness

Self-awareness doesn't necessarily require you to know why you do certain things. It is more important to be aware that you do certain things at all. Trying to answer the why is a philosophical exercise that gives you the appearance of self-awareness without actually being self-aware, at all. The reasons behind certain actions are often influenced by something seemingly unrelated—subconscious survival skills, lack of sleep, overstimulation, or you received bad news even days earlier. There are diverse scenarios that define why you do what you do, but the commonality is because it is what your brain thought would best serve you in the moment. Even when you logically know you "should" do something but don't have the energy to take action, not taking action is acting in line with what the brain thinks is best. It may be to conserve energy to heal; it may be because not taking action is what kept you safe from judgment in the past. The specific reason doesn't matter as much as asking what your brain is protecting you from and then assessing if that reason is true or not.

Asking why also often leads to judgment or justification. Neither are helpful for neutral self-awareness. Avoid asking why. Avoid believing the reason your brain gives for why.

For example, when you do something wrong, immediate thoughts may be "Why am I such an idiot?" "Why do I keep getting myself into these situations?" "Why can't I do anything right?" These thoughts are rooted in self-judgment and will be immediately followed by thoughts explaining why you are an idiot and can't do anything right. What you ask, the brain will answer. Asking judgment-based questions will get judgment-based answers.

More important than the awareness of *why* is the awareness of *what*. What emotions are you feeling? What sensations do you feel in your body? What part did you have in creating your current situation? What habits led to this? What are your thought patterns? What is destructive and what is helpful? Becoming aware and using what you know about the brain enables improved view of self, quality of life, and mental and physical health. Awareness decreases the brain's more natural inclinations to focus on the negative, perceived threats where they don't exist and lead you to internalize external beliefs and stigma.

Self-awareness is paying attention when your needs change, when resistance arises, or when you are tempted to engage in self-sabotaging behavior. Self-awareness is recognizing when you push through resistance, when you choose value-aligned behaviors, and when you meet your own needs.

Self-awareness can be improved by including others' feedback, but it depends greatly on who is delivering the feedback and how you measure its relevance. If it is someone whose perspective aligns with your interests and they have the ability and desire to give the truth with kindness, then you should take their feedback. If they are missing any of those factors, be cautious with their feedback.

Self-Accountability

It is incredibly easy to believe that everything that happens to us is because of external factors, especially when discrimination, bias, inaccessibility, inequity, abuse, and many more damaging acts exist in the world. These are real factors that have undeniably real impacts. Discrimination and social stigma increases self-stigma and shame. Self-stigma and shame negatively affect self-esteem, self-efficacy, quality of life, and mental and physical health (Dubreucq, Plasse, and Franck 2021).

There is an additional truth that there are ways to increase stigma resistance, or the ability to deflect or challenge stigmatizing beliefs (Dubreucq et al. 2022). Developing disability acceptance, personal trait acceptance, and overall self-acceptance mitigates discrimination and stigma (Jansen-van Vuuren and Aldersey 2020). This is promising because it isn't discrimination and stigma that have the most significant negative impacts on well-being—it is the *self-stigma*. This does not mean it is your fault. This just means you have some control. If you can protect yourself from letting discrimination and stigma become internalized as self-stigma, you can mitigate the negative impacts.

Examples of Acceptance in Daily Life

Self-acceptance is a moment-by-moment process. Each moment is an opportunity to choose again. While the choice is moment-by-moment, the impact is not. Every moment of acceptance affects what occurs after the acceptance, how you react in future similar experiences, and your brain plasticity (Meier et al. 2020).

Here are examples of self-acceptance in everyday life:

- Respecting your need for frequent breaks to manage fatigue or pain
- Using mobility devices even when it draws attention
- Letting feelings arise without judgment, resistance, or added stories
- Recognizing where you have internalized stigma
- Accepting compliments rather than dismissing or downplaying them
- Owning your right to exist without minimizing yourself or apologizing for existing
- Admitting where you are limited and asking for support or accommodations

Each time you choose self-acceptance is a successful moment. Each time you recognize and accept that you didn't choose self-acceptance is also a successful moment. It isn't diminished in value even if it is preceded by 100 moments of self-rejection and followed by 100 more. Self-acceptance one more time a day than the day before is valuable improvement. Eventually, you will get to the point where you are choosing acceptance 20% of the day. Then it gets easier, and you are soon choosing self-acceptance 50% of the day. Continue the same pattern, and you will eventually practice self-acceptance in all situations except new situations where you haven't yet built the self-acceptance habit or in moments where you're feeling a bit low. It doesn't require perfection. Self-acceptance is the culmination of small mindset shifts and small consistent actions.

16

Accept Others

PSYCHOLOGY 101 TEACHES that humans project onto others their own fears, insecurities, and judgments. Your ability to accept others directly hinders or supports your ability to accept yourself. Conversely, your ability to accept yourself directly hinders or supports your ability to accept others. Whether you are consciously aware of it or not, the two can't be separated. Building the habits of recognizing that others get to be who they are inevitably enables you to be who you are.

For some, accepting others is going to be a more effective next step in increasing self-acceptance than focusing on self-acceptance itself. Especially if you are already overly concerned with others' actions and perceptions, this can be a strategy to focus these habits in a positive way.

The acceptance addressed here is a neutral acceptance of what is, not necessarily an approval or tolerance of others' behavior. Accepting that the person is who they are allows you to navigate the situation better than trying to fight, deny, or attempt to change who they are.

Not accepting others is usually a desire to control our emotions by judging and controlling others rather than dealing with the emotions that come from acceptance of what is. It may be a way to avoid addressing the parts of yourself that you judge, or it may be a way to avoid accepting that what others say may be true. Accepting others means accepting that you don't have any control over who they are or how they treat you. Judging others is the easy way out in the moment, whereas accepting them and taking the necessary action on your own side is much harder, yet it makes your life easier in the long-term.

Accepting others at the most basic level is not making up stories about what their actions, words, or appearance mean. Accepting others means turning the focus back to you when you catch yourself judging and recognizing how it makes you feel and how you want to move forward yourself.

Accepting others means accepting their humanity and that they have every right to have their own opinions and to make their own decisions. It means accepting this even when it is inconvenient or uncomfortable.

For me, it means accepting my clients may cancel last minute. If I didn't accept that as a reality of working with clients with disabilities, I would provide subpar experience for my clients, judge them based on stigma, and be frustrated every time it happened. Instead, I build it into my processes and work around it so no money is lost, my day isn't negatively affected by the schedule change, and my peace of mind remains.

Acceptance of others also means accepting that others get to develop their own opinions of you. Others are allowed to feel inconvenienced by your disability. It may be rooted in stigma, or it may be rooted in their energy levels or personal needs. Either way, accepting their feeling as is and then deciding how to respond to best serve you is far more beneficial than judging them as wrong for having their opinion.

Non-Judgment

As always, awareness is the first step. Become aware that you judge. Then dig a little deeper and become aware of why you are judging. Is it because you are projecting onto them something you are judging about yourself? Or are you judging someone else's perception as wrong to avoid the pain if they were right? Is it judging them according to a standard you hold for yourself?

Just like it's not helpful to add judgment and meaning to your own circumstances, actions, and feelings, you would do well to not add judgment and meaning to others'. Judgments are always biased. Always. Biases are ways that our brain simplifies all the data it takes in to make sense of the world. The brain doesn't only see what is there; it uses information from past experiences to make assumptions based on patterns, relevant or not. Your brain projects your own fears, insecurities, and opinions onto others. It can lead you to focusing more on the negative and disregarding the positive when fears and insecurities are prominent, or focusing on the positive and disregarding the negative when you have high opinions of a person. These are just a few ways our brain enacts biases in everyday judgments of others. We all have cognitive biases and always will. But what we can do is become more aware of them, recognize when they cause harm, and try to focus on what is true rather than what a bias makes you believe to be true.

Outside of biases, we still are not likely to know the whole truth about someone else, especially if we are making up stories based on the limited facts we know. If somebody doesn't respond to you, it's easy to interpret that it's because they are mad or you did something wrong. If someone uses similar language that a previous ableist boss used, it is easy to tell a story that this new person is acting from prejudice even if the language isn't ableist in itself and there is no other indication of prejudice. It is easy to get mad, annoyed, or hurt when others don't act how we think they should act. It could be something as simple as not moving quickly when you are in a hurry or crying when you don't think it's appropriate or not crying when you think they should be. Why are you putting your definition of "correct" or "appropriate" onto others? Your life gets much calmer when you stop having judgmental and unpleasant thoughts and feelings about others' circumstances, actions, and feelings.

Life becomes much easier when you are able to avoid attaching meaning when people do what you don't like or when they do what you do like. They did what they did. That is all. There are a millions of reasons that could be behind it. It is highly unlikely you know the accurate reasons. Don't assume. If you can't help but to assume something, at least choose an assumption that helps your mental state while supporting you living your values and reaching your goals.

This means not tying judgment to their actions, but it also means not coming up with reasons to justify or explain their actions. Both are falsely created. Especially, don't attribute a diagnosis or trauma to their behavior that they didn't disclose to you. The reason doesn't matter because all you can address is the behavior. Also, why spend so much time analyzing someone else's behaviors? It may be that intellectualizing a problem helps you avoid accepting an uncomfortable truth about the person. It may be that finding justification to excuse their behavior or blame them allows you to avoid looking at yourself.

So stop.

Or don't, because you don't have to do what I suggest just because I think it's helpful. But maybe you'll start to become more aware and stop giving energy away to analyzing things that you will never figure out.

Some people won't change. Some people don't want to learn or change. Accept that and act accordingly. Be freed by it instead of trying to change it.

It's also okay to not like other people. It doesn't mean they are wrong, or bad, or anything negative. It simply means that you don't like them. That is okay. Just as it is okay for other people to not like you.

Because you are human and you can't be completely free of judgment, err on the side of positive assumptions. Even when you're wrong, the positive assumptions promote psychological well-being. If you are someone who doesn't do well when someone acts in a way that you didn't expect, you can prepare for a less than ideal situation while assuming the best—the old "hope for the best, prepare for the worst" adage. It works because it ensures you are prepared either way but aren't dwelling on something that may or may not ever even happen.

Non-Resistance

Resisting what is true about someone else is just a distraction from what actually matters. Others' beliefs and behavior can be pretty convincing distractions that lead you away from what matters most to you. One common example is people not believing you. Whether you have an apparent or non-apparent disability, you have probably had people who didn't believe your disability, your needs, or your capabilities. In these situations, it is easy to focus on changing the other person's belief. It is easy to think you need to over-explain or prove yourself. You can convince yourself that changing their belief requires disclosure of personal information and engaging in exhausting conversations.

But if someone has made up their mind that they don't believe you, you don't know that nothing you say is going to change that disbelief.

What matters is getting the access you need, the support you need, the job you qualify for, and so forth. What matters is being in environments you belong where you don't have to convince someone that you belong. Is there a way to reach that goal while accepting that you aren't being believed? If you accept that you aren't believed, what would you do instead of trying to fight it, change it, or deny it? Accepting reality immediately resolves a lot of the energy you exert trying to justify and prove yourself. Accept that a lot of people may hold untrue beliefs about you. And accept they may have those beliefs despite you clearly explaining or showing why they are wrong. This way, you at least get to protect your energy. This is the essence of non-resistance.

Accountability

Acceptance without judgment or resistance does not mean you let people go without accountability, even after you add compassion into the mix. In fact, holding others accountable gets far more effective when done without judgment or resistance. Instead of operating with frustration, judgment, and assumptions, you lead with neutral facts and traits that are more likely to lead to real solutions and understanding. Even if the solution is leaving the situation or person behind.

Self-Prioritization

Accepting others is prioritizing yourself. It isn't for their sake; it is for your own benefit. You conserve energy by not engaging in judgment or resistance of others. You strengthen your ability to accept yourself every time you practice acceptance of others. You improve relationships and connection by not letting judgments lead.

Beyond the general self-prioritization that comes from accepting others, you can further prioritize yourself by prioritizing your values, goals, and needs. When someone acts in a way that you don't agree with, decide whether you engage or not based on your goals. If engaging is aligned with your goals, decide how to best engage based on your values. Further decide how and when based on your needs. When it isn't aligned with your values and goals, let it go. In most cases, not engaging is going to be the appropriate response. And if you're not sure, err on the side of not engaging. You can always deal with it later if necessary, but you can't take back engaging in a way or on a matter that you regret.

Overall, the act of accepting others only serves to support you in accepting yourself. Acceptance practiced in one area strengthens your ability to accept in all areas. Accepting others is not to benefit them (though it does)—it is to benefit and support you in being your best.

17

Practice Being You

Now IS WHEN theory and thought get put into action. You can call this the exciting part, the fun part, or the hard part, whatever you decide is the lens through which your brain will interpret it, so you might as well define it as something that supports you.

Being you requires vulnerability, letting go of overactive survival skills, and building trust in yourself. The brain will interpret this as scary just because it is new and different and the opposite of what has kept it safe up to this point, but the results of pushing through are worth it. It results in improved self-confidence, self-efficacy, and resistance to stigma and shame. Self-efficacy is your belief in your ability to reach a goal, complete a task, or navigate life. It is more than just confidence in who you are—it is a true belief in your ability to make it through. You will have less stress and therefore improved mental and physical health. Your quality of life will improve, as well as your sense of connection and belonging. Even if nothing external changes, the benefits of being you far outweigh the risks.

If you get scared to be vulnerable and feel the need to enact survival skills that prioritize others at the risk of yourself, do something to regulate your nervous system (see Chapter 13) and remind yourself that what your brain really wants is on the other side of vulnerability. This is where acting boldly comes in. It will take courage. It is a risk. But you can do it. You can *boldly belong*.

Boldly: In a confident and courageous way, willing to take risks

Belong: To be suited to and accepted in a group or environment as you are

Boldly belong: To confidently and courageously find the relationships, groups, and environments that are suited for you

Improve Trust in Your Body

"First things first" is what I typically say when introducing this concept to my clients. It may have taken 16 chapters to get here but this is really the key to everything. If you didn't deconstruct any beliefs, but you learned to trust your body, your beliefs would naturally shift. If you didn't go through thought exercises to identify who you are but you learned to trust your body, you would naturally find who you are.

No matter who you are, the level of trust in your body can be improved. Even if your body or brain can't be trusted in some ways, you can improve trust in ways that matter. Everyone has some level of disconnection from their body's needs. It results in some level of questioning, not responding to, and eventually not even feeling the body's prompting. How many times do you avoid using the bathroom because you don't feel like it, or don't want to inconvenience someone else, or don't want to be seen going through that group of people? How many times have you pushed through pain or fatigue unnecessarily instead of giving your body what it needed? There are times to delay, and there are times to push through, but that isn't as often as it might initially seem.

We all have our excuses:

- But I have kids.
- But I have a deadline.
- But I might get fired!
- But a have to reach this goal.
- But they will judge me.

Or we have justifications (or procrastination):

- I'll relax when I get the raise.
- I'll sleep after I finish this project.
- I'll eat when I get home.
- I'll ask for accommodations next time.

There will always be reasons to push off your needs. There will always be convincing reasons to prioritize something external over yourself. There will always be justification to stay with the status quo just a little longer and meet your needs later. Those reasons don't go away when the situation changes; they don't go away ever. They just get less priority when you choose to give them less priority.

Kids are a priority, meeting deadlines is a priority, keeping your job is a priority. Avoiding judgment from others is not so much a priority, but I know your brain may convince you it is. Improving trust in your body means prioritizing your body over everything else. It means listening to your body over everything else. It doesn't mean not prioritizing those other things; it just means you recognize that all the other things wouldn't be possible and will be threatened by not prioritizing your body. It means recognizing that your body was built with highly efficient systems to communicate your needs to you, and listening to your body is the best way to get those needs met.

Give your body sleep when it says it needs it. Give your body food when it says it needs it. Go to the bathroom when your body says it needs it. Learn to distinguish between fear of something new and discomfort because something is actually wrong and your body is telling you to leave the situation.

This may seem impossible for the environments and situations many of you are currently in. Those situations are the ones most vital to listen to your body. Those are the situations that your body is likely in a state of constant stress that is harming both the body and the brain. Eventually you will burn out if you haven't already, which in the worst cases can lead to severe medical complications. I know many people who thought they couldn't take sick time because they needed the money only to get so sick they couldn't work for six months. Or people who thought they could push through a slight injury and then ended up making the injury so bad they couldn't walk or drive. Those situations aren't the exception—they are the norm. Putting stress on your body without also giving your body what it needs to heal and grow from that stress is asking for disaster.

Immediately after writing that paragraph, I opened an Internet browser and saw the headline: "I worked nights, weekends, and holidays after being put on a performance improvement plan. I saved my job, but it wasn't worth it" (McCollum 2024). A brief glance over the article showed that the author was put on a performance improvement program (PIP) just a few days after making a complaint. While there was no mention of disability, those of you who have disclosed a disability, asked for an accommodation, or made a related complaint likely know how it feels to get put on a PIP, let go, or otherwise treated differently as a result. In the author's case, the hard work resulted in successfully completing the PIP but also resulted in being hospitalized for heart palpitations and an irregular heartbeat. Upon successfully completing the PIP, she was given a promotion and the opportunity to lead an important project. This "promotion" would result in more hours but no additional pay. This experience is not uncommon. Your reward for successfully navigating harsh conditions is more of the same harsh conditions. Successfully getting through by de-prioritizing your needs seems to give even more reason to deny your needs. The cycle will continue. Eventually, it has to end. And you have more power to end it on your own terms than you may think.

Is it true that you have to work late? Do you have to stop taking your meds? Do you have to not use your assistive device? Do you have to work without accommodations? Do you have to accept the hotel that doesn't have any accessible rooms? Maybe you do. But most likely, you don't. In moments of stress, we are much more likely to feel that it is as serious as life or death and feel trapped into one option. Knowing this, we can work with our brain in a way that identifies the real threat level and then prompts the brain to look for other solutions.

The human body can do amazing things when exposed to stress if given what it needs to heal. Look at ultra-marathon runners who run 100 miles at a time. They put their body through consistent stress to get to the point they can run a distance most humans won't walk, let alone run. If you try to do that without the proper training or without giving the body what it needs, you will seriously injure yourself. But with the proper rest, hydration, nutrition, and physical care, the body grows stronger and able to withstand more and more stress without harm.

The way to get where you can do more is by not pushing yourself too far too fast. It isn't by ignoring your needs. It is by attending meticulously to your needs. It is by recognizing the difference between healthy discomfort and harmful discomfort. It is by ensuring proper care, which facilitates necessary recovery from stress. Intentionally pushing your body to its limits for it to grow is a good thing. You can't do it without trusting your body or without building your brain's trust in you to meet your body's needs.

Improve Trust in Yourself

Your relationship with yourself is a relationship like with anyone else. Your communication and actions have an impact. If someone tells you they are going to do something but then they don't, you lose a little trust in that person. If they do it repeatedly, you learn to expect them to not do what they say. Eventually you may not trust their words at all and stop taking them seriously. If someone repeatedly tears you down, you may try to earn their respect or affection, or you may lose respect for them.

Every time you tell yourself you are going to do something but then don't do it, you reinforce to your brain that it can't trust you to follow through. Every time you call yourself names or shame yourself, you teach your brain to feel the same way about yourself that you feel about others who call you names. Your own actions can make your brain feel unsafe.

Trust yourself to be able to handle what comes up. Trust yourself to remove yourself from situations that aren't good for you or don't meet your needs. Trust yourself to advocate. Trust yourself to handle it when you don't have it in you to self-advocate. Build your trust by doing these things. You build trust by showing up for yourself even in the small ways that are in line with your intentions and values. If you told yourself you'd get up after snoozing the alarm once, then respect yourself enough to stick to that. If you told yourself that you'll act in line with your value of treating others with respect, do that or apologize when you don't.

As you are making these efforts, trust in your ability to improve confidence. Confidence doesn't come from being the smartest, strongest, best looking, or any other external metric. Confidence comes from belief in yourself. Belief stems from trust. The more you show your brain that it can trust you, the stronger it gets in supporting you.

Teach Your Brain Your New Beliefs

Embrace your new identity and let go of the past identity based on shame, fear, or external input. Let go of letting past trauma define who you are in the present. Yes, past traumas, patterns of treatment, and other experiences affect who you are today. But they don't *define* you. Past experiences may help explain certain parts of your behavior and beliefs, but that isn't even close to the whole story. It is certainly not the best or most interesting parts of your story.

Leaving behind old stories and embracing your identity free of stigma and shame require retraining your brain. To embrace your new identity, choose to act in line with your new identity. Prioritize the new identity more than past habits, fears, and avoidance of judgment. This will strengthen neural pathways aligned with your values while letting connections based on past faulty beliefs weaken from disuse.

If your identity is a fighter, fight even when winning isn't certain. If your identity is never settling, don't accept less just because it is the easy choice. If your identity prioritizes family, don't let even your own goals distract you from family. If you prioritize professional growth, don't let others' priorities convince you that you're selfish or wrong. If you value bravery, push through fear. If you value curiosity, answer perceived threats with a desire to understand. If you value tenacity, build tenacity by doing the things you don't want to do. If you value integrity, tell the truth even when it means admitting fault. If you value honest communication, have even the hard conversations. As you do so, be open to shifting as you learn more about yourself.

Every action you take in line with your values and goals shows your brain that doing so is safe, possible, and rewarding. You make it easier by training your brain that it is safe to be you. You make it easier by training your brain that you are no longer prioritizing external feedback. While anything new entails some discomfort, the more you do it, the easier it gets. Then the easier it gets, the easier it keeps getting. Momentum works the same both ways. Just as the more shame you feel, the easier and more natural it is to feel more shame, the more pride you feel, the easier and more natural it is to feel pride.

Intentionally strengthen your brain to make it act in new ways. The more you act as if you already believe the new belief, the more your neural networks will back that up. Gradually, self-protective instincts loosen their grip and the brain structurally changes to support the shame-free identity. Practice doing hard things. Practice failing. Do things you don't want to do. Practice handling rejection by getting rejected on purpose. Ask to be included. Admit to mistakes and feel the discomfort. All of these actions strengthen various aspects of the brain that will provide protection against stigma, discrimination, and external judgment.

Be compassionate with yourself in this process. Old habits and fears may continue, and you will stumble. But with consistent effort you'll gradually feel more and more that you belong.

Be You

Don't judge your worthiness based on what you do or don't do; instead choose what to do or not to do based on the knowledge that you are already enough.

How would you treat yourself if you believed you were enough just as you are? How would you know someone accepted you? How would you know someone respected you? What actions would they take? Start treating yourself in that way. Even if you don't love yourself. Even if you don't even like yourself. Start treating yourself with even basic respect, and your brain will realize that you are enough and that you have been all along.

If you know someone accepts you by letting you be you even at your weakest, then let you be you without judging yourself even at your weakest. If you know someone respects you when they provide for your needs without question, provide for your own needs without question. Being you doesn't just mean being you externally; it means being you to yourself. It means acting in line with your own values and goals in your relationship with yourself. It means advocating for your needs to yourself. If you can't be you to yourself, it will continue to be hard to be yourself around others.

It really isn't hard to be yourself once all the junk beliefs are removed. Is a decision in line with your values and goals? Do it. Is your decision rooted in fear or avoiding discomfort? Don't do it. Acting in line with who you are even in the face of discomfort and fear is the biggest act of self-love that there is. Every action you take that is true to you reinforces self-trust, self-confidence, and self-efficacy. All of these individually decrease depression, anxiety, and self-doubt. Eventually the changes add up, and being you becomes so natural that you don't have to logically assess your thoughts or decisions as often. Eventually you will do what you want to do when you want to do it because you know exactly who you are.

You don't have to be perfect for this to become reality; in fact, you can't be perfect. Your new beliefs and actions will work together to support your improved efforts, just like all the previous mindsets and actions worked together to support self-sabotage.

PART

IV

Self-Advocacy

IN THIS PART you will learn how to effectively self-advocate using your values, goals, and needs as the guide. You will learn when to self-advocate for change from others, when to self-advocate by holding others accountable to relevant laws, and how sometimes the best way to self-advocate is by leaving a situation.

Advocacy doesn't have one look or one right way. The only right way is doing what meets your needs while staying true to your values. This will present differently for every person, and will present differently for the same person in different situations or on different days. Some days you may have the energy to advocate for yourself in real time. Other days you may need to preserve your energy, leave the situation, and advocate for yourself after the fact. Other times the best form of self-advocacy is leaving a situation that actively harms you or doesn't support your values, goals, or needs.

Part of self-advocacy is also learning to advocate for yourself to *yourself*. It is recognizing when external judgments and expectations are relevant or not. It is learning to prioritize what you know matters most while deprioritizing and even tuning out others' judgments.

Self-advocacy means preparing for the resistance that is to come instead of avoiding or succumbing to it.

And finally, Chapters 21 and 22 provide specific actionable guidance around how to stay true to yourself in two situations in which it may seem impossible to stay true to who you are:

- You can stay true to yourself even in the workplace where you are asked to fit into a specific mold. You can find a way to fit into a mold while living your values and meeting your needs. And when you truly can't, self-advocacy is leaving as soon as possible and finding somewhere that does not require you to lose your values and deny your needs.
- You can stay true to yourself even when everything sucks and it feels as if you were losing everything. You don't have to lose yourself.

More is possible. Better is possible. It is easier and more effective in the long run to be who you are rather than trying to be someone you're not. It requires up-front effort, but once established turns into a much easier version of life even if all existing external struggles remain.

18

Advocate for Yourself

TEACHING PEOPLE TO advocate for themselves is what I believe to be the most important work that I do. It is more powerful than any of my work trying to change external stigmas and biases. Are both types of work necessary? Absolutely. But even with the most inclusive environments, if you don't know how to articulate and ask for what you need or want, you're less likely to get it.

Knowing how to effectively self-advocate very quickly reveals environments where you may belong versus environments that will not be accepting or even safe for you. While much of my work is focused on guiding organizations to be more inclusive, I strongly believe as individuals it will always be vital to determine which environments will meet your needs, allow you to belong, and facilitate safety. There will always be people and places that don't meet your needs or that are unsafe for you. This doesn't mean these people or places are inherently bad, like a boat not belonging on a road and a car not belonging in the water. Knowing how to identify the people and places that can't or won't meet your needs, believing better is possible, and respecting yourself enough to advocate means less time spent in those unsafe or inaccessible environments.

Lead with Values, Goals, and Needs

Advocacy is far more than just advocating for your needs. While getting your needs met is often necessary for survival, you are more than your needs and you can do more than merely survive. Whether it originates with you or others, a focus on needs alone will inherently make you feel needy. A focus on needs that are perceived to be tied to deficits or differences can naturally make you feel less-than or othered. You are more than your needs. You get to have desires in life (goals). You get to have personal standards you set for yourself (values). You get to live a life where you have peace, success, or satisfaction, even if only in your mind. You get to prioritize and advocate for your goals and values along with your needs.

A goal is anything you want out of life. This could be a feeling, a tangible item, an achievement, or experience (addressed in depth in Chapter 14). Your goals help you decide what to focus on and what to let go. Having clarity on your goals helps you recognize things that detract from your goals as distractions. Conversely, when you don't have goals to guide you, your focus is more susceptible to be influenced by the opinions, judgments, and expectations of those around you.

To achieve your goals in a way that is true to you, you'll let your values guide you. Values are what most motivates you. Whether it is family, accuracy, serving others, safety, or any other value identified in Chapter 12, your values guide how you achieve your goals, how to interact with others, how to live in times of comfort and ease and in times of struggle and pain.

Values also drive how you advocate for yourself. Advocacy often feels unnatural or wrong when you have been denied your needs for so long, belittled because of your needs, or somehow made to feel less. As a human, advocacy is necessary. It becomes even more so when you have a disability, especially when advocacy is uncomfortable. Advocacy becomes more comfortable when you learn how to do it in a way that is true to you. That is, through identifying and acting in line with your values.

When you don't consider your values in your advocacy and actions, you may react with defensiveness, avoidance, or people-pleasing—all natural human tendencies. It takes intention to overcome your natural reactions, yet it is possible. With your values as a guidance system, you can take action proactively instead of reactively. The shift may not happen immediately, but the more you prioritize acting in line with your values, the more it becomes your natural tendency, even in situations where you previously reacted without much conscious thought. The more you practice advocating in ways aligned with your values, the more advocating for yourself becomes a natural extension of who you are.

Acting according to your own values will get you further and lead to more successful advocacy than acting according to an expert's guidance. Even mine. I have a lot of evidence to show that if you follow my steps for self-advocacy, you will get great results. However, there is a significant difference in following my guidelines when applied to your goals and values versus following my guidelines exactly how I would. If you aren't naturally assertive, not afraid of conflict, and don't prioritize accuracy, you would be incredibly uncomfortable doing it how I do it. You'd simultaneously judge yourself for not being good enough because you didn't measure up to the "expert's" standards, while also judging yourself for acting in a way that felt uncomfortable or wrong (which is always how it will feel when you act in a way that isn't true to yourself). Judging yourself according to my values is completely irrelevant and would almost certainly make the situation worse. Alternatively, judging yourself according to your own values is relevant and sets a signpost to not engage in any behavior that you can't be proud of.

One client of mine said one of his values was "compassionate curiosity." That is something that I would not have thought of on my own and definitely don't enact in my day-to-day. I don't know that I have ever thought about compassion accompanying curiosity. However, because that is how he strives to be, the suggestions I gave for advocating were based on compassionate curiosity. He outlined the facts, knew his rights, and asserted them, but the tone was drastically different because he did it asking questions to understand the treatment he was being subjected to. He did it asking to better understand why treatment toward him had changed after disclosing disability. This worked well for him as the conversation with his manager went very well, despite conversations on the same topic not having gone well for months before.

Advocating goes well when you know the facts and look at your part and the other party's part objectively. It goes really well when you then apply your own values and goals. For someone else, understanding the why would have been a distraction, not a means to reach the goal. For another, being that curious would feel invasive because they don't naturally ask questions about past reasoning and focus more on the now. It doesn't matter what your values or goals are. There is always a way to enact them. There is always a solution. The solution may mean doing something uncomfortable or going through hard times. It doesn't remove discrimination, mistreatment, human disagreements, or natural ebbs and flows of life. But it does ensure that you don't lose who you are in the process.

If you do nothing else but start acting according to your values, you will start accepting, maybe even loving, yourself more. Acting according to your values shows respect for yourself. It gives you something to be proud of. Maybe most significantly, it provides you evidence that you don't have reason to feel shame—especially as it relates to being different. Acting in line with your values is acting more in line with you. When you act in ways you are proud of no matter the situation, you will start to feel connected to you again. This is true even if you act in a way you are ashamed of and then recognize it, accept it, and act in line with your values to correct and make up for it. By acting in line with your own values, you are giving yourself a new basis to judge yourself rather than going by others' judgments and expectations of you.

You also will almost certainly start having better results. Most of my clients, regardless of gender, race, socioeconomic status, or disability, get better results when they feel permission to be who they are, to advocate for their needs to be met and their rights to be granted, while being confident in doing so. Getting better results doesn't mean you will always get what you thought you wanted, but what you wanted may very well change when you see what is possible by allowing and advocating for who you really are.

Articulate Your Needs

Have you ever disclosed your disability to someone and they responded awkwardly? Have you ever disclosed your disability so that they would know your needs, only to have them not support you or make any adjustments to their behavior to accommodate your needs? Or have you been frustrated when you obviously have a disability and people don't respond accordingly? Many of my clients have told a story about how they disclosed their disability to their boss or a coworker who then responded awkwardly and didn't make any of the necessary adjustments. Or how they obviously have certain needs made evident by an apparent disability, but they weren't offered the relevant accommodations. The clients are frustrated and feel a lack of support or even disrespect.

Telling someone your disability does not tell them how to interact with you or support you. Telling someone your disability does not tell someone what you need or what you expect from them moving forward. The same is true if you have an apparent disability. The disability being apparent does not tell others how to interact with you or support you, nor does it make it obvious what you need and how you need it. A diagnosis on its own says nothing about your specific needs or how you prefer your needs to be met. It's well known in the disability community that two people with the same diagnosis can have different ways of meeting their needs, different preferences of accessibility tools, and other differences related to the disability. Because of this, you cannot expect others to know your needs simply by making your disability known. What is obvious to you is not obvious to others. You will get much better responses if you speak directly to your needs instead of expecting others to figure it out.

But what if you are in a new situations and aren't yet fully aware of your needs? Then that is a need itself, and you can clearly articulate that. If you need their patience while you figure it out, or if you need their support in figuring it out, communicate that, as well. Regardless of how much or little you know, clearly articulating what you do know and what you want from the other person is going to benefit all involved.

If you aren't sure how to communicate your needs, come up with a go-to script that is in line with your values and goals. It doesn't have to be extravagant and detailed. Simple and direct is often better. You may feel the need to justify your request, but you don't have to in everyday conversation. You deserve to get your needs met. You may have legal rights to get your needs met. Aim to communicate in a way that matches the fact that you deserve to get your needs met. You aren't asking for a favor; you aren't asking for special privileges—you are asking for a need to be met.

If you are getting anxiety even thinking about articulating your needs, practice with a friend, a family member, or by yourself. Do whatever it takes to push through the discomfort. Push through even when your needs get denied. The discomfort won't last forever, and the more you do it, the more the discomfort will decrease, while the support and acceptance from others will increase.

Advocating for your needs, especially when you aren't yet used to it, can feel very serious and like it's a big event. But it can be as natural as you let it be. How you originally make the request sets the tone. You can't control the response, but you can control how you start. If you ask in a really awkward way, not really sure what to say, obviously hesitant and insecure, it is natural for the recipient of the request to also feel awkward. There are some people who have the skill of always responding in the ideal way and making anyone feel comfortable, but that isn't common. If someone responds awkwardly to your awkward request, it is probably less about them being awkward about what you said and them feeling awkward because they can tell you are. Don't internalize their response. Similarly, if you make it seem like a really big deal that you need your accommodation when it could have been a simple ask, it's going to seem like a big deal. This doesn't mean you're to blame, but it does mean that how you ask sets a tone, and you can control that.

Learn to Say No

Sometimes, the most effective self-advocacy is a two-letter word. It may be a literal "no," or it may be using more words to articulate the same meaning. Saying no is completely appropriate when declining offers that are invasive, not in your best interest, or are not aligned with your values, goals, or needs. You can also say no just because you don't feel like it. By saying no, you increase your autonomy, satisfaction, and happiness.

If you find it hard to even imagine saying no, start with something inconsequential and do it consistently. Once that becomes more comfortable, add another circumstance. Then keep adding until you are able to say no more regularly and more confidently.

Saying no does not mean you are rude, selfish, or ungrateful, even if the other person sees it that way. Others being bothered that you aren't acting the way that they want is not indicative of your worth. You don't need to take their opinion on as discomfort of your own—especially in the form of doing something you don't want to do. Somebody else's expectation does not equate to an obligation. You still get to choose for yourself.

Set Boundaries

Boundaries are a line that shows where the other party has influence on you and where that influence stops. Boundaries are a line that shows what you will allow and what you will not. Boundaries are not a means by which you get to control others. It doesn't mean changing the other person's behavior but taking your own action when a boundary is crossed.

Boundaries on a map show the line between countries, boundaries on a football field show the line between inbounds and out of bounds, and boundaries on a sidewalk show where the sidewalk is about to end and a road begins. Boundaries don't say what you are or aren't allowed to do; they simply define a line between two things, each having different rules and different consequences.

You can't define boundaries for other people. You get to define your boundaries and what it means when someone crosses them. You get to define the rules of your game. There may be some boundaries, such as the bumps on a sidewalk that show it is about to become a road, that act as a warning of potential danger. There are some boundaries, such as the rules in various sporting environments, that clearly define the result when you cross the boundary line. It is up to you to identify your boundaries based in need, as well as your boundaries based in preference.

Most of your boundaries are going to be related to things you learn about how you work best, your preferences, and your energy drains versus energy sources. This is where it is vital to know your own needs so that you can communicate them to others. It is when you communicate them to others that you are able to identify those who will respect your boundaries and those who will not.

Some of your needs may directly apply to their own boundary. For example, you have a severe allergy to something; that allergen can't be in your home, and you won't go into any home or place that has that allergen. However, part of having a boundary is considering what would happen if you do unknowingly come into contact with that allergen, for example, you immediately leave when you learn the allergen is present, or if it's too late for that, you or someone else will need to get the EpiPen from your purse and use it. Maybe you also decide not to go to that place again. It is important to define and communicate that part of your boundary, as well.

In essence, boundaries are personal principles that delineate where you end and others begin, what you will tolerate, and how you choose to respond when those limits are tested. They are not tools for manipulating others' actions but for guiding your own responses to preserve your well-being and respect. Just as physical boundaries in the world around us establish distinct areas with their own set of rules and consequences, personal boundaries establish the perimeters of your emotional and physical space, signaling what you deem acceptable or unsafe for you.

Know Your Rights and Responsibilities

Most countries have laws granting rights and protections to people with disabilities. These laws can include public accessibility, patient rights, anti-discrimination, and employment rights. For the purpose of this book and section, I will focus on rights relating to employment, especially regarding reasonable accommodations.

> *Reasonable accommodations* are necessary and appropriate modifications and adjustments not imposing a disproportionate or undue burden, where needed in a particular case, to ensure persons with disabilities the enjoyment or exercise on an equal basis with others of all human rights and fundamental freedoms (United Nations n.d.).

Out of 193 countries, 160 have some legislation that prohibits discrimination in the workplace based on disability, 113 countries have laws that require employers to provide reasonable accommodations to employees with disabilities (also referred to as reasonable adjustments in some countries), while another 6 countries have laws that encourage reasonable accommodations to be extended (World Policy Analysis Center 2023). While the specific laws differ, there are significant similarities as the Americans with Disabilities Act (ADA) signed in 1990 in the United States acted as the blueprint for many other laws and definitions, including those adopted by the United Nations General Assembly in 2006 with the Convention on the Rights of Persons with Disabilities.

It is imperative that you know your rights. After learning their rights, many clients who come to me realize they unnecessarily allowed violations of those rights. A common example in the United States is at-will laws that allow either the employee or the employer to end an employment relationship with no cause. This means an employee can quit or an employer can terminate an employee at any time for any reason or without reason. However, at-will laws do not cover terminations that are related to discrimination or retaliation. Just because you live in an at-will state does not mean you can be reasonably fired for asking for an accommodation, for making a discrimination claim, or for any other protected act. Similarly, being asked to sign a nondisclosure does not mean you can't make a claim of discrimination, retaliation, or ADA violation to the EEOC. You have certain protections that no document can take away.

Beyond enhancing your ability to self-advocate, I have found that knowing your rights also serves as tangible evidence that you deserve to have rights, that you deserve to get your needs met, and that you don't deserve to be discriminated against. Many of my clients come to me when they are struggling through an accommodation request process and not only improve in confidence and ability to self-advocate but also end up recognizing and internalizing more of their own value and worth. This knowledge can act as a catalyst for those who haven't been comfortable with self-advocacy or can act to reinforce the resolve of those who already do self-advocate. Even the law recognizes and upholds your right to fair treatment and protections, not as a matter of charity or pity but as a matter of justice, equity, and protecting basic human rights.

Maintain Balance

Knowing when to push harder and when to take a break is an important aspect of self-advocacy, especially when mental or physical disability is present and can be exacerbated. While it can be challenging to find a balance, or to know when to do what, it's important to understand and accept that sometimes it may be correct to push harder, while sometimes it may be necessary to rest and prioritize your health and well-being. Overall, it is important to listen to your instincts and take care of yourself while advocating for your needs.

Here are a few signs that it may be time to push harder:

- Your employer or another organization has not responded to your accommodation request, or they have responded negatively without providing reasonable alternatives.
- You are being excluded from opportunities or job duties due to your disability.
- You are being subjected to harassment or discrimination because of your disability.

In these situations, it may be necessary to seek additional support, such as contacting the Job Accommodation Network (JAN), the EEOC, or other disability advocacy organizations in your area that can help ensure that your rights are protected. You don't have to do this alone.

Here are some signs that it may be time to take a break:

- Feeling increasingly overwhelmed and stressed by the advocacy process.
- Your mental or physical health is taking a toll, maybe even experiencing exacerbated symptoms.
- You feel as though your advocacy efforts are causing strain on your relationships with family, friends, colleagues, or supervisors.

In these situations, taking a break from the advocacy process can be helpful to recharge and reevaluate your approach. It may also be helpful to seek support from colleagues, family, or mental health professionals to manage any stress or anxiety related to the situation. Your self-advocacy will always be more effective with a de-stressed mind and body.

Take Accountability

People can't read your mind. People cannot be expected to know what you need if it hasn't been communicated to them. A key aspect of self-advocacy is taking accountability for your own needs and how you communicate your needs. Despite how obvious you may believe your needs are, the truth is that people can't be expected to know what they don't know. The assumption to the contrary is not only unrealistic but potentially harmful to yourself.

Beyond being less likely to get your needs met, this unspoken expectation can lead to misunderstanding and frustration on both sides. One party may see the other as unsupportive and uncaring when needs aren't met, while the other may perceive a lack of gratitude when they make a lot of effort that is met with passive aggression. This cycle of miscommunication undermines your own self-advocacy and your ability to get your needs met, while also inhibiting your ability to connect and feel as if you belong.

Taking accountability is not just making vague requests or setting tentative boundaries; it is being clear on your needs and what you need or want from the other person. Even if you don't know your need or what exactly you want, you are responsible for articulating what you do know. For example, you could articulate that you aren't sure what you need, explain the situation, and then tell the other person what you are hoping to receive from them.

Not everyone will react in the way that you hope. Some may not know how to respond, some may refuse, and some will want to support but be unable to. Part of self-advocacy is learning to accept where needs can't be met, being willing to work with the other party to find solutions, or accepting what someone else is able to give when it is enough, even if not ideal.

Taking accountability comes down to owning your part in the communication process from the communication of the need, your expectation of the other party, and any follow-up. By doing so, all other steps of self-advocacy become more effective, your needs are more likely to be met, and you foster more supportive and accepting relationships.

19

Tune Out Others' Judgments

A WORLD WHERE you don't care what others think of you is a world where you are free to be yourself, express yourself, and pursue your dreams. It is a world where others' opinions, expectations, or judgments don't impede your confidence, happiness, and belonging. It is possible. It may not be as simple as the flip of a switch, but all that has preceded in this book set a foundation to make it possible sooner than you think.

So far, you have learned common faulty beliefs and how to deconstruct them, and how to identify, accept, and be who you are free of stigma. But stigma isn't going to stop. Faulty beliefs from others aren't going to stop. People are still going to judge, discriminate, or underestimate you. All the internal work won't change the fact that external opinions on how and where you should exist are going to continue. What you can do is accept that it is going to happen and plan accordingly.

You can accept that others' judgments are based on their beliefs, experiences, and expectations of themselves. You can practice awareness, acceptance, and self-regulation to not internalize others' judgments. Ideally, you get to the point where you truly are able to tune out others' judgments. Your brain already tunes out input it deems irrelevant; you can train it to see judgments as irrelevant, too.

Tuning out others' judgments is not about ignoring feedback or advice that could help you improve or grow. It's not about being arrogant, rude, or disrespectful to other people or their perspectives. It's not about isolating yourself from others or avoiding social interactions. And it's not impossible, unrealistic, or impractical in today's world.

Tuning out others' judgments is about ignoring, dismissing, or rejecting the opinions, evaluations, or criticisms that are not helpful, relevant, or accurate. Such judgments only serve to undermine your well-being and happiness. It's about respecting yourself and your choices, and acknowledging that you do not need to please, impress, or conform to anyone else. It's about choosing who you surround yourself with and seeking out people who support, encourage, and appreciate you for who you are.

You Are Bigger Than Any Judgments

"No one can make you feel inferior without your consent." This quote by Eleanor Roosevelt is often used to portray a message of self-empowerment and resilience. It puts the feelings of inferiority on the individual and highlights your power to resist the belief regardless of others' actions toward you. I believe with some added nuance, the point becomes even more powerful for those who have been made to feel inferior at a subconscious level after years of consistent negative external feedback. The nuance missing surrounds the fact that repeated exposure to stigma and discrimination inevitably have a negative impact on an individual's sense of self, feelings of shame, and confidence. Enough repeated exposure to negative input can eventually erode even the most confident person's self-perception. As consent requires conscious awareness, and feelings of inferiority often occur subconsciously, this erosion of confidence most often occurs without the consent implied in the original quote.

Eleanor Roosevelt made a similar point in another way by saying, "I think it is the effort of a person who feels superior to make someone else feel inferior. First, though, you have to find someone who can be made to feel inferior." And with that, I fully agree. However, more distinctions will aid the point. Conscious awareness again comes into play, as there are very few people, if any, who consciously choose to be made to feel inferior. People who can be made to feel inferior are often those with lower self-confidence, sense of self, and sense of worthiness. People who are reliant on those in positions of power to get their needs met are also those more susceptible to being made to feel inferior—especially by those who truly see them as inferior. Those who have been treated as inferior for so long that it is hard to believe otherwise are also more likely to be those who can be made to feel inferior. This makes people who are stigmatized by society the perfect target. Just because you may be the perfect target does not mean you are destined to feel inferior, even if you currently do.

Once the appropriate nuance is added to both of those quotes, the truth can be extracted—that the feelings of inferiority occur internally. The influence of others may have been the catalyst, but no one can make you feel something about yourself without you feeling it inside of yourself. Even if the internal feeling developed subconsciously, it is through processing the external negative feedback internally that it becomes a judgment you hold yourself. In this way, it is true that no one can make you feel inferior without you feeling inferior in the first place. This concept can be extrapolated beyond inferiority to any feelings about yourself.

You are stronger than any judgment in the sense that what you believe to be true about yourself is what decides which external judgments you internalize (or don't). If you are six feet four and someone calls you short, you can easily disregard that judgment. Maybe you even see it as humorous in its ridiculousness. If you are criticized for not being intelligent because your brain works a little differently, but you know you are intelligent, then their judgment can be easily disregarded. However, it is when you believe a judgment even *might* be true that the judgment begins to have power. If someone insults your intelligence and you yourself are insecure about it, then their insult has an impact. You may retreat into yourself in shame, you may get defensive, or you may act as if it didn't affect you while trying to subtly prove your intelligence. In this way, it is your feelings about yourself, not the other person's judgment of you, that are affecting you. In this realization, there is power and control. You can weaken the impact of someone else's words by knowing more of who you are. You can weaken the impact of others' opinions by knowing how you see yourself.

Once you become aware of where these feelings originate, you can develop an armor against the judgments and take steps to keep external judgments from becoming internal feelings and beliefs. You can then begin to resist the impacts of repeated exposure. While the roots of the belief first occur subconsciously, it eventually is something you consciously accept as a belief about yourself. By building protective mechanisms, you become someone who can't be made to feel inferior or anything that you don't believe yourself to be.

Judgments Aren't Actually About You

When you internalize others' judgments, it isn't their actual judgment that you are internalizing but your interpretation of that judgment. If you didn't believe it at all, it couldn't be internalized. Your brain wouldn't allow it. But enough similar judgments will eventually cause you to question what is true. Once a doubt creeps in, it becomes easier for that doubt to grow into a fully formed belief. This is what you want to avoid.

Others' judgments can influence your thoughts, feelings, and behaviors, both consciously and unconsciously. Depending on how you perceive and respond to them, they can have positive or negative effects on your well-being and happiness.

Allowing others' judgments, positive or negative, to guide your beliefs and actions leads to you not being your truest self. While giving credence to the obviously harmful judgments creates equally obvious harmful results, giving too much credence to the positives can also be harmful. Valuing external approval beyond what supports your values and goals leads to actions related to perfectionism and people-pleasing. It leads to chasing the approval and validation of others instead of yourself.

As a disabled person, you are more vulnerable to receiving harsh judgments and more vulnerable to the negative effects of others' judgments. Add to it any other marginalized identity, and there are increased vulnerabilities related to stigma, discrimination, or ignorance. You may internalize these judgments and believe that they are true or that you deserve them. You may also externalize these judgments and resent or avoid the people who make them. You may start to avoid the situations that trigger them. These reactions can be helpful if aligned with your values and goals, but those reactions not aligned with your values and goals can harm your self-esteem, self-confidence, and self-respect, as well as your relationships, opportunities, and happiness.

One of the most common pieces of advice from people looking back at what they would tell their younger selves is to stop caring about what others think. A curious pattern that I notice is that even people who have learned this lesson in one area of life often don't recognize that it can be applied to all areas of life. It is easy to disregard what you already don't care about. It is easy to not care about things you know aren't true. Where it matters most is applying that mindset to the insecurities and areas where you do really care. Not caring about what others think will have the most impact when applying it to the areas of your life in which you are most influenced by others' judgments.

What Tuning Out Others' Judgments Is Not

Tuning out others' judgments does not mean ignoring feedback or advice that could help you improve or grow. It is discerning between constructive and destructive criticism, and accepting or rejecting it based on your own criteria and standards. You can still listen to and learn from feedback or advice that is helpful, relevant, or accurate and that comes from a place of respect, care, or expertise. You can also ignore, dismiss, or reject feedback or advice that is unhelpful, irrelevant, or inaccurate or that comes from a place of ignorance, bias, or hostility.

It is not true that tuning out others' judgments means being arrogant, rude, or disrespectful to other people or their perspectives. The simplest way to tune out judgments is by saying, "Okay." You don't need to argue it or even humor it beyond a simple "okay." In some situations it would be completely reasonable to not respond at all. Tuning out others' judgments means respecting yourself and your choices, and acknowledging that you do not need to please, impress, or conform to anyone else. You can still respect and appreciate other people and their perspectives, and agree to disagree or compromise when necessary. You can also assert and protect yourself and your choices, and say no or stand up for yourself when necessary.

Tuning out others' judgments does not mean isolating yourself from others or avoiding social interactions but rather being more intentional in choosing who you surround yourself with and seeking out people who support, encourage, and appreciate you for who you are.

You can still enjoy and benefit from social interactions and connect with people who share or value your identity, interests, or goals. You can also avoid or limit social interactions that are harmful or draining and distance yourself from people who judge, criticize, or undermine you.

Tuning out others' judgments is possible, realistic, and practical in today's world, even if you have *rejection sensitivity*. There are many who have done so successfully using the types of tools and self-acceptance outlined in this book.

> Rejection sensitive dysphoria (RSD) is when you experience severe emotional pain because of real or perceived failure or rejection. This is linked to ADHD, autism, and other neurotypes, and experts suspect it happens due to differences in brain structure. Those differences mean your brain doesn't effectively regulate rejection-related emotions and behaviors, making them much more intense and painful (Cleveland Clinic 2022).

Strategies for Navigating Others' Judgments

First, become aware—aware that you are affected by a judgment of you. Be aware of your feelings and thoughts related to others' judgments. If you act in response to it, be aware of the fact that you are letting external judgments guide your decisions. A sub-step to becoming aware in this context is to become aware that their judgment is separate from you. Even if it feels as if it were about you, it is someone else's judgment, not yours. It belongs to them. They can keep it.

Of course, this is easier said than done. It isn't others' judgments themselves that affect you but your thoughts about their judgments. By changing your thoughts, you can change your beliefs. By changing your beliefs, you can tune out others' judgments more effectively.

Here are some examples of common thought patterns, as well as various ways to address the faulty thoughts.

Prioritize your values and goals over others' opinions:

- *Immediate thought*: "What will they think of me if I do this?"

- *More relevant thought*: "What will I think of myself if I don't do this?"

Prioritize what is true:

- *Immediate thought*: "They are right; I am slow."
- *More relevant thought*: "I may take longer, but I get everything done."

Remind yourself that their judgment has nothing to do with you:

- *Immediate thought*: "They are judging me because they are better than me."
- *More relevant thought*: "They are judging me according to metrics they use to judge themselves."

Challenge assumptions:

- *Immediate thought*: "They are judging me because they hate me."
- *More relevant thought*: "They are judging me, and I don't know why."

To challenge other thoughts related to external input, you can ask yourself, "Is this true? Is this relevant? Is this based on fact or assumption? What is more true?"

You can also challenge the thought by questioning the external source. If it is someone you don't respect, who isn't an expert in the field, or who doesn't know you well, you can immediately dismiss the input. If it is someone whose input you may want to consider, you can run it through your values and goals to assess if the feedback could add value.

There are a lot of uncomfortable thoughts that stem from others' judgments that may be true. It is these times that instead of challenging your thought, it may be most effective to accept it and the related discomfort. This is going to apply when a thought is true or perceived to be true. It will also apply when you know the thought isn't true, but your body isn't yet letting it go. When it is true, or seems to be true, letting it be without resistance can be the best course of action.

Another way to tune out others' feedback is by proactively seeking out relevant feedback. To ensure you are getting external feedback to help you improve in areas you may not recognize on your own, intentionally seek out feedback, support, or guidance from those who share or respect your values and goals. You can also seek out or create opportunities to meet, interact, or collaborate with people who have similar or complementary values and goals, and who can support, encourage, or inspire you. When you know who to go to for constructive feedback, other external feedback loses its perceived value and relevance.

Even when you solicit input from others, always ask yourself if their feedback is to support you living your values and reaching your goals, or is it feedback based on what they believe your values and goals should be. Even well-intentioned and expert feedback can be misguided if not relevant to you.

When you solicit feedback from others, it helps all involved to be specific about exactly what you are looking for. Specify if you want a factual critique, an honest opinion on your behavior, or tips to help you calm your nerves. Specify where you are open to feedback and where the feedback is not welcome. The better you communicate your needs and expectations, the better the other person is able to provide constructive feedback. It still may not be perfect, but setting up both parties for success leads to more peaceful mishaps if they do occur.

A last, but vital, tip is to seek out support from others. Seek out places where you are safe from judgment. Seek out people and places where you aren't always having to protect yourself against stigma, discrimination, and irrelevant opinions about how you live. It isn't the opinions of these people and communities that is most helpful; it is the lack of judgment and opinions. Being in places where you can let down your armor is vital to maintaining your energy. Fighting to not internalize others' judgments can be exhausting. Give yourself some reprieve when and where you can.

20

Inevitable Resistance

IN THE WORLD of professional sports, athletes don't just practice their craft, but they also prepare for the inevitable physical and mental barriers they may experience. Gymnasts learn how to fall safely to prepare for the inevitability of falling. In a sport that marks success in part by not falling, why do they practice the very thing they want to avoid? They accept that falling is going to occur as they train and prepare for it so as not to let it be more than what it is.

Professional baseball teams have mindset coaches for their athletes. There are going to be times pitchers make a bad pitch, outfielders stumble while running to catch a ball, or batters experience a non-hitting streak. Imperfection is inevitable. The best at their craft both physically train to reduce the likelihood of imperfections while also mentally training to ensure one mistake doesn't turn into many.

These are people who are the best at what they do, yet they prepare for resistance, both mental and physical. Preparing for the inevitable falls reduces the risk of injury. Preparing for the inevitable mental blocks reduces the risk of debilitating stress and anxiety that is common at that level of performance. Even the best at what they do prepare for inevitable resistance.

Resistance is the internal or external challenges that emerge during a journey of significant growth. Resistance is a natural response to transformation. Resistance can further support growth and increase strength, or it can hinder and even stop progress. The difference is how rooted, supported, and otherwise prepared for the resistance you are. Allowing the resistance to win results in resistance to growth, whereas recognizing that resistance is inevitable and preparing to grow despite it results in being strengthened in your resolve and identity.

Resistance, even at the highest levels of performance, is something everyone will face. This chapter aims to address some of the most common forms of resistance that come up when any human is attempting to make changes, especially changes that include the identity or changes that depart from lifelong beliefs or behaviors. Some of these forms of resistance originate externally, while most originate inside your own mind. Both are natural. You may think you are the only one dealing with your specific struggle, or you may think that it is a sign of weakness, especially when the struggle is psychological. Both beliefs are incredibly common when striving to make improvements in life, but both are flawed. You are never the only person to experience a specific struggle. Sure, there is no one else going through the exact same experience, but there are always others who can directly relate. Experiencing resistance, even in your own mind, is never a weakness. It is human.

Identity Crisis

As discussed in Part II, identity is in part shaped by stigma and the resulting shame and related faulty beliefs. One of the first and most powerful forms of resistance when on a journey of being more true to who you are is feeling that you don't know who you are. You may feel as if you've lost your identity. Who are you without being defined by stigma, inaccessibility, and how horribly others may treat you? Who are you when you stop people-pleasing to survive? Who are you when you drop the identity tied to struggle, shame, and learned helplessness? Who are you when your likes and dislikes aren't based on others' preferences? Who are you when you choose what you want instead of waiting to be told what you want?

The process of self-assessment is a necessary part of intentional transformation. Identifying and letting go of core parts of your previous identity can leave you confused, conflicted, and afraid. It can feel as if you've lost who you are. It can be terrifying, but it also can be freeing. You get to find who you are free of external judgments and expectations. You get to stop playing small for the comfort of others and start prioritizing yourself. It's okay to not know who you are.

An identity crisis is not a dead end; it is a sign that transformation is happening. It is the equivalent of a caterpillar losing who it was in a chrysalis to become the butterfly it is meant to be. It is correct in the life cycle to start as a caterpillar and then to shift to a butterfly. Neither forms are wrong. Both are necessary. The shift may seem uncomfortable and at times appear as if no change is happening, yet it is. You can trust the process, even if it doesn't seem to make sense. You'll find yourself along the way.

Fear, Doubt, and Guilt

When you are striving for something new, discomfort in the form of fear may be present. This is both a fear of the unknown as well as an internal conflict between your current state and what you aspire to be.

When hoping for something that goes against all your existing beliefs, doubt may be present. This doubt is rooted in your brain denying conflicting beliefs that pose a challenge to your existing worldview. The doubt itself serves as a sign that you are questioning the beliefs that have long held you back, pushing the boundaries of your comfort zone, and opening yourself up to more possibility and growth.

When you improve while others still struggle, guilt may be present. This guilt is not evidence of wrongdoing or undeserved success but evidence of your empathy and connection to the human experience.

It may feel safer to stay where you are now than to face fear, doubt, and guilt in all its forms. You are not, however, in as much danger as fear, doubt, and guilt might make you believe. You are not better off staying where you are now. Embracing fear, doubt, and guilt as natural forms of resistance allows them to be catalysts for growth rather than barriers.

Achieving Success: Fear of Losing It

Achieving success of any kind is a significant milestone. It is equally significant whether it is one of the more standard measures of success such as financial or professional achievements, or more personal measures of success such as being more assertive and finally being comfortable saying no. Once you achieve success, a new form of resistance often arises—the fear of losing what you've gained.

The fear of losing what you've achieved and backsliding to where you used to be is another natural response to change. It stems from an instinctual desire for security and stability combined with what you've known to be true up to this point. Before you experience success in a new way, you have little evidence that it is possible. All previous evidence you do have is to the contrary, so your brain reasonably has fear around the longevity of the success.

Acting from this fear may look like acting as if the success is going to be short-lived, or obsessively working to maintain the success. Living this way will only hold you back. Even if you do lose it all, you achieved success once—you can achieve it again.

To overcome this fear, you must accept it. Enjoy what is while it is. Recognize that you did this. That you got here once. There is not a lot of action to take other than recognizing when you are in this fear and avoid acting from the fear. You can see this fear as a natural result of achieving something new. You can feel the fear without believing it. You can accept it instead of fighting against it or acting on it.

Feeling Unsafe with Peace and Safety

Because your brain is wired to perceive what is familiar as safe, anything unfamiliar is going to feel unsafe. The unfamiliarity can make peace feel uncomfortable and safety feel unsafe. This is especially true for those who have spent much of their lives in hypervigilance or survival mode.

Because you aren't used to these experiences, your brain will look for ways to explain them through what you already know. You might see threats where none exist or not enjoy what you have because you are maintaining vigilance for the threat you believe to be inevitable. People who are kind and accepting of the "unacceptable" parts of you may immediately feel fake. You may wonder what their motives are, when they are going to leave, or when they are going to show that it was all a joke. This fear and doubt is a result of your brain explaining something unfamiliar with patterns you've previously learned to be real.

Finding it hard to relax or feel comfortable in safe situations and relationships does not mean the situations aren't safe. It just means your brain is interpreting them as such. This is where learning to trust your body is key so you can differentiate between real signals of danger and signals of perceived danger rooted in mental fear. Mental fear can be confronted and defeated. Real warnings of danger you want to respect and respond to appropriately. Practice differentiating between the two by taking chances in situations it is reasonably safe to do so.

Feeling Guilty While Others Still Struggle

When you know how miserable it feels to be where you used to be, it can be hard to know others are still struggling as your life gets easier and happier, with less stress and shame. Resistance in the form of guilt can be strong, especially when you know through experience the hardships that others are still enduring. It can make you feel as if you were a bad person for no longer struggling, or for not saving those who still are. You may start to question whether you are deserving or whether you are wrong for not staying in your previous state.

This guilt stems from empathy and compassion. Empathy and compassion do not come with prescribed responsibility to save those who you feel empathy and compassion toward. Empathy-related guilt is another normal human emotion. Guilt can make you believe you have responsibilities you don't have. Dealing with this resistance is most effectively done by remembering who you are in the form of your values and goals. You can act out of empathy without acting as a savior. You can foster a sense of community and show others that there is a way out while respecting them to find their own way. While you don't want to deny the guilt and empathy, you also don't want to become captive to it. You can accept and acknowledge those feelings while letting values guide your actions instead of guilt.

Progress Isn't Evident

What about when you have been trying very hard, doing everything right, yet still nothing seems to be changing? The pain, depression, and shame feel the same. It isn't getting any easier to self-advocate. There are few things as disheartening as trying your hardest, giving your all, yet still experiencing the same. You're ready to quit and go back to the way it was. At least you knew what to expect then. At least you won't be wasting energy anymore. Right?

There is a human tendency to focus on failures rather than successes. This tendency is often the cause of progress not feeling evident, but it doesn't mean real progress is not actually occurring. Change is often imperceptible in real time, but when you are making effort, long-term growth is inevitable.

To better recognize progress, reconsider what your goal is. Is it an end result? Or is being a little more you every day your goal? If you chose to be you when you normally wouldn't have, that is evident progress. When you feel judgment from a stranger and then a day later become aware that you let a stranger's judgment affect you, that is evident progress. When you wake up feeling happy, or not quite happy but not miserable, that is evident progress.

Being frustrated, discouraged, and disappointed may be completely reasonable feelings throughout this process. Feel them. But don't let those feelings drive your decisions. Take a break if you need to, but don't give up on yourself. If the lack of external evidence is causing you to lose interest, do something to create external evidence. Track how many times you said no instead of yes. Track how many times you did breathing exercises when you were stressed. See how many days in a row you can go without denying your own needs. Then, when you miss a day, see if you can make a new personal record. There are many ways to create external evidence based on what you can control that will keep you motivated long enough to see the progress you are hoping to achieve.

Judgment

Judgment is an inherent part of being human. It is a cognitive process that plays a crucial role in our survival and social interactions. The ability to assess the environment using all available senses combined with knowledge built from past experience is what allowed humans (and you specifically) to survive in various environments and situations. It helps you differentiate between what is helpful and what is harmful. While judgment is natural and necessary, it can also act as resistance when it goes beyond its purpose of assessing for safety and instead hinders growth. Judgment can be directed internally or externally, and it can be sourced internally or externally. You will judge yourself and others just as others will judge themselves and you. Being aware of judgment as a form of resistance and preparing to identify when it goes beyond helpful to harmful is key to not letting judgment stagnate you.

Judging Your Mistakes

You are going to make mistakes. You are going to fall back into old patterns. You are going to unintentionally hurt others or you might say or do the wrong thing while trying to figure out new patterns. These mistakes may result in frustration and self-blame. You may wonder why you can't ever get it right, and why you always screw things up.

Have you ever learned to do something new without making even one mistake? I don't think so. When you internalize a human mistake as a personal flaw, you incorrectly turn a natural human experience into a moral or value indicator specific to you. You aren't special in your ability to make mistakes; it just seems that way because you are present for all of your mistakes while you are only aware of a minute percentage of others' mistakes. Maybe you have made some mistakes that have had a larger impact, but you as a human aren't to blame for the fact that you make mistakes. That blame goes to your humanity.

Mistakes are feedback, not failure. Judgment is going to happen, but judgment doesn't have to be bad. You can assess (judge) your effort and progress based on the fact that you did it rather than the result. Effort and progress deserve to be celebrated. Yes, even when it results in mistakes or seeming failure. Judgment is inevitable, but you get to choose which parts of the situation are relevant to judge. Even when it isn't obvious to anyone else, you know how hard you are trying. Recognize yourself for that.

Increased Judgment from Others

As you become more confident being who you are, you will draw more attention to yourself. More attention means more judgment on its own, and judgment will increase as you become someone others don't recognize. You could be judged as selfish as you stop people-pleasing. You could be judged as lowering your standards as you stop perfectionistic actions. You could be judged as needy, demanding, or selfish as you start communicating your needs and acting accordingly when they aren't met. These judgments aren't accurate reflections of who you actually are, but they take place because the new you is behaving differently than past versions of you. Because your new actions are conflicting with who they understand you to be, their brains will make up explanations to reconcile the new you with the you that they knew.

There may be people who celebrate your growth who also have opinions about how you should have done it sooner or should be changing more. There are going to be some people who judge your efforts as never enough. Others may be jealous.

Judgments aren't going to stop and will likely increase the more you choose to be you instead of shape-shifting to fit in. But they can have less power over you and mean less as you prioritize your values, goals, and needs over irrelevant judgments from others.

Being Judged for Not Being Stressed

You might expect others to be impressed when you aren't stressed in seemingly stressful situations, but instead I have learned it isn't uncommon to receive judgments for not being stressed. It can be perceived as not taking a situations seriously enough. I once missed my first deadline at work and met with my boss's boss to address it. He said, "I am concerned you aren't taking this seriously enough." I had acknowledged the missed deadline and stated what I would do to resolve it. Because I wasn't exhibiting evident stress, my words were not deemed to be enough. I wasn't sure what else to do as I felt I had responded verbally in a respectful way to the situation. Upon asking for clarity on how I could improve, he stated I said all the right words but that "my flat tone and lack of distress was concerning."

When someone sees you in a stressful situation yet you aren't behaving in a stereotypical stressed out manner, they may judge you as not taking the situation seriously, not caring enough, or being irresponsible. Somewhere stress became the sign of responsibility and the appropriate level of respect and consideration for a high-pressure situation. This is false. What is common is not necessarily what is best.

Being stressed is not an accurate indicator of how seriously you are taking the situation.

You can reduce your stress response and still respond with an appropriate level of concern. In fact, by reducing your stress response you improve cognitive function and allow more energy to be utilized for actually navigating the situation instead of navigating your reaction. Stressing doesn't help a situation. Judging yourself for not stressing appropriately doesn't help a situation. Shaming yourself for not responding how others expect definitely doesn't help a situation. Don't let anyone lead you to believe otherwise, even if it is your boss accusing you of not taking the situation seriously enough. Let your actions speak louder than your lack of apparent stress. Recognize yourself for responding calmly even when others judge you. And find people who also recognize the benefit to your calm responses to stress.

Increased Judgment of Others

As you strive to be less judgmental and more accepting, you are likely to experience an increase in judgmental thoughts toward others, at least at the beginning. As you become more self-aware and strive to improve yourself, your brain will start to apply that awareness to what you see in others as well. You may start to notice the areas where others aren't self-aware and staying stuck. If you don't prepare for this experience, you can end up being the pious person preaching to others about how they should improve, but all you end up doing is showing how you still need significant growth. We've all met the person who just started a new protocol or learned a new way of life and started to become judgmental of any who didn't also believe it. We've all been that person at some point, as well.

Seeing in others the exact thing you are trying to improve is not an invitation to correct them or outwardly judge them. Judgmental thoughts will happen, but the less you feed them, the less they will continue. Alternatively, if you feed the thoughts, you will be more likely to act on them, and you can become bitter, cynical, and end up alienating others and isolating yourself. Just like others' judgments of you are based on their own beliefs and perceptions, your judgments of others are based on your beliefs and perceptions. Your judgments are projections of your own experiences, insecurities, and assumptions, not truth. And they are not relevant to the other person unless they ask.

Decreased Tolerance of Others

As you improve your beliefs about yourself and start treating yourself better, you will rightfully become less tolerant of those who don't treat you well. You will become less tolerant of those who lead with stigma, who see you as too much, or who maintain inaccessible environments. The decreased tolerance may reasonably lead to leaving situations and people that drain your energy, harm your self-perception, and treat you poorly. This is not a bad thing, but it can feel uncomfortable.

Instead of withstanding the mistreatment, discomfort, and inaccessibility, you will find yourself prioritizing you even when it disrupts the peace. You'll start putting an end to treatment you previously would have endured, while advocating for improved treatment of yourself and others. While this can be good and healthy, taken too far it can cause unnecessary harm. A decreased tolerance of treatment that affects you and others is healthy. A decreased tolerance of others making honest mistakes and expecting perfection from them will only serve to alienate yourself from others instead of protect you. There is a balance that may not be obvious at first and may differ from situation to situation.

Increased Judgment of Self

As you learn and grow, you have new information to judge yourself against. You have new standards to meet. You have more ammunition to tell yourself what you should be doing. Self-improvement efforts without self-compassion will lead to increased self-judgment.

You can recognize that learning new ways of living and new ways of growing does not have to mean new and harsher standards of judgment.

Judgment will happen. You don't really get to choose that that is just how your brain functions. But you do get to choose what you do with that judgment. Do you believe it? Do you keep fueling judgments and letting them grow? Do you judge yourself for judging? Or do you recognize the judgment for what it is and let it pass? You get to choose. Then you get to choose again. There will always be a chance to choose again.

Loneliness

Loneliness is almost guaranteed along the path to true belonging. It seems counterintuitive to experience what you are trying to avoid in order to achieve the goal you want. But it is the reality. Anyone who has ever worked to improve themselves, reach lofty goals, break a bad habit, or just be happier will experience loneliness in the space between where you were and where you are going. As you outgrow old patterns and beliefs, you outgrow certain environments and relationships. Even if you don't fully outgrow a given environment or relationship, how others are able to relate to you may momentarily wane as you are in the midst of your transformation. This is normal and healthy. The fact that it is normal and healthy doesn't make it any easier but makes it possible to not fight against it.

You already feel alone in some ways. You know how it feels to fight battles that no one knows about. You know how it feels for others to have no idea how hard you are trying. This new loneliness is temporary and due to becoming more of who you are, not less.

Being Misunderstood

There will always be people who don't understand. The people who used to understand you may not anymore as you outgrow beliefs that were a previous source of understanding and connection. But there are people who can understand. The less you fight to be understood by those who don't understand, the more likely you are to find those who do understand.

While looking for those who will understand, don't assume the only ones who can understand will be those who went through the same thing as you. Understanding can come from people with completely different disabilities, and sometimes no disabilities at all. Sometimes people who have the most extreme difference in backgrounds are the people who understand the most.

I thought no one would ever be able to understand my experience of learning to interact in the world for the first time as an adult. After all, it isn't a common experience to hit your head and forget 20 years of your life.

I went years believing that I was the only one in the world who was an adult learning basic things about life and culture. Then I met someone who grew up in a different culture who had an almost identical experience in many ways. It didn't matter that their experience was from being raised in an Amish community and completely unrelated to disability. They knew what it was like to, as an adult, be naive to a culture that everyone else knew. They knew what it was like to be confidently oblivious to what you don't know and the awkwardness that obliviousness causes. They knew the same facial expressions from others that were a clear indicator that what you just said was somehow weird, inappropriate, or naive. They knew how it felt to recognize the facial expression that meant you did something wrong but having no idea what exactly that was. We had very similar experiences despite having very different circumstances that led to those experiences.

I learned that my experience wasn't as unique as I thought, and I wasn't alone as I thought. No one will be able to relate to every aspect of your life in the exact same way, but there are plenty of people who will be able to relate to even your most specific experiences and feelings.

Actual Rejection

As you risk putting yourself in new situations with new people, you will find that some people and places are not a good fit. It may hurt at first, especially if you are used to rejection in ways that have actually threatened your connection, safety, or needs being met. Experiencing rejection when you are being you in ways that you can stay safe is a different type of rejection. Instead of it being rejection that signals a threat, it is rejection that helps you identify what is best for you. The more you experience rejection while reminding yourself you are safe, the more you begin to realize rejection is okay and that you can handle it.

Preparing to deal with rejection is a better way to move through discomfort than fruitless attempts to avoid rejection altogether.

You will do some of the rejecting, and you will be rejected. Becoming more of who you are doesn't result in less rejection from others but less rejection from yourself. Instead of rejecting who you are to be someone that will be accepted by others, you embrace who you are and find where you are accepted. The risk is worth it and necessary to find where you do belong.

Loss of Relationships

The first time I lost a friendship after my brain injury, I was distraught as I had a childlike belief that friendships would last forever. I remember talking to my sister, who with a sad tone said that this was a moment she wished I remembered middle and high school. That is when many learn that relationships come and go and that it is natural. Sometimes people move away, sometimes priorities shift, and sometimes people grow apart. This is a natural part of life. Knowing this doesn't necessarily make it easier overall, but it makes it easier to not fight against it. This knowledge makes it easier to not make loss of relationships mean something about you personally.

People aren't guaranteed to grow at the same rate or at the same time. This means that some relationships become incompatible as one person grows at a different rate or in a different direction than the other. This can be true for friendships, family, or work relationships.

Friendships based on the shame-based you will no longer fit as you no longer base your identity in shame. As you focus more on what you want rather than people-pleasing, those who relied on your acquiescence will no longer fit. As you focus more on awareness and acceptance rather than blame, anger, or denial, connections based on outdated belief systems will lose commonality and understanding. Some people may not like the new you because they aren't growing in the same way. That isn't a sign that you are on the wrong path; it is just a sign that you are on a different path or at a different point on the path.

You may feel betrayed, rejected, or abandoned by those who don't like or accept the new, truer you. Mourning the loss is natural and necessary. You may feel moments of blame toward yourself or others when you are the one who chooses to move on from a relationship.

You might feel sad, angry, or bitter. That is okay. Growing away from a job that you thought was the perfect fit or a friend who was the one who knew you the best will be hard. Hard doesn't mean wrong.

Need for Rest

When hummingbirds sleep, they, like us, recover from the day before and prepare for the day ahead. Unlike us, they go into a state called torpor, where their heart rate and body temperature drop significantly, and their metabolism slows down almost completely. Torpor allows the hummingbird to conserve their energy for what matters most, while also allowing for the much needed rest that living things require. Torpor is a built-in function to ensure hummingbird survival.

While I wouldn't judge a hummingbird for needing to rest after flying around so speedily all day, it is common to judge humans for needing rest or for conserving energy for certain tasks. If rest is taken at the "wrong time" or in the "wrong way," judgment is not uncommon. But human bodies need rest, too. And human bodies also have built-in systems to signal when it is time to rest. Rest is necessary when you exercise new muscles, or when you do something that requires more conscious thought. Intentionally being a new version of you requires more energy and, as a result, more rest. Like any need for rest, it is important to respect any related signals as a sign from the body telling you what you need.

Self-Advocacy Exhaustion

Constantly advocating, explaining, assessing for safety, and taking the measures to ensure your needs are met can be exhausting. There may be some days you just don't have it in you to deal with it all. That is fine. Meeting your needs is the priority. Improving accessibility in the world around you is secondary. What you don't want is to let it get to the point of burnout or to exacerbate burnout if you are already there.

Requirements to consistently self-advocate create states of prolonged stress and demands. It can be physically, mentally, and emotionally draining. Exhaustion will happen. Rest. Avoid unnecessary situations and people where self-advocacy is required. If that isn't possible, do what you can to avoid it even if only for a day. Call in sick if you need to. Taking care of momentary exhaustion not only avoids burnout but also avoids it growing into full-blown hopelessness and depression.

Sometimes the only way to avoid self-advocacy is by staying isolated. Temporarily that can be beneficial, but long-term it will add a different type of stress. Another solution to reduce self-advocacy exhaustion is to have someone with you who is willing and able to advocate for you in certain situations. If you are extremely exhausted and require rest, you could go a few days only advocating for your most urgent needs and not putting energy into advocating for other needs. I know this goes against some of what I've said in other chapters, but sometimes meeting your need of reducing self-advocacy-related exhaustion means prioritizing only your most pressing needs for a day or two. It is prioritizing your energy for what needs it most, and sometimes that is rest.

General Exhaustion

When the brain detects that a threat is no longer present, the parasympathetic nervous system activates to bring the body to the necessary resting state required to heal. After a short threat, it may only take 40 minutes to recover. After a longer period of stress, it may take a full 24 hours to recover. After chronic stress for months or even years, the recovery period may be quite long. Recovery from severe burnout can be a multiyear-long process (Cherniss 1990).

Recovery happens in rest. It is why sleep is required every night. It is why the body sleeps longer after surgeries, sicknesses, or long periods of physical exertion. General exhaustion after chronic stress is your body finally feeling safe enough to rest. This is a good thing. Recognize the exhaustion as your body communicating its need to you, and give your body the rest it needs. The key factors in burnout recovery are getting out of the environment that facilitated the burnout as much as possible, balancing external demands and internal needs, and taking control where possible (Toker and Melamed 2017). Meaningful relationships and connection are also contributing factors to recovery. Find support with those who understand and those who let you rest without requiring you to raise your defenses.

Lack of Motivation

Many people who have been in survival mode for a long time have become used to shame, fear, and external pressure as sources for motivation. Once you start to heal and release the shame and stress, some of that pressure no longer exists. While it may feel scary to lack motivation, it is actually a great sign. While it may be annoying or frustrating to lack motivation, know that it is only temporary. It is a significant sign of healing and change in your belief systems to no longer be motivated by shame and fear to the degree you were previously. The shift just means you get to find more healthy sources of motivation.

You can identify motivators that add excitement instead of stress. You can identify tasks that you enjoy doing but never realized previously because of the external pressure you felt. Motivation will return as you continue to act in line with who you are, coming from a place of acceptance instead of shame. Have compassion and respect for this stage of being free from motivation in the form of shame, fear, and externally sourced pressure.

As you identify what pressure feels good for you, there may be some externally sourced pressure that is actually helpful, healthy, and effective. Maybe you are your most efficient when you are timed or on a deadline. Maybe you get your house the cleanest the fastest when someone unexpectedly tells you they are stopping by in 30 minutes. This external pressure is different than expectations and judgments imposed on you by others in areas that you don't actually care about. It isn't the source of the pressure that makes it helpful or harmful but the motivation in yourself that comes from the pressure. If it is self-hate, shame, or appeasing somebody else, it is likely harmful. If an external event creates a desire or surge of energy to get something done, that is helpful. Some neurotypes benefit from a specific balance of stress. Working with this is helpful and only gets easier when you have removed maladaptive sources of internal and external pressure.

Resistance is inevitable. Knowing you are making changes in ways that will raise the challenges in this chapter might feel counterintuitive. But by being prepared for what is to come, you increase your belief and trust in yourself to get through challenges. Addressing the hard parts before they come helps to calm the stress before it starts.

Preparing for the hard parts before they come helps to strengthen your resolve and tenacity to continue despite the inevitable resistance. During the resistance, you may question if this is all worth it. You may wonder if it would be better to stay where you were to keep what you know. Preparing for resistance preemptively strengthens your resolve, plans for difficulties and how to navigate through them, and reminds you that you are not the only one experiencing what you are going to experience. You aren't doing it wrong.

21

Stay True to Yourself in the Workplace

ONE OF THE most common places to feel the need to hide who you are is the workplace. Despite legal protections for employees with disabilities and a legal right to accommodations, the workplace can be a place where you may be expected to conform. There may be cultural norms, expectations, and rigid rules (some of which are unspoken) that don't align with who you are. You may encounter discrimination, stigma, or exclusion. The fear of being judged, overlooked for opportunities, losing your job, or enduring threat to your mental or physical safety is real and oftentimes valid. Because of this, it is easy to believe that diminishing yourself, changing aspects of your identity, or minimizing disability-related limitations and needs is the most promising way to navigate the workplace. Changing yourself to fit in will not work long-term, however. It never does. It will lead to burnout, loss of sense of self, and probably won't even avoid the experiences you are trying to avoid.

Staying true to yourself in the workplace is not only possible but is the most promising path. This doesn't mean ignoring real threats to your safety or even potential threats. It is navigating those threats in a way that stays true to who you are. When you aren't worried about changing who you are, you will perform better, enjoy your work more, and open up to the possibility of feeling a sense of acceptance and belonging. There are steps you can take to be more true to yourself while also advocating for your needs and protecting yourself against mistreatment.

Identify Safety Measures

Because discrimination is an unfortunate reality, proactively identifying safety measures can help you avoid potential issues, while also empowering you with the knowledge and resources to address any challenges as they arise and before they escalate. Identifying safety measures does not mean becoming hypervigilant about possible safety risks; it just means proactively identifying how to stay safe in the event that something unsafe does occur. Identify policies for reporting discrimination, retaliation, or ADA violations. If there isn't a policy, identify the appropriate team who handles claims. Identify whether there are anonymous ways to report. If there are employee resource groups, join relevant ones and ask about the culture and ways the members have found to effectively manage disability and accommodation-related topics.

Document everything. This is not necessarily in anticipation of wrongdoing but as good business practice in general just as keeping good medical records, tax records, or any other important records is helpful. Specifically, keep records of any discussions or actions that have to do with disability, accommodation requests, or performance in the workplace. Documentation helps you and the organization stay accountable and on the same page, while also ensuring there can be no mistreatment that is made possible when documentation is lacking. Documenting everything is one of the most important safety measures there is.

Prioritize Your Values and Goals

Your values and goals are your guiding principles, even more so than company policies, avoiding judgment, or other external factors. Let your values and goals lead over fear, perceived threat, and external judgments. Plan for how to act according to your values and goals when disclosing disability or asking for accommodations. Plan for how to act according to your values and goals when you get judgmental comments about your disability, pushback on your accommodation request, or when you are struggling. Plan for how to act according to your values and goals if your employer or supervisor's definition of "professional" puts expectations on you that require you to hide parts of who you are. Maybe it is aligned with your values and goals to advocate by educating on how their policy is discriminatory, maybe you find a balance of how to technically meet the requirement while maintaining the core of who you are, or maybe you decide to test the policy's validity and show up as you are anyway.

Values and goals can act as your reminder of what matters most to you. If what matters most to you is working for or with companies who share your values on inclusion and mental health, then you probably won't want to stay with a company who has started discriminating against you regarding your disability. If what matters most is making money and not letting others take advantage of you, then you will advocate for a raise when you are asked to take on significantly more responsibilities.

Your values and goals are just as much a sign of how to act and respond as they are ways to judge environments where you belong. If an organization requires that you act in ways not aligned with your values or goals, that is a sign that the environment is not for you. I once had an organization ask me to overlook illegal practices they were engaging in. I couldn't do it. I addressed it with the CEO, who after looking into it decided that it wasn't illegal enough to cause concern, so he told me that I needed to work with it. When I refused, I was laid off. I was making the largest salary I had made up to that point and suddenly had no income. What I thought would be extreme stress turned out to be extreme relief. The next morning I woke up with peace. While the job loss significantly affected my livelihood for the next few months, the shame of not acting in line with my values likely would have been detrimental to my mental health and sense of self for much longer.

If you learn that you don't belong in a role or at a company, accept it and take the necessary steps to move on. It might not be easy, but it is easier than continuing to do something that will cause shame or self-judgment.

When you are tempted to compromise your values or goals, ask yourself why. Is it to please others, fit in, or avoid conflict? Is it the only way you see to stay free from discrimination or harassment in the workplace? Even when it is tempting, resist the desire to compromise yourself. If it is truly necessary to compromise your values or goals, do it in the minimal way possible, and immediately plan to leave that environment. A place that requires you to compromise who you are is not a place that is healthy for you long-term. No amount of money or other security changes that fact.

Advocate for Your Needs

To be your best you, you require the best support. Just as it is expected that you will have the necessary technology or safety gear to do your job, you can reasonably expect to get your needs met. I use the word "expect" intentionally. Some have told me I act entitled to getting my needs met, and they aren't wrong. I believe more people should act entitled to getting their needs met. When you know you deserve to get your needs met, you don't take no for an answer. You ask in a way that is certain rather than hesitant. You ask as if your need truly is a need rather than as if the other person would be doing you a favor. This requires differentiating between true needs and mere preferences, but you deserve to get your needs met. You may even have a legal right to get your needs met. Act like it.

Speaking to your specific needs rather than your disability is most effective when advocating for your needs in the workplace. In many countries it is not a requirement to disclose your specific disability, and often mentioning the specific disability can be more of a detractor than a help. Disclosing the disability often leads to a focus on the disability itself rather than a focus on identifying the best accommodations for the situation. This doesn't mean you should hide your disability, but do what is most necessary and helpful to reach your goal—in this case, an accommodation. What is necessary is disclosing that you have a disability, how the disability affects you, what limitations or barriers you are experiencing, and what accommodations may be effective. The most important piece of this process is identifying and securing the accommodation that will be most effective. That is where the main focus should lie.

When defining how your disability affects you, it is most effective to define it in a neutral way highlighting the affected areas of function, not the deficits. Immediately following the disclosure, state what helps mitigate the issue. For example, instead of saying you have trouble concentrating, you can say your disability affects your focus, which is improved when x. Instead of saying you have executive function issues, say that certain tasks require increased mental capacity and are supported by y. Instead of saying, you can't endure long periods of sitting, say that your mobility is affected and do best when you are able to move your legs every two hours. Presenting it like this presents to the listener what you need from them rather than presenting to them a deficit that they need to fix. They don't need to fix you; they just need to support you.

By framing your situation in a neutral and factual manner, you avoid much of the deficit-focused stigma that accompanies disability discussions. It changes the focus from deficit to tangible solutions. This approach also avoids triggering assumptions, biases, and misconceptions. While the deficit-focused stigma can't be avoided completely, communicating it this way is effective at decreasing its likelihood. Disabilities are not inherent flaws or shortcomings, and this presentation reflects that.

Be prepared to push back in a way that is in line with your values. This can be when your accommodation is denied, when your disability or ability to do the job is questioned, or when you are asked invasive or inappropriate questions. Be prepared to encounter ignorance, assumptions, or indifference. Being prepared for it does not mean expecting it. Expect the best, and assume the best in their actions, but be prepared to advocate further when necessary.

Know your rights. Advocate for them.

Practice Acceptance

Sometimes there are managers who do not know how to manage. Sometimes people have no idea how to navigate the accommodation process. Sometimes people have completely pointless or inaccessible processes. Accepting what is allows you to identify what you can control versus what you can't. It allows you to identify steps you can take to make relevant improvements and where holding on to frustration, annoyance, or anger is pointless and only harming your own mental health.

Even if someone is discriminatory, feel the feelings that arise and accept that it happened. When deciding how to handle it, reflect with as much of a neutral lens as possible. Dealing with mistreatment is more effective when you don't add your own stories or meaning beyond what actually happened. The experience of discrimination is bad enough without added stories. Staying neutral (or as close to neutral as possible) in your response improves your credibility if it needs to be escalated to human resources or higher. Staying neutral helps your mental state, and the external results. You can stay logically neutral while being emotionally hurt, frustrated, or angry.

Of course, also practice acceptance of yourself with a neutral lens. Accept when you made a mistake and then respond accordingly. Accept when you need support. Accept all of you, including the parts you may feel you need to hide.

Tune Out Irrelevant Judgment

Any feedback that doesn't affect your employment or help you live your values or reach your goals is irrelevant. It doesn't matter whether it comes from the CEO of the company or the person who sits right next to you. It is irrelevant.

If somebody's opinion or feedback does have the potential to affect your employment, values, or goals, identify how and then identify how to respond in accordance with your values and goals. If your boss thinks you aren't capable and brings in human resources, maybe you show human resources evidence that you are capable and meeting expectations rather than trying to change your boss's opinion.

If human resources thinks you are making up your disability, you can refer them back to the relevant doctor's note. If that doesn't work, maybe the next step is to escalate it inside the company or engage an outside organization. Distinguish between responding because you are protecting your job versus responding to defend yourself or prove yourself.

It is possible to maintain who you are in the workplace, and it is an ongoing journey. The path may not be easy, especially initially, and you may encounter ignorance and resistance along the way. By being choosy about what workplaces you allow yourself to stay and spending as little time as possible in unsafe environments you remove many of the barriers that you can't control. By taking the steps to advocate for your needs, act according to your values and goals, and protect yourself, you remove many of the barriers that you *can* control.

22

Stay True to Yourself Even When Everything Sucks

Sometimes life just sucks. There is no way around it. Denying, resisting, or fighting against the reality won't change it and will make it suck even more. Maybe you lost a pet, got denied a promotion, lost a job, or all three within a short period. Maybe you're experiencing something more serious such as losing everything in a fire when you were weeks away from giving birth. (Something that happened to my sister just before I wrote this book.) You may have such extreme pain that it's hard to leave the house, meet expectations at work, or enjoy anything that you used to enjoy as is the case with many of my clients. How can you possibly be expected to maintain yourself through it all? You don't have to maintain your best self, your most positive self, or your most hopeful self. The only goal is to not lose yourself. And that is possible.

True Acceptance

True acceptance when life sucks means accepting that it sucks. It doesn't involve denial or toxic positivity. It doesn't involve adding story or meaning to make it worse mentally than it already is. While avoidance has been shown to be effective in various circumstances when applied temporarily, it is not an effective strategy for the long term. Being in situations where everything seems to be going wrong does not speak to your value, your abilities, your morals, or any other meaning you may be inclined to assign.

True acceptance is acceptance of the reality as it is. It is accepting your emotions as they are. It is accepting that you can't control what you can't control and taking control where you can. When things are their worst, it is helplessness and the feeling of no control that makes it feel so bad. If you can find even a small area of your life where you can exert control, you can improve your mental state even slightly and strengthen your resolve.

When you don't feel like tolerating something, true acceptance is accepting that. It is accepting when you may have a tendency to self-sabotage, or give up, or act in a way not in line with your values. It is accepting your feelings without making them mean more than just signals from the brain. You don't have to act on the feelings, though you can. Then true acceptance is accepting that, too.

The Valley of Despair

In change management, there is a model called The Valley of Despair, which describes what happens to performance when a new change is implemented. Anything that requires a learning curve, adoption of new habits, or adaptation to a new way of doing things goes through a similar process. While this models describes performance patterns in large groups, I find there is a lot of relevance to any change in life, personal or professional.

When change is first introduced, it is normal to feel some anxiety around it. Then, acceptance enters and turns to happiness, even excitement. You have the hope of something better, belief in the effectiveness of what you are implementing, and are excited to see the results of change. There are endless possibilities as you try something that you haven't yet seen fail.

Then struggle begins as you learn something new, try to incorporate the new process into what already exists, and you make mistakes. While a learning curve is normal for anything new, it still becomes frustrating, and your start to doubt whether it is going to work at all. The more you seem to keep failing, the more defeated you become.

The excitement that you had at the beginning is just a memory, and any hope is fleeting as you start to wonder whether you should have implemented the change at all.

Then at the lowest point of the valley, depression enters and may even turn to anger. It is at this point that hopelessness can begin. If hopelessness is allowed to take more control than persistence, you may feel inclined to give up, and in fact, this is where many people quit. You've been consistently decreasing in performance and mood, so it becomes harder to believe that there is any way it can get better. If you are unaware that this is a natural pattern in change management, then it seems to be a logical conclusion to accept that in fact, it won't improve.

Curiously enough, it is pushing through the moment you feel like giving up that improvement becomes inevitable. The Valley of Despair is called that because a valley has a decline and incline on both sides. The only way you stay in a valley is by not going out one of the sides. You can revert back to the previous way of doing things, which takes effort and comes with its own frustration. Or you can choose to go out the other side of the valley, which only requires you continue moving forward. Eventually, the learning curve levels out, and your performance starts improving again. Now you are on your way up and out of the valley. Mood slowly improves until eventually you reach acceptance. It is right after acceptance that you surpass the level of performance you were previously in and begin moving forward confidently again at a higher level than you were when you began the journey of change on the other side of the valley.

While the valley of despair is likely to occur, it is not an end destination but a part of the normal ebbs and flows of life and learning. The valley of despair is a point on the path of adaptation and growth. If you are in the valley, it's okay. Feelings of fear, denial, guilt, depression, defeat, and anger are all natural and expected. You don't have to fight against them. Just keep moving forward even in small ways.

When applying this model to business or personal situations, it is important to have clear expectations and values to guide you even when it gets hard. Even if you don't have the energy to care about your goals, acting in line with your values as best you can is still enough to ensure you don't lose yourself in the valley.

Resist Acting Against Your Values

When everything sucks, nothing is working, and you don't see any solution other than one that isn't aligned with your values, it may be tempting to reject your values. Even if you don't have the energy or care for anything else, try to care just enough to not reject your values and in doing so reject yourself. Even when you lose everything in life, you still have yourself.

When life seems at its lowest, it is common to feel the lowest about yourself, too. You may wonder what is the point of acting in line with your values when everything sucks anyway. Acting in line with your values may mean staying in a situation that you could get out of if you just decided to lie or cheat or steal. You may feel selfish for sticking to your values in this way. I have not met anyone who regretted acting according to their values even in their times of great-est struggle, but I have met many who regret acting in a way they aren't proud of when they thought it was their only option. Doing something that brings you shame is rarely, if ever, your only option. You don't need to add more guilt and shame to any feelings that already exist. If nothing else, act in line with your values to avoid the discomfort of guilt and shame.

If you do choose to act out of line with your values, that's okay, too. You are never too far gone to turn back to who you truly are. It may be harder, but you are never a lost cause.

Meet Your Basic Needs as Possible

If everything sucks, that probably includes your ability to meet all of your needs. While that can be true, it is still important to prioritize what you can. What are your absolute basic needs to survive? Which ones can you meet, even partially? Prioritize those needs every day. Your body has enough stress. Meeting any needs, even drinking water, will aid in your well-being and ability to continue. It isn't just your physical needs but mental, social, and spiritual, too. If it helps you to pray, do it. If it helps you to stare at the stars, do it. If it helps you to talk to someone, anyone, prioritize that. Even the seemingly small needs can have a huge impact. Prioritize meeting whatever needs you can.

Practice Nervous System Regulation

If somebody told me to breathe, tap, or name five things I could see or smell when I was at my lowest point, I probably would have wanted to punch them. I would have probably yelled at them that regulating my nervous system wasn't going to change my situation and that they were an idiot and insulting for even suggesting it. Even knowing the impact of mental state on physical health, I would have been annoyed at the suggestion. But it works, so I am including it.

That being said, I get it. This is not going to change your external situation. It isn't going to make you have money if you have none. It isn't going to bring someone back who you've lost. It isn't going to completely remove the chronic pain you feel or the new diagnosis you received. What it will do is equip your body to take better care of yourself while you go through whatever you're going through.

Regulating your nervous system will allow your body to prioritize energy to the areas that need it most (refer back to Chapter 13). It will also reduce your anxiety and depression levels. While it may not completely remove your pain, it can reduce it. It will put you in a better mental state to see the situation for what it is, not for more than what it is. It will help you to avoid tying stories to the reality. While it won't directly change anything externally, it may help you see possibilities that you didn't previously see in the state of despair. Or it may help you to accept the lack of possibility and make the most of what you have. I don't know the specific result it will have for you, but it will benefit you mentally, physically, and emotionally.

Even when you lost everything else, you don't have to lose yourself, too. You are worth fighting for.

References

Adolphs, R. 2013. "The Biology of Fear." *Current Biology* 23(2), pp. R79–93. https://doi.org/10.1016/j.cub.2012.11.055.

Akinrodoye, M. A., and Lui, F. 2022. "Neuroanatomy, Somatic Nervous System." [Updated 2022 Nov 7]. In: StatPearls [Internet]. Treasure Island (FL): StatPearls Publishing; 2024 Jan-. https://www.ncbi.nlm.nih.gov/books/NBK556027/.

Bakaeva, Z. V., Shumov, D. E., Yakunina, E. B., et al. 2022. "The Influence of Music with the Binaural Beat Effect on Heart Rate during Daytime Sleep in Humans." *Neurosci Behav Physi* 52, pp. 218–222.

Balban, M. Y., Neri, E., Kogon, M., Weed, L., Nouriani, B., Jo, B., Holl, G., Zeitzer, J. M., Spiegel, D., and Huberman, A. D. 2023. "Brief Structured Respiration Practices Enhance Mood and Reduce Physiological Arousal." *Cell Reports Medicine* 4(1), p. 100895. https://doi.org/10.1016/j.xcrm.2022.100895.

Barron, K., and Gravert, C. 2018. "Beliefs and Actions: How a Shift in Confidence Affects Choices." MPRA, Munich Personal RePEc Archive, WZB, University of Gothenburg, Paper No. 84743. https://mpra.ub.uni-muenchen.de/84743/1/MPRA_paper_84743.pdf.

Beetz, A., Uvnäs-Moberg, K., Julius, H., and Kotrschal, K. 2012. "Psychosocial and Psychophysiological Effects of Human-Animal Interactions: The Possible Role of Oxytocin." *Frontiers in Psychology* 3 (January). https://doi.org/10.3389/fpsyg.2012.00234.

Booth-Kewley, S., and Friedman, H. S. 1987. "Psychological Predictors of Heart Disease: A Quantitative Review." *Psychological Bulletin* 101(3), p. 343.

Brooks, A. W. 2014. "Get Excited: Reappraising Pre-performance Anxiety as Excitement." *Journal of Experimental Psychology: General* 143(3), p. 1144.

Calhoun, C. D., Stone, K. J., Cobb, A. R., Patterson, M. W., Danielson, C. K., and Bendezú, J. J. 2022. "The Role of Social Support in Coping with Psychological Trauma: An Integrated Biopsychosocial Model for Posttraumatic Stress Recovery." *The Psychiatric Wuarterly* 93(4), pp. 949–970. https://doi.org/10.1007/s11126-022-10003-w.

Charles, S. T., Mogle, J., Chai, H. W., and Almeida, D. M. 2021. "The Mixed Benefits of a Stressor-Free Life," *Emotion* 21(5), pp. 962–971. https://psycnet.apa.org/doiLanding?doi=10.1037%2Femo0000958.

Cherniss, C. 1990. "Natural Recovery from Burnout: Results from a 10-year Follow-up Study." *Journal of Health and Human Resources Administration*, pp. 132–154.

Chervonsky, E., and Hunt, C. 2017. "Suppression and Expression of Emotion in Social and Interpersonal Outcomes: A Meta-Analysis." *Emotion* 17(4), p. 669. https://psycnet.apa.org/doi/10.1037/emo0000270.

Clear, J. 2022. "How to Master the Art of Continuous Improvement." (August 2022). https://jamesclear.com/continuous-improvement.

Cleveland Clinic. 2022. "Rejection Sensitive Dysphoria (RSD)." https://my.clevelandclinic.org/health/diseases/24099-rejection-sensitive-dysphoria-rsd.

Connors, M. H., and Halligan, P. W. 2022. "Revealing the Cognitive Neuroscience of Belief." *Frontiers in Behavioral Neuroscience* 16 (July), p. 926742. https://doi.org/10.3389/fnbeh.2022.926742.

Deci, E. L., and Ryan, R. M. 2014. "Autonomy and Need Satisfaction in Close Relationships: Relationships Motivation Theory." In: Weinstein, N. (ed.), *Human Motivation and Interpersonal Relationships*. Dordrecht: Springer.

Dickerson, S. S., Kemeny, M. E., Aziz, N., Kim, K. H., and Fahey, J. L. 2004. "Immunological Effects of Induced Shame and Guilt." *Psychosomatic Medicine* 66(1), pp. 124–131.

Dickerson, S. S., Gruenewald, T. L., and Kemeny, M. E. 2004. "When the Social Self Is Threatened: Shame, Physiology, and Health." *Journal of Personality* 72(6), pp. 1191–1216.

Dickerson, S. S., Gruenewald, T. L., and Kemeny, M. E. 2009. "Psychobiological Responses to Social Self Threat: Functional or Detrimental?" *Self and Identity* 8(2–3), pp. 270–285. https://doi.org/10.1080/15298860802505186.

Dubreucq, J., Plasse, J., Gabayet, F., Faraldo, M., Blanc, O., Chereau, I., Cervello, S., Couhet, G., Demily, C., Guillard-Bouhet, N., Gouache, B., Jaafari, N., Legrand, G., Legros-Lafarge, E., Pommier, R., Quilès, C., Straub, D., Verdoux, H., Vignaga, F., Massoubre, C., . . . Franck, N. 2022. "Stigma Resistance Is Associated with Advanced Stages of Personal Recovery in Serious Mental Illness Patients Enrolled in Psychiatric Rehabilitation." *Psychological Medicine* 52(11), pp. 2155–2165.

Dubreucq, J., Plasse, J., and Franck, N. 2021. "Self-stigma in Serious Mental Illness: A Systematic Review of Frequency, Correlates, and Consequences," *Schizophrenia Bulletin* 47(5), pp. 1261–1287. https://academic .oup.com/schizophreniabulletin/issue/47/5.

Eisenmenger, A. 2019. "Ableism 101: What It Is, What It Looks Like, and How to Become a Better Ally." Access Living. https://www.accessliving .org/newsroom/blog/ableism-101/.

Elison, J., Garofalo, C., and Velotti, P. 2014. "Shame and Aggression: Theoretical Considerations." *Aggression and Violent Behavior* 19(4), pp. 447–453.

Fisher, M. H., Sung, C., Kammes, R. R., Okyere, C., and Park, J. 2022. "Social Support as a Mediator of Stress and Life Satisfaction for People with Intellectual or Developmental Disabilities During the COVID-19 Pandemic." *Journal of Applied Research in Intellectual Disabilities* (JARID) 35(1), pp. 243–251. https://doi.org/10.1111/jar.12943.

Gaertner R. J., Kossmann, K. E., Benz, A., Bentele, U. U., Meier, M., Denk, B., Klink, E. S. C., Dimitroff, S. J., and Pruessner, J. C. 2023. "Relaxing Effects of Virtual Environments on the Autonomic Nervous System Indicated by Heart Rate Variability: A Systematic Review." *Journal of Environmental Psychology* 88, p. 102035.

Gausel, N., and Leach, C. W. 2011. "Concern for Self-image and Social Image in the Management of Moral Failure: Rethinking Shame." *European Journal of Social Psychology* 41(4), pp. 468–478. https://doi .org/10.1002/ejsp.803.

Gross, C. A., and Hansen, N. E. 2000. "Clarifying the Experience of Shame: The Role of Attachment Style, Gender, and Investment in Relatedness." *Personality and Individual Differences* 28(5), pp. 897–907.

Haft, S. L., Greiner De Magalhães, C., and Hoeft, F. 2022. "A Systematic Review of the Consequences of Stigma and Stereotype Threat for Individuals with Specific Learning Disabilities." *Journal of Learning Disabilities* 56(3), pp. 193–209. https://doi.org/10.1177/00222194221087383.

Hiroto, D. S., and Seligman, M. E. 1975. "Generality of Learned Helplessness in Man." *Journal of Personality and Social Psychology* 31(2), p. 311.

Inagaki, T. K., and Eisenberger, N. I. 2016. "Giving Support to Others Reduces Sympathetic Nervous System-Related Responses to Stress." *Psychophysiol* 53, pp. 427–435.

Jansen-van Vuuren, J., and Aldersey, H. M. 2020. "Stigma, Acceptance and Belonging for People with IDD Across Cultures." *Current Developmental Disorders Reports* 7(3), pp. 163–172.

Kox, M., Van Eijk, L. T., Zwaag, J., Van Den Wildenberg, J., Sweep, F. CGJ, Van Der Hoeven, J. G., and Pickkers, P. 2014. "Voluntary Activation of the Sympathetic Nervous System and Attenuation of the Innate Immune Response in Humans." *Proceedings of the National Academy of Sciences* 111(20), pp. 7379–7384. https://doi.org/10.1073/pnas.1322174111.

Lester, D., and Dadfar, M. 2022. "Sociotropy, Autonomy, Depression and Suicidality." *Suicide Studies* 3(4), pp. 2–10. https://www.researchgate.net/publication/359146221_Suicide_Studies_2022_34.

Li, K., Chen, Y., Wu, D., Lin, R., Wang, Z., and Pan, L. 2020. "Effects of Progressive Muscle Relaxation on Anxiety and Sleep Quality in Patients With COVID-19." *Complementary Therapies in Clinical Practice* 39 (May), p. 101132. https://doi.org/10.1016/j.ctcp.2020.101132.

Li, W., Mai, X., and Liu, C. 2014. "The Default Mode Network and Social Understanding of Others: What Do Brain Connectivity Studies Tell Us." *Frontiers in Human Neuroscience* 8 (January). https://doi.org/10.3389/fnhum.2014.00074.

Lutwak, N., Panish, J. B., and Ferrari, J. R. 2003. "Shame and Guilt: Characterological vs. Behavioral Self-blame and Their Relationship to Fear of Intimacy." *Personality and Individual Differences* 35(4), pp. 909–916. https://doi.org/10.1016/s0191-8869(02)00307-0.

Macfarlane, R. 2013. *The Old Ways: A Journey on Foot.* Westminster, London: Penguin Books.

Maier, S. F., and Seligman, M. E. P. 2016. "Learned Helplessness at Fifty: Insights from Neuroscience." *Psychological Review* 123(4), pp. 349–367. https://doi.org/10.1037/rev0000033.

McCollum, N. 2024. "I Survived a Performance Improvement Plan, But It Wasn't Worth It." *Business Insider*, Jan 2024. https://www.businessinsider.com/survived-performance-plan-wasnt-worth-hard-work-2024-1.

McLeod, C., and Sherwin, S. 2000. "Relational Autonomy, Self-Trust, and Health Care for Patients Who Are Oppressed." Western University, Philosophy Department, *Philosophy Publications* 345, pp. 259–279. https://ir.lib.uwo.ca/philosophypub/345.

Meier, S. K., Ray, K. L., Waller, N. C., Gendron, B. C., Aytur, S. A., and Robin, D. A. 2020. "Graph Theory Analysis of Induced Neural Plasticity

Post-Acceptance and Commitment Therapy for Chronic Pain." *medRxiv* 2020.10.19.20212605, pp. 2020–10. https://doi.org/10.1101/2020.10.19 .20212605.

Murad, A. 2010. "A Neurological Mystery from History: The Case of Claudius Caesar." *Journal of the History of the Neurosciences* 19(3), pp. 221–227.

O'Connor, D. B., Thayer, J. F., and Vedhara, K. 2021. "Stress and Health: A Review of Psychobiological Processes." *Annual Review of Psychology* 72, pp. 663–688.

Oxenham, M. F., Tilley, L., Matsumura, H., Nguyen, L. C., Nguyen, K. T., Nguyen, K. D., Domett, K., and Huffer, D. 2009. "Paralysis and Severe Disability Requiring Intensive Care in Neolithic Asia." *Anthropological Science* 117(2), pp. 107–112. https://doi.org/10.1537/ase.081114.

Pennington, C. R., Heim, D., Levy, A. R., and Larkin, D. 2016. "Twenty Years of Stereotype Threat Research: A Review of Psychological Mediators." *PLOS ONE* 11(1), p. e0146487. https://doi.org/10.1371/journal .pone.0146487.

Pineles, S. L., Street, A. E., and Koenen, K. C. 2006. "The Differential Relationships of Shame–Proneness and Guilt–Proneness to Psychological and Somatization Symptoms." *Journal of Social and Clinical Psychology* 25(6), pp. 688–704.

Raub, J. N. 2022. "Knowledge, Fear of the Unknown, Opinion, and the Pandemic." *American Journal of Health-System Pharmacy* (AJHP) 79(5), pp. 400–401. https://doi.org/10.1093/ajhp/zxab323.

Richards, J. M., and Gross, J. J. 1999. "Composure at Any Cost? The Cognitive Consequences of Emotion Suppression." *Personality and Social Psychology Bulletin* 25(8), pp. 1033–1044. https://doi.org/10.1177/ 01461672992511010.

Russell, A. L., Tasker, J. G., Lucion, A. B., Fiedler, J., Munhoz, C. D., Wu, T-y. J., and Deak, T. 2018. "Factors Promoting Vulnerability to Dysregulated Stress Reactivity and Stress-Related Disease." *Journal of Neuroendocrinology* 30(10), p. e12641. https://doi.org/10.1101/2020.10.19.20212605.

Salleh, M. R. 2008. "Life Event, Stress and Illness." *The Malaysian Journal of Medical Sciences: MJMS* 15(4), p. 9. https://www.ncbi.nlm.nih.gov/pmc/ articles/PMC3341916/.

Salmon, P. 2001. "Effects of Physical Exercise on Anxiety, Depression, and Sensitivity to Stress: A Unifying Theory." *Clinical Psychology Review* 21(1), pp. 33–61. https://doi.org/10.1016/S0272-7358(99)00032-X.

Sandmire, D. A., Gorham, S. R., Rankin, N. E., and Grimm, D. R. 2012. "The Influence of Art Making on Anxiety: A Pilot Study." *Art Therapy* 29(2), pp. 68–73. doi:10.1080/07421656.2012.683748.

Sapolsky, R. M. 2004. *Why Zebras Don't Get Ulcers*. Third edition. New York City: Holt Paperbacks.

Satô, T., and Gonzalez, M. A. 2009. "Interpersonal Patterns in Close Relationships: The Role of Sociotropy-autonomy." *British Journal of Psychology* 100(2), pp. 327–345. https://doi.org/10.1348/000712608x331009.

Schaefer, L. M., Burke, N. L., Calogero, R. M., Menzel, J. E., Krawczyk, R., and Thompson, J. K. 2018. "Self-Objectification, Body Shame, and Disordered Eating: Testing a Core Mediational Model of Objectification Theory among White, Black, and Hispanic Women." *Body Image* 24, pp. 5–12.

Seligman, M. E., and Maier, S. F. 1967. "Failure to Escape Traumatic Shock." *Journal of Experimental Psychology* 74(1), p. 1.

Shukla, A. 2020. "A 5-Step Mindfulness Grounding Technique to Ease Anxiety & Why Mindfulness Works." *Cognition Today*. March 27, 2020. https://cognitiontoday.com/5-step-mindfulness-grounding-technique-to-ease-anxiety-why-it-works/.

Simons, D. J., and Chabris, C. F. 1999. "Gorillas in Our Midst: Sustained Inattentional Blindness for Dynamic Events." *Perception* 28(9), pp. 1059–1074. http://www.chabris.com/Simons1999.pdf.

Sippel, L. M., Pietrzak, R. H., Charney, D. S., Mayes, L. C., and Southwick, S. M. 2015. "How Does Social Support Enhance Resilience in the Trauma-Exposed Individual?" *Ecology and Society* 20(4). http://www.jstor.org/stable/26270277.

Smith, M. M., and Arnett, P. A. 2013. "Perfectionism and Physical Disability Predict Depression in Multiple Sclerosis." *Journal of Psychosomatic Research* 75(2), pp. 187–189.

Smith, M. 2023. "People-pleasers Are at a Higher Risk of Burnout, Says Harvard-trained Psychologist—How to Spot the Signs." CNBC, May 22, 2023. https://www.cnbc.com/2023/05/21/harvard-trained-psychologist-people-pleasers-are-at-higher-risk-for-burnout.html.

Smith, M. M., and Arnett, P. A. 2013. "Perfectionism and Physical Disability Predict Depression in Multiple Sclerosis." *Journal of Psychosomatic Research* 75(2), pp. 187–189.

Steele, C. M., and Aronson, J. 1995. "Stereotype Threat and the Intellectual Test Performance of African Americans." *Journal of Personality and Social Psychology* 69(5), pp. 797–811. https://doi.org/10.1037/0022-3514.69.5.797.

Toker, S., and Melamed, S. 2017. "Stress, Recovery, Sleep, and Burnout." *The Handbook of Stress and Health: A Guide to Research and Practice*, pp. 168–185.

United Nations. n.d. "Convention on the Rights of Persons with Disabilities, Article 2." Department of Economic and Social Affairs. https://www.un.org/development/desa/disabilities/convention-on-the-rights-of-persons-with-disabilities/article-2-definitions.html.

Viktor E. Frankl Institute of America, The. n.d. "The Life of Viktor Frankl." viktorfranklamerica.com.

Volchan, E., Leal Souza, G. G., Franklin, C. M., Nórte, C. E., Rocha-Rego, V., Magalhães De Oliveira, J., David, I. A., et al. 2011. "Is There Tonic Immobility in Humans? Biological Evidence from Victims of Traumatic Stress." *Biological Psychology* 88(1), pp. 13–19. https://doi.org/10.1016/j.biopsycho.2011.06.002.

World Policy Analysis Center. 2023. "Disability data download." https://www.worldpolicycenter.org/maps-data/data-download/disability-data-download.

Wouters-Soomers, L., Van Ruysseveldt, J., Bos, A. E. R., and Jacobs, N. 2022. "An Individual Perspective on Psychological Safety: The Role of Basic Need Satisfaction and Self-compassion." *Frontiers in Psychology* 13 (August), p. 920908. https://doi.org/10.3389/fpsyg.2022.920908.

Zhang, T., Harrington, K. B., and Sherf, E. N. 2021. "The Errors of Experts: When Expertise Hinders Effective Provision and Seeking of Advice and Feedback." Harvard Business School, Harvard University. http://www.ting-zhang.com/uploads/2/1/7/3/21738392/zhang_harrington_sherf_2022.pdf.

Acknowledgments

WRITING THIS BOOK has been a collaborative journey only made possible by the unwavering support and contributions from a remarkable network of intelligent, accepting, and accommodating individuals.

I am immensely grateful to the team at Wiley, particularly Christina Rudloff, who saw value in my words beyond what I saw myself, and Gus Miklos, who freely provided calm, clarity, and wisdom. Thank you for your support, which was critical in bringing this book to completion.

I thank those in my community, especially Alyssa Harris, Laren Goldberg, Colleen Giblin, and Nidhi A, who each played a significant role in helping me through the many mental blocks I couldn't navigate alone.

I thank my parents whose unconditional love and acceptance of me is why I am who I am. You give an example of how people can and should be accepted for who they are.

Thank you to the readers who choose to read this work. I hope this book offers valuable insights and helps you to be a little more you every day.

To each person who has contributed, directly or indirectly, to this collaborative effort, thank you for being part of this journey.

With gratitude,
Julie Harris

About the Author

After experiencing complete memory loss due to a brain injury, Julie Harris quickly defied doctors' expectations as she found success in secondary education and the corporate world. Drawing from personal study and formal education in neuroscience, process improvement, and disability inclusion, she consults with individuals and organizations around the globe.

Despite having less than 16 years' worth of memory and knowledge, Julie's expertise has been sought after by numerous Fortune 500 companies, where she has delivered compelling speeches and invaluable consultation on disability inclusion, workplace rights, and reasonable accommodation process improvement. She has guided hundreds of employees to successfully advocate for their needs to be met in the workplace, and has educated thousands more on their legal rights and improved self-advocacy skills.

Julie's goal is to demonstrate that success can be achieved through unconventional paths that defy rules and expectations.

Index

and autonomic nervous
system, 134–6
being judged for not
showing, 220–1
and fear of being perceived, 112
from perfectionism, 89
stress-related illnesses, 89, 112, 139
subjective helplessness, 93
subjective social disconnection, 90
success, fear of losing, 215–16
supplements, 159
support, social, 105
sympathetic nervous system, 134, 139

T
tapping, 144
temporal lobes, 6–7
threats, 137–8
tolerance of others, decreased, 222
true acceptance, 237–8
Truman, Harry S., 44
trust
in your body, 184–7
in yourself, 187

U
United Nations, 44, 201
urban planners, 32

V
The Valley of Despair, 238–9
values
acting against your, 240
core human, 151
identifying your, 150–3
leading with, 194–6
in the workplace, 232–4

W
why, asking, 173
Why Zebras Don't Get Ulcers
(Sapolsky), 138
workplace, 231–6
needs advocated for in the,
234–5
practicing acceptance in
the, 235–6
safety measures identified
in the, 232
tuning out irrelevant judgment
in the, 236
values and goals prioritized in
the, 232–4

Y
"you are enough," 89,
148–50, 189–90